Running From
H.E.L.L

By JC Rowe

ISBN-13: 9780473625047
eBook ISBN-13: 9780473648893
Paperback cover design by: Holland Power
eBook cover design by: Batimaqui
Edited by: Kristen Mackay

Written in New Zealand

This book is dedicated to everyone who said to me 'is your next book out yet?' or 'I need the second book now.' Well here it is. Thank you for wanting to see what happens with Elsie and Lu next.

Foreword

Please be aware that I have written this book loosely based on my past (very exaggerated). I wrote it with the intention to explore my own feelings, sexuality and impulses. This is for the age range of 17 and older, as there will be explicit sex scenes.

Trigger warnings include: Child abuse, murder, mentions of rape, violence, drugs, alcoholism, suicidal thoughts, depression, anxiety, food disorders.

THIS IS BOOK 2 OF THE *THEY ARE H.E.L.L* SERIES.
Please read *We Are H.E.L.L* first, as this book is a
continuation.

Prom night was meant to be the best night of Elsie and
Lu's senior year of high school. Instead, it turned out to
be the worst after a series of unlucky events.

Now, wanted for murder and escaping police custody,
Elsie and Lu are on the run from both the law and the
retaliation of the mafia after killing one of their own.

Plagued with awful memories, regrets and worry about
being caught and having to go to prison for the rest of
their lives, both girls have to rely on each other to get
through each day.

It seems as though Elsie's wish definitely did come true,
when she wished she didn't have a boring life. Now she
has to keep running, so she doesn't end up in hell.

Chapter One

Lu

Out-driving the cops was a lot easier than I thought. Since I was only using the streetlamps as my light source, I didn't think they could tell what direction we went. It wasn't long, until I was satisfied that we were nowhere on their radar. I flicked on the headlights, turned off the main road and headed into a residential area.

I had to get Elsie to Maria. I had no choice. There was no way we were going to a hospital. Elsie hadn't made a sound since we zoomed away, so I was pretty sure she had passed out.

I parked the car a few houses away from Maria's, not wanting to make it obvious if someone reported the car stolen and an alert was broadcast. I got out of the car and opened the back door to find Elsie awake, but pale and shivering.

"Elsie," I breathed out, taking off my jacket and carefully putting it over her shoulders.

"It hurts," she told me, her voice shaking.

"We're at Maria's. I'm going to go get her, okay?" I told her and lowered myself down to kiss her on her forehead.

"Okay," She whispered back and my heart pounded against my chest at the thought of having to leave her, even if I was only going for a few minutes.

"I'll be right back," I promised. I shut the door and ran to Maria's house.

Once I got to the door I banged on it repeatedly until it opened. Raúl, Maria's husband and my father's best friend, stood on the other side, not even remotely surprised to see me.

"Lucita, where is she?" He asked me, grabbing his jacket as he rushed out the door.

"In the car, follow me," I told him and hurried back down the pathway with him at my heel.

"How did you know?" I asked as we rushed to the car.

"Your father called and told me to expect you. He was told everything by Mateo," he explained and my heart skipped a beat at the thought of my dad.

"The Italians have already retaliated by sending their people to your father's clubs. But he told me to tell you not to worry and just get out of here as soon as you can. He said to go to the safe house and he will meet you there," he told me as we reached the car. I wanted to ask more, but now wasn't the time.

I opened the door to find that Elsie had passed out and she was sweating.

"What happened?" He asked. I told him about the car accident and how her hip was dislocated.

"Maria has set up the spare bedroom and is waiting for us," he told me. I stepped aside as he carefully grabbed Elsie under her arms and pulled her out of the car, placing her on his shoulders like she weighed nothing. I guess that was a perk of being one of the strongest men in Los Dragones.

We rushed back into the house and into a bedroom where Maria was waiting for us. She let out a gasp when she saw the state of Elsie and watched in horror as Raúl gently put her down on the bed.

Elsie's jacket had come apart and Maria could see her torn dress. She looked at me, then back at Elsie and started checking her over.

I hurried to the other side of the bed, feeling déjà vu, but I couldn't help but think that this was ten times worse. The previous time was just a wound that had now healed, only leaving a scar. But this time, not only had Elsie dislocated her hip, she had also been violated in a way that would probably never heal.

"Go now, Raúl, we will be fine," Maria told her husband and he just nodded before leaving the room. It wasn't long until I heard the garage opening and a motorcycle start up, which made me look at Maria, questioningly.

"He was waiting until he saw you, so he could update your father," she explained, before turning her attention back to Elsie. "What happened?"
I told her, including what Dante had done to Elsie.

Maria paled at my explanation as she moved to her medical bag. She loaded up a syringe with what I assumed was a pain killer and injected it into Elsie's arm.

"Morphine," Maria confirmed, as she capped the needle and put it in a medical waste bag.

"I need to reset her hip and it's going to be very painful," she continued. She got out a cloth and wiped the sweat from Elsie's face as I brushed Elsie's hair out of the way.

Elsie stirred slightly and opened her eyes. I smiled down at her.

"Hi, babe," I whispered.

She smiled softly and whispered back, "hi."

Maria gently rubbed Elsie's arm, which caused Elsie to turn from me to look at Maria.

"What I am about to do is going to be very painful. I have given you morphine, but you're probably still going to feel it," she explained and then she looked at me.

"I'm going to need you to hold down her shoulders. She needs to be still for this," Maria told me.

I gulped as I nodded. I didn't know if I was going to be able to do this. I put my hands on Elsie's shoulders and gently held her in place. Maria moved her hands under Elsie's leg, lifting it up slightly. Elsie closed her eyes tight, letting out a small cry of pain. I gritted my teeth and I watched Elsie, focusing on her rather than what Maria was doing because I didn't think I could bear to watch.

"Three. Two. One," Maria counted down. I felt movement behind me, then suddenly a loud pop sounded before Elsie started screaming. I had to hold her down firmer, but it only lasted a second before she fell back down again, completely passed out.

"She's not going to be able to walk on it properly for a few days. So wherever you go next, make sure she can rest," Maria stated and I looked at her, tears filling my eyes as I nodded.

Maria pulled out a bottle of pills from her bag and handed them to me.

"The strong stuff, so be careful with these," she noted. I nodded my head again as I pocketed them. She then pulled out a little bottle, popped out a small plug and put it under Elsie's nose. Elsie stirred and then opened her eyes, blinking a few times before focusing on me. I smiled at her, moving my hand into hers and gave it a comforting squeeze.

"I know you probably don't have long before you have to leave, but I need to check you over," Maria told Elsie, which made Elsie turn her head to look at her.

"You mean, down there?" Elsie asked, so quietly that I almost didn't hear her. She sounded petrified. Maria gave her a look of remorse as she nodded her head.

"If it comes to it, your defense council will need any evidence they can use to reduce your charges," Maria explained softly. I could feel Elsie's hand shaking, so I moved a little closer to her so I could run my fingers through her hair. She looked at me and I could see her eyes filling up with tears.

"I'll be here, every step of the way," I whispered to her, leaning forward to kiss her on her forehead.

"Okay," Elsie whispered and looked back at Maria.

Maria gave Elsie a reassuring smile, then moved to push her skirt aside. Since it was already torn, there wasn't much to move. I gasped when I saw the blood between her thighs and I laid myself down so I could put my head in the nook of Elsie's neck. I kissed her gently on the shoulder.

"I'm assuming this isn't from your period?" Maria

asked, as she moved to remove Elsie's underwear.

"It's not due till next week," we both responded at the same time. We both let out a small, uncomfortable laugh.

"We are on the same cycle," I explained, shifting my head so I was looking at Maria.

From this position, I couldn't see what was happening. Maria just nodded and gently moved Elsie's legs apart and made it so her legs were bent at the knee. I felt Elsie tense up and I looked over at her. Her eyes were tightly closed.

"I know it doesn't seem like it now Elsie, but it's going to be okay," I whispered to her. "I know that it's uncomfortable and I know that it's probably making you picture what happened but think of anything but that. Think of me if you have to," I continued, rubbing my thumb over the back of her hand.

I wasn't sure what Maria was doing and I wasn't about to ask, but I noticed that she had pulled out her camera.

"I'm going to have to take photos. I won't show anyone but the defense if they need it," Maria stated, and Elsie just nodded her head, her eyes still tightly shut.

Maria took the photos and then grabbed a packet of wet wipes from her bag and pulled a couple out. She wiped away the dried blood and then discarded them in the medical waste bag. She then lowered Elsie's legs, took the underwear completely off and put them in a plastic zip lock bag and then put Elsie's skirt back over her legs.

"I've finished my examination now. You have a tear, which caused the bleeding," She explained softly and I had almost stopped breathing.

"Is that why it's still so painful?" Elsie asked, as she opened her eyes and looked at Maria. She nodded back in response.

"How's the pain at the moment, overall?" she asked her.

"About a one. I want to sleep," Elsie admitted and I breathed out again, remembering how strong pain killers made her sleep.

"Well before you do that, you need to get out of this dress and Lu, you need to get out of those bloody clothes. I have packed a bag," Maria started, nodding to the duffle bag at the end of the bed, that I had only just now noticed. "Spare clothes, underwear and toiletries," she explained.

"When …" I started to ask, but Maria carried on talking.

"Your father called just after Mateo told him that Elsie had shot her father."

I just nodded.

"Get changed and then meet me in the family room," Maria told me. She got up, gathering up her supplies and then left the room.

I pushed up from lying next to Elsie's side and grabbed the bag, pulling out two t-shirts, two pairs of pants, a pair of underwear and a bra.

Elsie sat up, groaning slightly as she put weight on her hip. I reached over to her and pulled down the zip at her back. She stood, swaying slightly, but then removed her dress. I reached up and unhooked her bra, which she pulled down her arms.

I let out another gasp when I saw bruises on her left breast. She looked down, let out a groan and then burst into tears. I got off the bed quickly and pulled her into my arms and hugged her. She wrapped her arms around me and her head dropped on my shoulder while I was trying my hardest not to start crying with her.

We stood there for a minute, with me rubbing her back while she cried, until she stepped back from me, reached for my phone that was in my pocket and handed it to me.

"Take a picture. For evidence," she said.

I took my phone and nodded. I unlocked it, noting the twenty-seven text messages and missed phone calls, but ignored them and opened the camera. I took the photo and then threw my phone on the bed.

I grabbed the clean bra and handed it to Elsie and we continued getting changed in silence.

I pulled the gun I stole from Detective Swanson from the pocket of my pants and put it in the duffle bag.

I noticed a plastic bag left on the floor next to the bed, so I picked it up and put our dirty and ripped clothes in it, only keeping my bloody red shirt which I put in the duffle bag along with my phone. I flung the duffle over my shoulder, waiting for Elsie to finish dressing. She was quite a bit slower due to being zoned out on painkillers and probably still feeling the pain from her hip and between her legs.

Once she was done, I grabbed her hand and led her out to the family room where Maria was waiting on the couch for us.

"Thank you so much for helping us, Maria," I said as we approached her. "But what you've done is aided and abetted wanted criminals. I don't want to get you in trouble for this," I pointed out.

I unzipped the duffle bag and pulled out the gun. I made sure the safety was on, having learned my lesson from the last gun I had held.

"We have to make it look like I forced you to help

us," I declared, giving Maria a look that also said I didn't want to do this.

"I was going to suggest you punch me or something, but that would work better," Maria sighed and stood up from the couch. "Just make it look good." She closed her eyes tightly.

I grimaced as I raised the gun over my shoulder then brought it down on her face, pistol-whipping her. She swore and immediately backed away, placing her hand over her face.

"Fuck, I'm sorry," I moaned, putting the gun back in the duffle and rezipping it. Elsie was leaning against me, so I couldn't hurry to Maria's side, but she put her other hand up as she bent over.

"I'm fine. I'm good. You just have a wicked arm," Maria informed me. She let out a deep sigh and stood up and I winced when I saw the open cut on her forehead. I could also see that the skin around it had already started to bruise.

"Get out of here. Who knows how long it will be until they have a stolen vehicle report and it gets found here? You know where to go, right?" She asked, wiping the blood across her forehead. I gave her an ashamed smile.

"Yeah. To the safe house about three hours out of town," I replied, thinking of the house located in the middle of a forested area that my father used as a safe house, storage and cemetery when he didn't want bodies found. I'm pretty sure that's where some Moretti family members were buried.

Maria nodded, pulled out a bundle of cash from her pocket and handed it to me. I started to protest, but she started to push us out the door anyway.

"Is it okay if I grab a few things out of the garage?" I asked. "I need a gas can and a hose."

Maria nodded. "It should be open."

I quickly ran to the garage and grabbed the things I needed. When I got back to Elsie, I practically had to carry her back to the car as she was starting to fall asleep. I managed to get her in the front seat, where I gently rested her head against the window so she didn't hurt her neck, before she fell asleep for real.

I put the duffle bag in the back seat, placed the gas can and hose in the trunk and climbed into the driver's seat. I hot-wired the car again and then drove out of town.

Chapter Two

Elsie

My face felt numb, but cold and I swear it was wet. I opened my eyes to find my cheek sticking to the car window, surrounded by my drool. I blinked a couple of times before moving myself away and wiping my face with the sleeve of the top that Maria had given me.

I looked over at Lu, who was focusing on driving. She looked exhausted and I couldn't blame her. She had been worrying about me and I couldn't begin to think what she was going through, having to murder someone else to protect me. If I felt numb just at the thought of shooting the man that I once called my father, I hated to think what she felt.

She must have seen me move, because she turned her head to look at me, with a big grin on her face.

"Hello, sleepy head," she stated, moving her hand off the wheel and holding it out for me to take. I put my hand in hers and linked our fingers together.

"How long have you been driving for?" I asked, as she turned to focus back on the road. It was dark, with nothing but the headlights giving us light.

"About two hours. There is a small town coming up that we need to stop at. I think we should ditch this car.

I can't shake the feeling that they're looking for it," she explained and I knew without her saying it that she was talking about the cops.

"What are we going to do with it?" I asked, as we drove past the welcoming sign.

"Blow it up," Lu responded, her voice suggesting no room to argue.

"Okay," I gulped. She gave my hand a small squeeze.

"We're going to have to go to the gas station. Get hair dye and some other stuff," she said quietly and I just nodded my head.

We sat in silence for a few minutes and Lu pulled into a gravel track to the side of the road. We were at the edge of town, just before all the streetlights started.

"We'll walk from here. You can lean on me if it hurts too much - the station is only a few meters up the road," she explained and I nodded my head again. I wasn't in much pain. The painkillers I was given were working really well.

She parked the car when we were surrounded by trees, the road no longer in view. She let go of my hand to do something with the wires, then the car turned off and leaned back in her seat.

"I'm sorry I left you alone to go to the bathroom," Lu said quietly. I responded by grabbing her hand in mine again.

"You have nothing to be sorry about. It wasn't your fault," I replied, bringing her hand to my mouth to kiss it.

"I should have realized sooner that you were gone for longer than you said. I should have known that he was up to no good, being at a higher grade's prom," she stated, pulling her hand away from me, like she thought she didn't deserve my kiss.

"Lu, it's not your fault," I said again, my voice firm. I didn't blame her at all. I blamed myself because I told her not to follow me. I blamed myself because I wasn't strong enough to fight them off. To fight him off.

"I should have gone with you," she continued and I shook my head.

"If you had come with me, then he would have done something to you too. He had more of his friends with him, but he told them to leave when he cornered me. If you were there, they would have overpowered you," I pointed out and she hung her head. I lifted my hand and put it on her cheek and forced her to look at me.

"The only person to blame is the person that is now dead. I do not blame you for any of it. You saved me. You killed for me. And I love you," I told her and she let out a small sigh and put her hand on top of mine.

"I love you too, Elsie. We're going to get through

this. I don't know how, or what we're going to do from here, but whatever it is, we'll be together. I won't leave you alone again," she said, squeezing my fingers as she took them away from her face.

I gave her a small smile and nodded. I had no idea what would happen now either. I was scared. We were wanted criminals. She had killed two people, including Mr. Miller. I had killed Richard. I believed with all my heart that he was dead. There was way too much blood for him not to be. Not to mention, I had almost killed Olivia.

"We should go," Lu said softly, pulling her hand away from me again and grabbed the duffle bag from the back seat. I nodded, unbuckled my seat belt, opened the door and got out.

The fuel door and trunk clicked open, followed by Lu getting out of the car. She walked over to the fuel tank of the car and unscrewed the cap with one hand, while undoing the zipper of the duffle with the other.
She pulled out her blood coated shirt.

"Is there anything I can do to help?" I asked, which caused Lu to look up.

"Can you start walking to the road? I'm going to need you as far away from here as you can be and since you can't run…" she said softly and I nodded, knowing exactly what it was like being near a blast of a blown-up car.

"Be careful," I told her. I saw her walk toward the trunk and pull out a gas can and a hose.

"I'm going to syphon a little of the gas, to dip the shirt in. Then I'm going to put it in the tank and light it," she explained.

"Like a fuse?" I asked and she laughed.

"Yeah, something like that," she responded.

"Now, go," she insisted, so I turned and started walking back to the road.

I was a lot slower than normal because my hip felt like it was going to pop out of the socket again, but I managed to see the view of the road before I felt Lu's arms wrap around my waist. She pulled me close to her and I instantly felt the need to hurry so I lifted my leg and started hopping as she pulled me along.

The blast sounded and I turned my head to see a flame erupt from beyond the trees.

"Come on," Lu urged and I turned back to focus on where we were going. We continued running (well, I was hopping) along the road, until we reached the town.

We heard sirens of the fire station and could see lights flashing in the distance, coming closer by the second. Lu pulled me behind a parked car, ducking as the fire truck sped past, followed closely by a police car. We hid until the coast was clear and then started to walk to the gas station, which was the only lit up building in the street.

"Did your dad teach you how to do that?" I asked, as Lu took her arm away from my waist and slipped her hand in mine.

"Yeah. I also know how to build a bomb, but I don't ever want to do that," she explained, letting out a small laugh. My heart pounded against my chest. What couldn't she do?

Lu stopped just as we were coming up to the station and she unzipped the bag again. She took out two hats and hair ties. She zipped the bag up before handing them to me.

"Hide your hair under the hat," she explained and I did by tying my hair in a bun on the top of my head. I put the hat over it and pulled it down, shielding my eyes. Lu did the same. The one thing that made us stick out was our hair, especially Lu's and I knew we had to change it.

"When we're in there, I will grab the stuff we need. You go in first and head to the drinks. Grab us a couple of waters," she stated and I nodded. She pulled out the cash she was given by Maria and handed me a note.

"We shouldn't draw attention to ourselves so we're doing this properly," she added. I couldn't help but let out another laugh.

"Stealing is the last thing on my mind," I responded, and Lu just nodded with agreement.

"Good," she said. I couldn't help but smile when I saw her face light up.

We began to walk again, my hip giving me trouble as I felt the pain killer beginning to wear off. I sure hoped that Lu had more and a plan to get out of here in a vehicle. I didn't know how much more walking I could endure.

We walked past a parked pick-up truck with a for sale sign on the windscreen. I noticed Lu flicking her eyes over it and I wondered if she was going to get it. She looked back at me and nodded her head, which made me smile more, considering she just did her weird mind reading thing.

"Ready?" She asked as we approached the entrance, and I nodded my head. She walked a bit ahead of me then, which caused me to slow my walk down. As much as I wanted to be near her, I couldn't keep walking that fast.

When we got inside the station, I went to the back of the store towards the drinks. Lu did her thing, going to the middle aisle, so she disappeared from my view.

My heart pounded at the thought of not seeing her,

remembering what had happened the last time she wasn't with me. But nothing was going to happen this time. We were just buying stuff.

I walked to the fridge and opened it to pull out two bottles of water. I walked to the front of the store and put them on the counter. The man behind it watched me curiously.

He had the news on and when I glanced up, I noticed the TV had a picture of me and Lu on it. I gulped and lowered my head so he couldn't see my face. I pulled the money out of my pocket and slipped it towards him and he took it without saying anything. He handed me back the change and put my bottles in a bag and handed it to me.

"Have a good night," he said and I nodded my head.

"You too. Thank you," I replied, taking the bag and walked out the door.

My heart was pounding furiously in my chest and I felt like I couldn't breathe. The sudden fresh air helped only a little bit, but I could feel the dizziness taking over. Black spots went through my vision and it was difficult to breathe. Our faces were on TV. We were on the news. The picture had shown the two of us with the words 'wanted' and 'armed & dangerous' under it. Lu had stolen a gun, so we were armed. We had killed people, so we were dangerous. I doubled over, feeling bile coming up from my stomach.

I flinched when I felt a hand on my back, but when I felt it rubbing, I relaxed.

"It's ok, Elsie. He didn't recognize us," Lu stated. Immediately I started to feel better just from the sound of her voice. I stood up straight and looked at her, my breathing still fast. She moved her hands so they were on my shoulders and she forced me to look at her.

"He wasn't even watching it. He was playing a game on his phone and had the TV on mute. He had no idea what was going on and he was beyond happy to sell his truck," she explained and she jingled the keys that she had hooked on her finger to show me.

I slowed my breath down, breathing in and out slowly like Lu had shown me so many times before. I nodded and let out a relieved laugh.

"But we do have to be more careful. Our faces are out there now," she continued and I stopped laughing.

"It'll be ok," she said.

Lu pulled me to the parked truck. She opened the door, climbed in, then leaned over to open the passenger side. I walked over to it and got in, pulling out one of the water bottles and took a huge drink of it. Lu started the truck and I looked at the fuel gauge, sighing with relief that it was full. We didn't have to go back in.

"Did Maria give you any painkillers for me to take? It's getting unbearable again," I muttered and Lu nodded, pulling the bags over and putting them between us.

"In the bag. Only take one though, they're addictive," she stated as she put the truck in reverse and drove out of the gas station's parking lot.

I opened the zipper and rummaged around the bag until I found the small bottle of pills. I took one out, replacing the cap and throwing it back in the bag before taking the pill with my water. I leaned back on the seat and let out a small sigh.

"We have about an hour of driving left before we get to the safe house," Lu explained, as she got on the main road and headed towards the highway again.

"Feel free to drool all over the window again," she added and we both laughed.

~.~

When I felt the truck pull into park, I woke up, my face unsticking from the window as I pulled away. I turned to Lu just as she let out a huge yawn.

"We're here," she announced, unbuckling her seat belt. I stretched out my arms, blinking a few times before I was properly awake.

"How long can we actually stay here?" I asked as I

unbuckled my seat belt and grabbed the bag that Lu had bought at the gas station. I saw her bottle of water had been opened and was now lying half empty next to her.

"I'm pretty sure this place is secure enough that we should be able to stay here for a while. Techy has top of the range security here and everything is off the grid, so to speak," Lu explained and I nodded.

We got out of the pick-up truck and a few seconds later, Lu was at my side, holding me around my waist so I didn't put too much pressure on my hip. I had jumped at the sudden contact and I hoped like hell that she hadn't noticed.

"Thanks," I commented and she kissed me on my cheek lightly.

"No problem," she replied and started walking us towards the house.

It was dark, but we could see that there was a light on in the house. I recoiled slightly against Lu and we stopped walking. Who was it? Why was there someone in the house that we were meant to be safe and alone at?

"It'll just be Techy," Lu explained and I nodded my head, feeling slightly silly for reacting that way. I then realized she couldn't see me, so I cleared my throat.

"Right, of course," I answered and we began walking towards the door again.

The door flew open just as we reached the top of the step and Techy was indeed the person who was in the house.

"Didn't you check your phones?" Techy cried, running out the door towards us. Lu unwrapped her arm around me and I took a step back, hiding behind Lu as Techy advanced.

I don't know why, but the look on his face reminded me of the man I had just shot four hours earlier.

"We weren't exactly in the frame of mind to think about answering text messages, Techy," Lu commented. She put her hand in mine and gave it a squeeze.

"They've got the FBI involved. They hired the best hackers to track you," he explained, his voice giving away his anger.

"What? Better than you?" Lu countered, a small scoff sounding in her own voice.

"Yes," he answered, holding out a black bag in his hands.

"Even better than me. I tried to block them out of your GPS, but they got past the firewalls. You've probably led them straight to us," he snapped.

"Put your phones in here. If they haven't got to us yet, this bag will stop them from hacking you," he explained.

I pulled my phone out of my pocket. I couldn't help but check my phone first and I saw there were two messages from Mrs. Taylor.

Mrs. Taylor: He died on the way to the hospital. I don't blame you at all. Please keep safe.
Mrs. Taylor: I've gone into early labor.

I stared at the screen, wondering if the stress I had caused made her go into early labor. I hoped she and the baby were okay. Lu nudged me so I looked up at her. I could see the look on her face because the light from the house was shining on it. She looked sorry for me.

"I'm fine," I told her as I slipped the phone into the bag. Techy closed it up and then walked back into the house without another word.

"It's ok if you're not," she responded and I squeezed her hand in thanks. I knew I should be feeling a lot more than I was. Perhaps I was still in shock, or maybe the painkillers were still working. I felt a bit dazed.

I had killed the man that had raised me. I had never held a gun before, so knew nothing about them. I had shot him by accident, not knowing that I had taken the safety off the gun before pulling the trigger.

Now the man that had abused me for my whole life

was dead and I was his killer. I should have felt sick. I should have felt something. Instead, I felt nothing.

"Seriously. I'm fine," I replied and I leaned forward to kiss Lu's cheek. She gave me a small smile, then led me into the house.

When I walked in, I had to let out a gasp as the kitchen was surrounded by screens. Cameras were all around the property. I could see one screen showing the end of the driveway. One was pointing at the pick-up truck. There was one pointing out towards a lake, which made me wonder where we were. There were about five more, but Techy blocked my view.

"Your stuff is in the second bedroom on the right. If those hackers got past the firewall, you've probably only have about three hours before the cops show up, so I suggest you do what you've got to do then get out of here," Techy declared. I could tell by the sound of his voice that he was still annoyed with us.

"Cut the attitude, Kyle," Lu said in an equally annoyed voice. She stepped forward and clipped him lightly around the head.

"Not even five hours ago, Elsie was sexually assaulted, we killed two people and we were in a car accident. We're sorry we didn't check our phones, but we were too busy getting Elsie's hip fixed and getting the fuck away from the cops to even think about it," she stated, which made me gulp at the way she described our night.

Techy dropped his shoulders, a look of shame showing on his face as he looked from Lu to me, then back at Lu.

"I'm sorry," he announced, moving his chair slightly, so he was looking at the both of us.

"I think I'm annoyed more at myself than anything; I couldn't stop the FBI hackers. I guess I'm not as good as I thought I was," he explained and then looked at me.

"I'm sorry that happened to you, Elsie. All of it," he stated and I awkwardly hung my head.

"It's not your fault," I muttered, feeling my cheeks warm up.

"Seriously though, you two need to move. Do what you got to do and when you come back out I'll have a new phone and some other stuff to give you. Lu, your father is eagerly awaiting your phone call, so I would call him as soon as you're done," he suggested and Lu merely nodded her head and then grabbed my hand to lead me to the bedroom.

As we entered, I noticed that the trunk of wigs was in the room. Obviously this was also the stash house as well as a safe house.

"Even though we have the wigs back, we need to change our hair," Lu announced, taking her hand away from mine and moving it to the bag she was holding. She pulled out a box of black hair dye and some scissors. I looked at the box of dye and gulped. I only ever had black hair when I used the wig but the thought of going to that color permanently was daunting.

"What are the scissors for?" I asked, wondering if I had to cut my hair too. I have always had long hair.

"You're going to cut off the pink," Lu declared and I looked at her with wide eyes.

"It's the most stand out thing about me. We have no choice," she stated and I nodded in agreement.

"I know. It's just so much," I admitted.

Lu took my hand again and led me through the door at the back of the room and into the bathroom. Lu pointed at the toilet, gesturing me to sit down. I sat and watched as Lu opened the box of dye and started getting it ready. It wasn't long before she had finished working it into my hair.

"Now we have to let it set. In the meantime, you can give me a haircut," Lu told me, leaning forward and kissing me on the cheek. I closed my eyes, savoring the moment for a second, before I stood and traded places with her.

I picked up the scissors from the vanity and stood in front of Lu, my heart beating loudly in my chest. I felt like this was all my fault. She wouldn't have to cut off the pink hair if it wasn't for me.

"It's ok, E. Just get it over with and then it'll be done," Lu spoke softly, so I knew she was feeling just as conflicted as I was about it. Her hair was part of her identity.

"Ok," I gulped, then took a step forward and took a strand of her hair in my other hand and started cutting.

After what seemed like forever, Lu's beautiful pink hair surrounded us on the floor. I made sure her now shoulder length hair was even and then set the scissors back on the vanity.

"I'm done," I announced, still feeling guilty as hell. Lu stood up and walked over to the mirror to inspect my handy work.

"Not bad," she declared, turning to me to give me a grin. I knew she was just saying it to make me feel better, but it wasn't working.

"Time to wash out the dye," she announced which led me to let out a sigh of relief. I was itching to have a shower, as I couldn't help but still feel an unwanted presence down there.

I started to get undressed, pausing as I looked at the

finger-sized bruises on my breast. Why did I have to have a physical reminder there? Wasn't it bad enough I couldn't get it out of my head?

I took off my pants and underwear and gasped when I noticed the dried blood. Lu grabbed my hand, which made me move my eyes from between my legs to look at her. She passed a washcloth to me and I took it, with my eyes filling up with tears.

"Can you join me?" I asked and she nodded her head.

"Of course," she said quietly, before letting go of my hand to get undressed.

I moved to the shower and turned it on, waiting for the water to warm up before getting in. I put the washcloth under the water and put some body wash on it. I began to wash the blood away from between my legs, getting more frustrated by the second as the blood wouldn't come off. I started to cry and it wasn't until Lu took the washcloth from me, that I had realized it was no longer blood on my legs, but red from rubbing my inner legs raw.

Lu pulled me into a hug and I leaned into her and cried, watching as the black from the hair dye rinsed off me and down the drain. Lu continued to wash me and I was grateful as I didn't know if I was strong enough to continue.

After we were done, I realized I had even more of a reminder as we noticed that I had more bruises between my legs from where he had forced my legs open.

After the shower Lu and I got dressed using the clothes that we had first stolen. We grabbed the bags that were left for us on the bed and filled them up with more clothes and wigs. I picked up the locket we stole from the jewelers and put it around my neck. I grabbed a pillow, so we had something to sleep with in the truck, then we walked back out to the kitchen where Techy had set up a line of tech gear.

There was a phone, a card, a bracelet, a pile of cash and a bag of cannabis.

Lu walked over to the stuff, pocketing the phone and the card. It looked like the one we had used to get into the shops. Lu lifted up the bracelet.

"What's this?" She asked, looking back at Techy.

"It's a police detector. If they're within 200 yards of you, it will vibrate. The closer they get to you, the more intense the vibration will be," Techy explained. Lu nodded her head and put it on.

"Thanks," she muttered, before turning to the cash and the cannabis. She put those in her bag. She then yawned, which made me realize that she hadn't had any sleep at all.

"I'll drive to wherever we're going next. You need to rest," I said, grabbing onto her hand.

"How are you feeling?" Lu asked and I knew she was worried about the painkiller I had taken..

"I'm ok to drive," I told her, having felt the effects of the drug wearing off about a half an hour ago.

Lu nodded her head and smiled at me. She turned and grabbed two bottles out of a cupboard and filled them up with water.

"Right, we better get out of here then," she mumbled and I nodded, grabbing the keys off the bench.

"Thanks for everything, Techy," I said, turning to look at him.

"Stay safe girls," he muttered and I knew what he was really thinking: try not to get killed by the police. I'm sure they all knew by now that Lu had stolen the detective's gun.

"We will," Lu declared and then she grabbed my hand again and we walked back out to the truck.

Soon we were on our way to our next unknown location, with no clue what would happen next.

Chapter Three

Olivia

I woke up to the sound of beeping surrounding me. I tried to move, but the sharp pain in my chest told me I shouldn't. I opened my eyes, blinking to adjust to the sudden brightness.

There was a blurry figure in my line of sight and I had to focus on it to realize it was my mother.

"Oh, honey!" She cried, causing my head to pound. It felt like I had been hit by a truck. Or perhaps *I* had hit something with my truck?

I tried to sit up again, but there was a gentle push on my shoulders and I saw my mother shake her head.

"Lie still, Olivia. You've got cracked ribs and a concussion," she informed me and I frowned slightly, causing a sharp pain at my hair line. I brought my hand up to my head and felt a dressing around it.

"What happened?" I asked, glancing around and realizing that I was in a hospital room. I looked down and saw that I was wearing a hospital gown.

"You crashed your car into a tree," Mother replied, grabbing my hand with both hers and bringing it to her face.

"Elsie," I whispered, immediately remembering what

happened. I tried to get up again, but my mother gently pushed me back down.

"They escaped custody, honey," She told me and I leaned back against my pillow.

I was stupid for not having an officer come with me to the hospital. I knew it and by the way my mother was speaking, she knew it too.

"Has anyone told you anything?" I asked, my heart pounding against my chest.

This was not the way I wanted this to go down. Why did Elsie have to run? I would have gotten her a lawyer if she had just trusted me.

"I was told that they had escaped before back-up arrived. Thank heaven they got you out of the car before it blew up," she informed me and I could hear the fear in her voice.

"So you don't know if the girls were hurt?" I asked and my mother shook her head.

"Why didn't you wait for back-up?" She asked. I closed my eyes tightly, trying to ignore the pain in my head, my ribs and my heart. I opened them and looked down at my hands, noticing the faint lines of H.E.L.L written on my palm. I felt my heart jump.

"I didn't think it would be an issue. I stupidly trusted them." I whispered, feeling like an idiot just saying it out loud. I had gone against protocol and now there were two dangerous girls on the loose.

"You trusted two criminals?" she asked, her voice filled with doubt.

"I trusted one," I corrected, my heart skipping a beat as I looked at my mother.

"It's her, isn't it?" She asked and my eyes started tearing up. I hadn't told my mother about my suspicions. When I met Elizabeth - Elsie - Neilson two months ago, I developed a feeling deep in my gut that I couldn't ignore. It didn't help that her birthday was the exact date I had given birth to a beautiful baby girl. Which happened to be 18 years ago, today. I had gone against every protocol to find out that she was in fact my daughter and I hadn't even talked to my mother about it.

"You're a stickler for rules, Olivia. You've never done anything this reckless before. There is only one reason I can think of for you to go against protocol and take two girls who have just been accused of murder and attempted murder to the hospital, unaccompanied," she paused. "Is she my granddaughter?"

I let my tears fall as I nodded.

"When did you know?" Mother asked, as she squeezed my hand in comfort.

"About a week after she was first arrested." I was

crying in earnest now. She moved forward and gently put her arms around me. I rested my cheek on her shoulder as I continued to sob.

"She looks like him, Mom. She has his eyes. His nose. She has my hair," I told her through my crying, thinking of Elsie's birth father, my one true love.

"When I was investigating the car incident at the school, she was injured, bleeding. I took a cloth with her blood on it when no one was looking, got it tested against my DNA and it was a match. She's my daughter," I sobbed and then I pulled away and looked at the woman who had made me put my child up for adoption.

"He abused her, Mom. He physically and mentally abused her," I told her. I felt my heart and head pounding profusely. "You told me the family was a nice family, a loving family," I stated and my mother looked at me with wide eyes.

"They were *his* family," Mother explained, her voice sounding horrified.

I never knew to whom Elizabeth went. I was told only that she would be loved and cared for by a family who wanted nothing more than a baby. Because I was only sixteen and still thought my mother knew best, I didn't argue. But it broke me. My baby was the only thing left connecting me to the love of my life who had been killed eight months earlier.

"It was his sister. They seemed perfect, loving," she continued and I started to breathe in and out slowly, to calm my quickened heart and breath.

"She died when Elsie was twelve. She was in and out of the hospital most of Elsie's life. You didn't think to do a background check? Make sure she didn't have a terminal illness before you placed my child in the care of a dying woman and an abusive man?" I questioned, clenching my fists together.

"Olivia, they seemed perfectly fine when we met them. There was no indication that he was abusive, or that she was sick. Your father did a background check and there were no prior arrests for either of them," she stated, putting her hand on top of mine. I looked down at them and I closed my eyes tightly.

"He almost killed her when she was twelve," I pointed out and I heard my mother let out a gasp.

"I didn't know, honey," she whispered, squeezing my hand.

"She didn't have a loving childhood and now she's gone and fallen in love with the first person who showed her any kindness. She's fallen in love with a girl who taught her how to lie, steal, break and enter, how to kill,"

I continued and then I remembered how she looked the last time I saw her.

"She was sexually assaulted," I told my mother and she unclenched my hand, linking her fingers with mine before giving my hand another squeeze.

"That's why I was bringing them to the hospital," I whispered and I wondered where they went instead.

My mother didn't say anything for a moment. She just kept holding my hand and leaned over to the side table that had the remote on it. She pointed it at the little TV on the wall and turned it to the news channel. They were live at the school.

I didn't know how long I had been in the hospital, but it was daytime, so it had been at least eight hours. I leaned back against the pillows and listened carefully.

"It has been confirmed that the headmaster of Neilson High School, Richard Neilson, has died from being shot by his own daughter, Elizabeth Neilson," the anchor reported and my heart froze as her picture came up on the screen.

"She and her lover and partner in crime, Lucita Torres Alvarez, escaped police custody last night and are currently on the run," he continued and a picture of Lu came up.

"Both are considered armed and dangerous and

should not be approached. If you have any information of their whereabouts, please contact the number on the bottom of the screen," he told the viewers. My stomach lurched as the number of my station came up on the screen.

"Armed?" I asked, looking at Mother curiously. She looked away from me, avoiding the question, but I nudged her slightly, causing her to let out a sigh.

"They have your gun," she responded and I groaned. I wasn't going to get out of this with just a slap on the wrist.

"Please remember, viewers, that they may look innocent, but these two young women have murdered three people in the last two weeks. Leave the confrontation to the police and stay safe," he commented. With that, I leaned over to grab the remote from my mother, ignoring my protesting ribs and shut the TV off.

"Elsie's not dangerous," I whispered, looking back at my mother.

"She murdered someone, honey," she pointed out, but I shook my head.
"She shot the man who abused her all her life. She was devastated by it. I don't think she meant to do it," I said quietly. "She's a scared, broken girl who did a stupid

thing, but she's not dangerous. It's Lucita who is the dangerous one," I commented, but my mother looked at me, biting her lip.

"You're going to have to distance yourself from this. You're too emotionally involved as it is. Leave it to the rest of your squad," she urged, but I shook my head.

"I can't, Mom. I have to make sure that when they're found, nothing gets out of hand. I can't lose her again, Mom, I just can't." I squeezed her hand. "I promise, I won't let my emotions get in the way again," I added. My mother just shook her head.

"You have to tell your father," she pointed out and I let out a sigh. Being the captain's daughter was never easy, but maybe it would help me now. If he had known it was his granddaughter at the center of the prom incident, maybe he wouldn't have the calvary lead the search with guns blazing.

~.~

Being yelled at by your captain for misconduct is bad enough but being yelled at by your father is even more painful. I had been released from the hospital only an hour before and went straight to my station.

When I arrived I was told to report to the captain's office immediately. So there I was, standing in my father's office, with two broken ribs and a nasty cut on my forehead, getting told off for not following procedures. As difficult as it was to breathe, I stood at attention, taking in every word.

"Not only did you break protocol by taking those girls unescorted, but you shouldn't even have been involved with any of it to begin with! As soon as you found out who that girl was, you should have excused yourself. Instead, you let your emotions take over your judgement and now they've escaped custody and are armed with your service weapon!" My father, Captain Raymond Swanson bellowed.

I was glad the door was closed, but even then, the team that were still at the station working the case could probably still hear.

"And don't think I don't know how you got that information. Using police resources for personal use is a serious matter," he added and I couldn't help but hang my head. I hoped the lab technician didn't get in trouble.

"And now I have to suspend my own daughter for two weeks without pay for insubordination. You haven't been a detective for long. Do you know how that looks to the Commissioner?" He stated with a disappointed sigh.

He suggested that I sit down, which was a relief because the pain in my ribs was growing. I sat and he did the same, coming down from his 'I'm the Captain' high and becoming the man who loved me no matter what I did.

"Why didn't you tell me you found my granddaughter?" He asked, his eyes wide with curiosity.

"I didn't know how to approach it," I mumbled, feeling ashamed that I had kept it to myself. If I had known how supportive my parents would be about it, I would have been more open. Maybe then we wouldn't be in this mess.

"Do you know what led her to shoot her adoptive father?" He asked, though the look on his face told me he already knew.

"He was physically abusing her," I replied, my heart pounding at the thought of what my daughter had gone through. My dad grimaced.

"She tried to tell me it was an accident. I don't think she has ever handled a gun before. It definitely wasn't intentional, considering it wasn't even her gun," I pointed out. That much I had known from talking to the officers before getting in the car to take Elsie to the hospital. My dad nodded in agreement.

"Yes, the gun belonged to the dead boy's uncle. Seems the young Moretti stole it in order to intimidate the daughter of the man who murdered his father and brother. At least, that's according to one of Moretti's friends who spilled everything while the paramedics cleaned up a cut on his hand," he explained.

I shuddered, thinking that if only Elsie hadn't gotten involved with the young Lucita Torres, then none of this would have happened. Then again, I would have never met my daughter.

"She was sexually assaulted by the Moretti kid," I whispered quietly, as my dad looked away.

"I know. The 'friend' explained everything. He's currently in a cell downstairs on conspiracy to commit rape and murder," he stated.

"Lucita Torres reacted in defense of Elsie," I pointed out.

"But then she stole your gun after escaping custody. Any lawyer could have gotten them a good plea deal, due to the circumstances, but that ship has sailed," he said, pointing out the obvious.

"The investigation you were working on with Elsie's adoptive father, do you have all the files still?" he asked. I nodded.

"Good. Keep them and we can pass them onto her chosen lawyer once the girls come to their senses and turn themselves in," he commented and I couldn't help but be thankful for his optimism.

Unless he declared to the whole police force not to

use excessive force, there was a high chance that if they *didn't* quickly come to their senses, they would come under fire. They were considered dangerous. They were armed. And, though it pained me to acknowledge it, one of the girls wasn't white. That was one of the things I really hated about my work – that not all police officers thought the same when it came to different races.

I must have had a concerned look on my face, because my dad reached over and grabbed my hand.

"They're seventeen and eighteen-year-old children. As long as the gun isn't in view, there will be no need for the police or FBI to use their guns," he stated.

"The FBI is involved?" I gulped. This was the first I had heard of it.

"They have more resources than we do, when it comes to tracking. Besides, they've already crossed state lines with your gun, so it's beyond our jurisdiction," he commented.

"But that means we won't be able to keep in touch with the investigation," I groaned.

"*You* won't be doing anything with the investigation. You're suspended. Which reminds me, I need your shield and ID," he commented, dropping my hand and holding it out for me to hand them over. I complied and he put them in a drawer in his desk.

"I had to recuse myself, obviously, but the Commissioner is aware of the situation and is going to keep me informed. All we can do is wait and hope they turn themselves in," he explained and I nodded, letting out a sigh.

"Now, why don't you go to our house so your mother can look after you. She's been worried sick about you since the moment she heard you were in a car accident. Let her do what she does best and take care of you while you recover," my dad said with a laugh and I grinned.

"You just want her to keep an eye on me to make sure I don't get myself into any more trouble," I pointed out and my dad gave me a smirk and shrugged his shoulders.

"Am I that easy to read?" He asked and I continued to laugh as I nodded.

Then I stood up and waved goodbye as I walked out of his office. I couldn't help but think of Elsie as I left the precinct and did exactly the opposite of what my dad had just instructed me to do. I pulled up Maria Sanchez's address on my phone, knowing that was where the girls would have gone if either of them were injured in the crash.

~.~

Because I no longer had access to a police car, I had to go back to my apartment building to get my old beat-up but reliable Plymouth Horizon.

Soon I was parked outside Maria Sanchez's address and I walked up to the door. I was about to knock, when the door opened, revealing a puzzled, beat-up looking Maria. Like me, she had a cut on her forehead, but hers was darkened by the bottom of a gun shaped bruise. I cringed slightly, knowing that it could have only been my gun that had done that.

"Detective? What are you doing here?" Maria asked, looking behind me to my car, then back at me.

"Please. Call me Olivia. I'm not here on official business," I explained and Maria frowned slightly before stepping aside.

"Come on in," she said, glancing at my own cut as I stepped past her.

"Thank you," I murmured, walking into the entrance area. She walked past me and led me into the family room, which looked like a hurricane had ripped through it.

"What happened?" I asked, gasping as I looked to Maria. She studied me carefully before answering.

"You're not on official business?" She asked again and I shook my head.

"No, it's personal," I clarified and she nodded her head.

"The girls came here," Maria started and I looked around once more before settling my gaze on her bruise.

I couldn't help but wonder if it was a staged hit, considering I knew how much Maria loved her niece.

"And let me guess, they forced you to look after one of them," I asked, doubtfulness laced in my voice. Maria pressed her lips together.

"Look, I know how much you love Lucita. You don't have to pretend with me. I know you would have nursed either of the girls, no matter the consequences. Like I said I'm not here as an officer of the law. In fact, I was suspended because of my connection to them. I went against procedure because of it," I told her.

Maria relaxed slightly, then gestured for me to sit down on the couch, which was the only piece of furniture left untouched.

"Would you like a coffee?" She asked and I nodded my head with a smile.

"That would be lovely, thank you," I answered and she walked towards the kitchen.

"Make yourself at home. Sorry for the mess, I was in the process of cleaning up," she stated, before disappearing from view.

I sat back against the back of the couch, wincing

slightly at the pain in my ribs. I had been given pain killers, but I was trying to get by without them, because I wanted to be coherent while trying to find my daughter before anyone else.

A few moments later, Maria came back into the room with two mugs of coffee. She handed me one and then sat down next to me. I took a sip.

"You mentioned a connection to the girls?" Maria started, breaking the awkward silence. I nodded my head and lowered the mug.

"A connection to Elsie to be exact," I said quietly. I had never mentioned this out loud to anyone other than my parents before.

"She's my daughter," I explained and Maria looked at me with a blank stare before her eyes widened with realization.

"You gave her up?" She asked and I nodded my head.

"I didn't want to. I was sixteen years old and her birthfather had just been killed in a fire," I explained, my heart squeezing tight as I spoke about the one true love of my life.

"My parents made me, told me they had found a nice family. I had no idea that it was her birthfather's sister that they had let adopt her. I had no idea that Richard Neilson would go on to abuse her," I explained, my voice pitching slightly as I felt myself starting to cry. Maria set her mug down on a side table and put her hand gently on my lap in comfort.

"All those things I told you at the hospital… you didn't say anything," she said quietly and I hung my head slightly.

"I didn't actually know for certain then, but I had a strong suspicion. It took everything in me not to react to what you were telling me. Lucita was in the next room. I saw her sneak in when we started talking. I had to put my feelings aside to talk to her," I explained and Maria took a deep breath.

"Who was hurt? Why did they come here?" I asked, though I had a feeling I knew, considering Elsie had her legs in an awkward position when I crashed into the tree.

"Elsie. She dislocated her hip," Maria explained and I groaned.

"She doesn't seem to catch a break," I commented, my voice breaking even more.

I looked down at my coffee for a moment, wondering how I was going to word what I wanted to say next. Sexual assault wasn't something that was easy to talk about. I felt myself tear up just thinking about what Elsie had gone through.

"Did you, um… was there any evidence that could

help Elsie and Lu's defense if they need it?" I asked, looking back at Maria, my eyes so full of tears that they started leaking down my face. Maria took my coffee from my hands, putting it on the table next to hers and then put her hands in mine.

"Yes there was. It was clear that there had been an assault. Nothing could dispute that," she explained quietly and I let out a sob. Maria then moved her hands to my shoulders and pulled me into a hug.

"I just wish I had told Elsie sooner. Maybe then the girls would have known that they had someone in law enforcement on their side. That they would have known that I would do anything to get them the best outcome for their situation," I said quietly, as I hugged Maria back. She rubbed my back and I leant back to look at her.

"Do you have any way to contact them? I've tried both their phones, but it goes straight to voice message. I assume they've gotten rid of them by now," I stated. Maria let go of me and I moved back as she reached for our cups before answering me.

"I know someone who can get in touch with them," she told me as she passed mine back to me. I took another drink.

"But I can only pass on a message. It's up to them to contact you," Maria explained and I nodded my head.

"Anything will help. Thank you, I appreciate it," I said, finishing my coffee.

Maria took the cup from me, putting it back on the side table along with hers. She got a pen and paper and handed it to me.

"Write your message on here and I will make sure the girls get it," she told me and I nodded, gripping the pen tightly in my hand, as I hovered over the paper, thinking of what I wanted to write.

Elsie, I should have told you this when I first figured it out. I am your birthmother. I know it's a lot, but I wanted you to know that you have someone who is on YOUR side. Please contact me, so we can talk. Please know that I am going to do whatever I can to make sure you are safe. Please consider turning yourselves in, before it gets out of hand. Love, Olivia Swanson.

I folded the paper once I had finished writing it and gave it to Maria, who put it straight into her top pocket.

"I'll pass this on as soon as you leave," Maria promised and I nodded my head gratefully.

"Thank you," I said, smiling. I stood up and Maria did too. We started walking towards the door.

"I, um, I won't be arrested for aiding and abetting, will I?" Maria asked, her face reddening slightly. I couldn't help but laugh.

"As far as I'm concerned, I was never here, so I don't know anything. Besides, you helped my daughter, *again*. I have nothing but gratitude towards you, so rest assured no one will hear anything from me," I told her, as I took her hands in mine and gave them a reassuring squeeze.

"But, please, if you do hear anything, please contact me," I added, moving my hand to my pocket to pull out a business card, which had my cell number on it.

Maria took it and I smiled as she pocketed it with the note and nodded her head.

"Of course," she noted.

I grinned at her and walked back to my beat-up car, feeling closer to finding Elsie than I was before.

Chapter Four

Lu

When I opened my eyes, I was grateful that Elsie had thought about grabbing a pillow before we left the safe house, as it was the only thing shielding me from the blinding sun that was coming through the truck window.

I blinked a couple of times to orient myself, finding that we were parked in the middle of some trees. I looked over to Elsie, but I saw that she had used my legs as a pillow and was sound asleep. I put my hand on her shoulder to wake her and she jumped at my touch. I quickly brought my hand away from her, noting this was the second time she had done that.

"Sorry, I didn't mean to frighten you," I said quietly, running my fingers through her now black hair as she opened her eyes to look at me.

"I know," she responded, with a smile.

"I think I got us a four-hour head start, but I couldn't go on anymore," she explained, yawning as she sat up.

"I don't think anyone can see us from the road. I went quite a way in," she added, looking around then back at me.

"Do you know where we are?" I asked and she laughed as she shook her head.

"No idea," she replied and I pulled out my new phone and looked at the GPS.

"We're about 10 miles from the nearest town. We probably need to fill up," I said quietly. I heard Elsie take a deep breath and I looked at her.

"They'll be looking for two of us, so when we get to town, you need to drop me off somewhere and go get the gas. Will you be ok with that?" I asked. Elsie nodded, though I noticed the worried look on her face.

"As long as you're quick, no one is going to recognize you with black hair. They're looking for a blond, remember?" I pointed out and she nodded again.

"I know. I just can't help but think about the last time we weren't together," she replied. My heart skipped a beat. I grabbed her hand and brought it to my lips.

"Nothing is going to happen to you, E. If you drop me off just down the road, I will walk to the station and I will be there by the time you finish paying. You can keep the gun, if you think that will help you feel safer," I said quietly, but Elsie shook her head.

"No thank you, I'll be fine. I never want to touch a gun again," she said, shuddering. I gave her a knowing look, kissing her hand again.

"You had to do what you did, Elsie. He wasn't going to stop. Besides, you probably saved Mrs. Taylor's baby growing up being abused," I whispered, knowing that she was probably overthinking it in her brain like I had after I killed the jewelry store owner.

Elsie took her hand from mine and turned to start the truck. Clearly she didn't want to talk about it anymore.

She put the truck in reverse and maneuvered it until we were facing the opposite direction and then started driving towards the road.

"Who taught you how to drive anyway? Your father didn't seem the type," I asked quietly. Elsie let out a scoff.

"Drivers Education, plus I watched you," Elsie replied, as we made our way along the dirt track. It wasn't long until we met the road and Elsie signaled, making sure the road was clear before turning.

"Well you're good at it," I stated and she grinned at me, before focusing on the road again.

"What are we going to do once we fill up? Carry on driving?" Elsie asked, just as her stomach rumbled.

"Well, I was thinking we could find a motel," I stated quietly. Elsie looked at me for a second, frowning.

"I'm guessing not a five-star one," she said, with a hint of humor in her voice.

"Well, no. Maybe more like the ones that have a 'don't ask, don't tell' policy," I replied, giving her a slight smirk.

"I could do with a proper sleep and we need to eat," Elsie agreed, turning to look at the road again.

"Me too," I added, my own stomach rumbling.

Elsie moved her hand down between us and I took it in mine. We sat in silence as we made our way into the town. When, according to the GPS, the gas station was just a bit further along the road, Elsie pulled over to the side.

"Be careful," she said quietly, as she leaned over to close the distance between us. I met her halfway and we kissed.

"You too," I replied as I moved back from her. I opened the door and got out, taking the bag with the gun in it and pulling the strap over my shoulders.

"I'll see you soon," I promised and gave her a reassuring smile.

I closed the door and walked over to the side of the road, watching as Elsie drove the truck forward again towards the gas station. I walked slowly, looking around cautiously. The town wasn't overly busy, but I was watching people, looking for any signs of recognition as they looked at me. Many people just looked briefly at me, then turned their attention away. I breathed a sigh of relief, realizing that I wasn't on anyone's radar.

My bracelet vibrated and my heart skipped a few beats as it got more intense and quickly. I didn't have time, nor anywhere to hide as a police cruiser drove past me. I kept my gaze ahead, trying to look just like anyone else on the street, but I'm sure if they looked close enough they would see me sweating, not to mention they would probably hear my heart beating very fast and loud.

The cruiser drove past without slowing down, which made me breathe out a deep sigh of relief.
I looked back just as they turned the corner and I quickened my pace. I pulled out my phone to look up the whereabouts of a cheap motel, trying to memorize the route.

When I arrived at the gas station, Elsie was coming out of the shop with her arms full of drinks and food. She grinned when she saw me and we reached the truck at the same time. I opened the door for her and she put her groceries on the middle seat, before pulling me into a fierce hug.

"I saw a cop car drive past. I'm so happy to see you," she stated. I laughed as I hugged her back.

"They didn't even give me a second look. I don't have pink hair anymore," I stated and I rubbed her back just as she let me go.

"Let's get out of here," I exclaimed and she nodded.

"Do you want me to drive? I think I know where a no-tell motel is," I stated and she nodded. She walked around to the other side of the truck and got in. I followed suit and we were on our way again.

It wasn't long until we reached the hotel. I parked and Elsie started gathering our things. I grabbed a few hundred-dollar bills and looked towards the reception area.

"I'll be right back," I promised Elsie, grinning at her, as I started to walk towards it.

When I got there, I had to take a deep breath before going inside, because the smell was horrific. Clearly they didn't care about cleanliness

"One double room please," I said, pushing two hundred across the counter.

"I don't know how long we will be here, but we don't want to be disturbed," I stated to the man. He leaned forward and grabbed the money off the counter. He nodded and reached for a set of keys.

"Room 4," he stated and handed the keys to me.

"You've got enough here for 4 nights," he said. I nodded. I didn't think we would be there that long, but it was good to know.

I left the reception area, letting out my breath as I got into the fresh air again. I hated to think what the room would be like. I shuddered slightly as I walked back to Elsie and the truck. I grabbed everything else that Elsie couldn't carry and led her to our room.

When I opened the door, I gasped at the sight of it. There were left over cigarette butts on a plate on a table in the corner. The bed was not made and it looked like it had been used for some questionable sex games.

"Gross," Elsie exclaimed and I laughed. I picked up the plate of cigarette butts and put the stuff I was holding down on the table.

"Put the stuff here. I'll give it a quick clean up. I saw that they had fresh linen in the reception room," I explained. Elsie nodded and put her stuff on the table. I walked back outside and threw the contents of the plate out the door, adding to the thousands of butts on the ground.

I walked towards the reception again, putting the plate down on an outside table on the way past.

"I'm glad you clean up after guests," I stated to the man who watched me as I grabbed new bed linen. He just grunted in response. I saw that there was a few cleaning products and trash bags on the bottom shelf, so I grabbed those as well.

"At least make the beds, no one needs to see evidence that people had a good time," I said as I exited the room again. When I got back to our room, Elsie had already stripped the bed. She had left the old linen outside the door. I'm sure it was probably going to stay out there for the entire duration of our stay.

"I guess this is going to be the life we have to get used to?" Elsie asked, as she opened the bedside drawer. She wrinkled her nose and pulled out a used syringe, carefully holding it between her thumb and index finger.

"Unfortunately," I responded, holding out a trash bag, into which Elsie dropped the syringe. She shut the drawer and took the linen from me. I dropped the bag on the floor.

Elsie unfolded the bottom sheet and I went to the other side of the bed so we could start making it together.

Once the bed was made, I took the cleaning products to the bathroom. I gagged at the sight of it. Needles and cigarette butts were everywhere. I pulled on the gloves I had grabbed and started picking them up, carefully putting them in the trash bag. I wiped every surface and cleaned the toilet, while Elsie cleaned out the mini-fridge and cleaned the kitchenette area.

When we had finished cleaning, we were both starving and tired. We put the trash out the door next to the used bed linen and then we washed our hands.

When we sat down to eat the food Elsie grabbed at the

gas station, it truly felt like the first meal we had eaten in days. It didn't take us long to eat.

I decided it was best to call my dad at that point; no doubt he was worried because he hadn't heard from me yet. He answered on the first ring. I told him what had happened from my side of things and he told me he was going to do everything he could to keep me safe. He reminded me that I could turn myself in at any point and he would get the best lawyer that his money could buy.

When I hung up, I felt guilty about the position I had put him in, considering he had only just told me that he was afraid to lose me to the system.

I grabbed the gun from my bag and placed it on the bedside table, which Elsie tried to ignore. I grabbed her hand, pulling her to the bed. Soon we had settled in, with me using the pillow we had brought with us. Elsie had chosen to use her usual spot on my chest as her pillow and it didn't take long for the two of us to fall asleep.

~.~

I had thought that if anything was going to wake me up, it would be Elsie's tossing and turning. Once I realized that she was still fast asleep and wasn't having those 'throw you awake' kind of nightmares, I settled back to sleep myself. No, the thing that woke me up was the banging at the door.

"I told you we didn't want to be disturbed!" I yelled, as I begrudgingly sat up on the bed. Elsie had just awoken too and was rubbing her eyes.

"What's going on?" she mumbled, still in a sleepy state. I put one arm around her and with the other I shoved my phone down my bra and then grabbed the gun and pointed it to the door.

"I don't know, babe," I replied, as the banging got louder.

I shifted from the bed just as the door banged open, falling off its hinges. I flicked the safety off the gun, ready to start shooting at who ever came in, but for a split second, I considered whether shooting at armed police was a good idea. The moment of hesitation cost me, because it wasn't the police who came barging through the door. It was a gang of men.

They rushed in with their own guns cocked and pointing straight at us. We were outnumbered. Elsie cowered into me and gripped me close as I lowered my gun. I wasn't going to win this fight.

"What the fuck?" I demanded, my eyes locking on to the gun that the closest man was now holding towards my face.

"Think you would get away with killing my nephew

did you? *Dovrei farti saltare il cervello*," he stated and I gulped. This was the Morettis' gang. Somehow, they had found us.

"But I won't blow your brains out. My brother wants you alive," continued the man, who nodded at his other gang members. They walked past him and pulled Elsie and me roughly out of the bed.

The gun was forced out of my hand and then a sack was thrown over my head, blackness surrounding me. Elsie must have had one thrown over her head too, because she let out a scream. I tried to hold onto her, but I was pulled out of her grasp.

"Don't hurt her," I screamed, but all I got in response was a hit to the head with what felt like the bottom of a gun. Pain pounded from the spot it hit and stars came into view.

"Fuck!" I cried. I was roughly pulled towards what I assumed was the door, because my shoulder hit the door frame on the way out.

I could hear Elsie crying behind me and I tried to get out of the grip of the goon who held me, but he only gripped me tighter.

"If you don't stop fucking moving, I'll kill your girl right now. It's you the boss wants, not this bitch," he spoke in such a low tone, I knew he was whispering it in my ear. I stilled immediately. The man laughed and pushed me to the car.

"How did you find us?" I asked, as I was thrown against something hard. I winced as I tried to move my hand around to feel where I was.

"It didn't take a genius to think you would go to the nearest town first. Only took one bill to get the boy you bought the truck off of to start talking," the man who had first pointed the gun at us explained.

"Was my lucky day when he said he had forgotten to take his old man's GPS tracker off the truck before selling it," he added with a laugh. I groaned. Why didn't I think about searching it for a tracker? God damn it, my dad was literally going to kill me when he got his hands on my soon-to-be-dead body.

Elsie was still crying and I could hear the men talking amongst each other. I tried to listen, but my pounding head blocked most of it out. I did manage to catch someone say, "shut her up," which made my heart skip a beat. *Please don't hurt her, please don't hurt her.*

There was some ruffling sounds and soon Elsie's crying stopped.

"What did you do to her?" I cried, moving against the hands that were holding me tight again.

"She's fine. She's just having another sleep," the man holding me sneered, then I heard the trunk of a car open and I was pushed inside it.

I felt a body underneath me and all I could hope was that it was Elsie. My legs were pushed in behind me and the sack was pulled off my face. I squinted as I adjusted to the brightness and saw the man who had first pointed his gun at me.

"I hope you don't mind small dark places, because you're going to be in here for a while. Enjoy the peace while it lasts, because when Giovanni gets ahold of you, you'll wish you'd never been born," he sneered, slamming the trunk shut, plunging Elsie and I into total darkness

Chapter Five

Elsie

My head was pounding when I woke up. I tried to see where I was, but it was all darkness. I frowned, trying to remember what had happened and I gasped when I remembered the men bursting into the hotel room.

"Lu?" I cried out and I felt a hand move over to my mouth.

"Shh," Lu pleaded and I felt something being pulled from underneath my head, but it still didn't help with the darkness.

"They'll hear you and know you're awake," Lu continued. I nodded my head and she moved her hand away from my mouth and replaced it with her lips.

"What's happening?" I asked, when she lifted her lips away from mine and rested her head on my chest. I tried to move, but I could tell we were in a confined space, as I hit something solid on either side of me. Wherever we were, it was hot and our breathing seemed to be shallow.

"We are in a trunk of a car," Lu explained and I felt my heart stop. Lu moved her hand, patting around until it finally landed on mine and she linked our fingers.

"I'm sorry I hesitated," Lu whispered. I thought back to how she just lowered her gun as the men charged in.

"I thought they were going to be cops and I didn't want to you know, become a cop killer," she explained. I gave her hand a gentle squeeze.

"We would have been dead in seconds if you had taken that shot. I'm not sorry, so neither should you be," I replied, trying to move my leg ever so slightly to get it out from its current numb state.

"I never thought I would be in this situation, but I'm glad it's with you," I said softly after a moment of silence. Lu laughed and she moved her head closer to mine to kiss me again.

"What do you think they're going to do to us?" I whispered, my heart pounding faster just at the thought. If they were anything like the rest of the Moretti family, would they try and rape us again? I shuddered and I felt Lu squeeze my fingers reassuringly.

"It's me they want to hurt. I'm the one who killed Dante. They know I was involved with his father's and brother's murder too," Lu responded and I wished I could see her face. Instead, I lowered my head until I felt her head against my lips and kissed it softly.

"We have to get out of here," I pointed out the obvious.

"Do you still have your phone, or did they take it from you?" I asked, remembering how she put it in her bra before she grabbed the gun.

Lu swore and unlinked her fingers with mine and then suddenly there was a bright light bringing her face into view. We both blinked a couple of times to adjust ours. I then noticed she had a dark spot above her eye and I knew that was from a hit she got after telling them not to hurt me. I cringed.

"Techy has already messaged me," Lu informed me and she awkwardly moved over me so she could text with two hands.

"He says he's been tracking me and he is wondering why we were heading back to Sutton," Lu told me. She paused as she texted something back to him.

"I told him the Morettis have us and that we're in a trunk of an unknown car," Lu explained. Her phone vibrated and she didn't say anything as she read the new text.

"He's just said that my dad and the gang are on their way and not to worry," Lu replied and I could see the look on her face as she read something else and I could tell it wasn't something good. She shut the phone and put it back in her bra, darkness surrounding us once again.

"There isn't much battery left," she explained softly and she moved her hand back to mine.

"Now's probably not the best time to mention it, but

just in case there isn't another chance," Lu started, but then paused, making my heart pound with anticipation.

"What is it? Don't stop like that, just spit it out. Can't be as bad as finding out my father isn't my real father," I said with a slight laugh. Lu shifted uncomfortably next to me and I had to wince when her elbow dug into my stomach. I was about to say something, but she moved it.

"Well, maybe it is. It's about your birth mother," Lu stated and my heart stopped pounding.

"Did Techy tell you who it was?" I asked, wondering if he had been looking, because Mateo had told him what Richard Neilson had told everyone in the school.

"Yes. And I don't think you're going to like who it is," Lu responded. I groaned slightly.

"Come on, L, the anticipation is killing me. Just tell me," I pleaded. Lu squeezed my hand.

"It's Olivia," she declared. I blinked a few times wondering if I had heard the name right.

"As in Detective Swanson?" I asked, picturing her in my mind. I mean she did have blond hair like me. And blue eyes. I frowned.

"Why didn't she tell me?" I whispered, tears forming in my eyes. Lu squeezed my hand again.

"It would explain why she was so anxious to get you back on her good side," Lu pointed out and I remembered back to the day before prom.

"Why she called you 'our girl'," Lu continued. "Why she kept giving you the disappointed mother look when she arrested you," she added. I remembered back to all those times. It kind of made sense now.

"Ok, maybe she was trying to tell me, without actually telling me?" I said quietly.

"It makes sense," Lu replied, just as my head hit the side of the trunk as the car turned a corner.

"Ow," I announced, wishing I could move my hand to rub it.

"We're off the straight road, we must be close to wherever we are going," Lu said and my mind shifted from the blond detective who was my mother, to consider worst-case scenarios.

"Are we going to die?" I asked, my voice breaking as tears flowed down my cheeks.

"Not if my father gets to us first. He will never let that happen," Lu told me, squeezing my hand.

The car stopped and we could hear gravel moving under the feet of the men as they exited the car. The trunk opened and two men looked down on us. We squinted at the sudden brightness, but we didn't have time to adjust as we were brutally pulled from the car.

My leg stopped me from exiting gracefully and I ended up falling face first into the gravel. The man who had grabbed me laughed and pulled me roughly to my feet.

"Clumsy, this one," he said. I glared at him as I spat the loose stones out of my mouth. Blood splatted on the ground next to me, so I knew my mouth was bleeding. He moved his sleeve over his thumb and he wiped the blood away from my lips, causing Lu to let out a growl.

"Don't touch me," I snapped, though my tears and squeaky voice betrayed the bravado I was trying to show.

"Maybe a little bit feisty too?" he added, a look of interest in his eyes. I felt like I was going to be sick. Not again. Before I could get a good look around, the sack went back over my head.

"Don't say a word, or you'll go for another little sleep," the man told me, gripping onto my upper arm forcibly.

"That goes for you too," said the other man who had Lu. We stayed silent as we were escorted to wherever we were going. I wasn't going to give those men any reason to think we were easy targets. I'm sure Lu was thinking the same thing.

It wasn't long until we were forced down onto what felt like chairs. My arms were tied around something behind me and my legs were tied to the chair legs. The sacks were ripped off our heads.

From what I could tell we were in a basement. I looked over my shoulder to find that Lu was behind me and our chairs had been tied to a pole.

"Giovanni will be here in a moment. He's just returning from burning down your father's last club. He won't have any more products left to sell and nowhere to sell it from. Isn't that a shame," he mocked, as he slapped Lu across her face. I let out a cry, but Lu kept her brave face on and spat at the man's feet.

"He'll bounce back," Lu bit back and I closed my eyes just as I heard another slap. This time Lu let out another growl in pain.

"Now's not the time to be a mouthy bitch," the man who had been hitting her said.

The other man who had been watching carefully walked up to his friend and slapped him on the shoulder playfully.

"Maybe we should teach *la cagna* a lesson," he said, a smirk rising on his face as he looked at me. The other man turned his attention to me also, which Lu noticed.

"No, leave her alone, I'll behave, I promise," Lu started, but it didn't matter. The man who had hit Lu came closer to me and punched me in the stomach. I cried out as I tried to double over but being tied down made it difficult.

"Please! Stop it!" Lu begged, but the man laughed and did it again, this time nearer to my ribs, winding me completely. I couldn't breathe. Darkness blotched my eyes as I struggled to breathe again. The men must have noticed this, because they stepped away.

"If we hear a peep out of either of you before Giovanni turns up, we'll add more cuts and bruises to your bitch's pretty face," the man who punched me promised. I wasn't sure if he was talking to me or Lu, but I had a feeling that promising to hurt me made more of an impact on Lu than it did if he had promised to hurt her.

"We'll be good," Lu promised and I let out a sigh of relief as I started breathing again. The men left, shutting and locking the door behind them.

"Where is your father?" I whispered as quietly as I could.

"They can't be too far away. They still haven't taken my phone, so they'll know our exact location. It won't be long now," Lu replied just as quietly.

I tried to move my fingers to see if I could reach for Lu's, but they must have tied our hand up in different places around the pole, because I couldn't feel anything but air. I felt a poke in my back and I relaxed, knowing that at least there was some kind of touch between us.

"Are you ok?" she asked. I nodded my head, but remembered she couldn't see me, so I cleared my throat before answering.

"Just a bit winded," I replied. He had punched me right where I was missing one rib, so of course the hit landed on my half lung.

"I'm sorry," she whispered, I could tell from the sound of her voice that her own bravado was breaking.

"Stop apologizing. We both got ourselves in this mess. It's not just your fault," I reminded her. I tried to turn my head to look at her.

"Look at me," I said, even though it was near impossible, considering we were tied back-to-back. I could sense her awkwardly turning her head, so I could just see her from the corner of my eye.

"This is not your fault," I said again and she closed her eyes but nodded in agreement.

"Ok," she noted quietly and I could tell she didn't believe me.

"This would never have happened if I just let you come to the bathroom with me. If it's anyone's, it's mine," I continued and her eyes flew open and she tried to move her neck more, but she couldn't.

She let a small cry of frustration and I felt her fingers

poke further into my back like she was trying to squeeze my fingers like she normally did.

"Don't say that. I should have gone with you anyway," Lu replied and I just shook my head.

"Let's not play the blame game again," I told her and she pulled her fingers from my back slightly.

"You're right. It's not going to help the situation," she replied.

I was about to speak when the door flew open once again and in walked a new man followed by the two other men that brought us in here. This must be Giovanni.

The man walked up to Lu and grabbed her face roughly in his hands, forcing her to look at him. I cringed, but Lu kept her brave face on and stared at the man in front of her.

"So this is the girl that has brought several members of my family down. Almost a whole family. The only one left is a broken widow and childless mother," spat Giovanni. My heart pounded in my chest and I felt hopeless as I was forced to listen.

"Get the girl," ordered Giovanni to his men and within seconds, I was free from my ropes and I was being held against the man who had wiped the blood from my lips, with a knife to my throat. My back was pressed hard against his body and I cringed the moment I realized that he was turned on by this.

"Maybe we should take away the one you love, huh? An eye for an eye?" Giovanni suggested, letting go of Lu's face so violently that the back of her head hit the pole. My heart pounded so ferociously against my chest that I was scared it was going to cause a heart attack.

He walked closer to me and grabbed the knife from his goon and pushed the sharp blade into my throat.

"Both my nephews were killed by a stab wound to the throat," Giovanni mused out loud.

Lu let out a muffled groan as the other man had made his way over to her, to force her to look in the direction of us.

"Please, don't hurt her. She has done nothing wrong," Lu was no longer stoic as she cried out her plea.

"Neither did my nephews," Giovanni commented, in the same musing tone.

"They were rap-," Lu started, but she stopped talking when she saw that Giovanni had pressed deeper into my skin and I was now bleeding.

I whimpered, trying my hardest not to let the fear overtake me. If I struggled, I knew that I would be satisfying both of the men and there was no way I could let that happen.

"Please. They killed my mother," Lu cried.

I closed my eyes tightly as I felt the sting of the blade.

"And you killed my brother. My nephew. Then you had to go and kill my youngest nephew. That's three. Now, don't worry, after I've killed your girlfriend, you'll be next," Giovanni explained and I felt the knife plunge in deeper. Lu screamed and I opened my mouth to start screaming too, but then the door blasted open and shots rang out.

I felt warm liquid spray over the back of me and the man who was holding me fell by my feet. A second later Giovanni's blood squirted over my face and he dropped down also. The third man was down too. I blinked, shocked at the sudden change in my situation.

I slowly pulled my hand up to my throat and put my hand around the handle of the knife.

"Don't!" cried Lu, who had been cut free by Mr. Torres. He tried to hold onto her, but she had already pushed him aside and ran to me.

"Don't pull it out," she told me, her face full of tears, bruises and blood. I didn't know if any of the blood was hers. She put her hand around mine that was around the knife.

"We have to keep it steady. It might have hit an artery," she explained and I could see the panic in her eyes.

"Am I going to die?" I asked her, remembering the way Dante had died.

"No," she replied, as she gently lifted my fingers off the handle.

"We have to move," Mr. Torres bellowed after a second, putting his hand gently on Lu's back. He looked at me with concern, but then pointed at the door.

"I take it you can walk yourself out of here?" He asked, taking off his sweater, folding and twisting it until it looked like a round donut which he put around the knife handle. Some of the blade was still sticking out, so I didn't think he had pressed the knife hard enough to cause any real damage, so I was sure I could walk without causing more.

"I think so," I whispered and he nodded his head once before taking Lu's hand and pulling her out the door. Lu quickly grabbed onto mine just before they left me completely.

I was glad that the sweater/knife holder was working well, because it was more like a run than a walk. I was sure my bouncing up and down wasn't doing me any good, but I was still conscious so that was a win.

When we got out of the building, we continued to run towards a line of motorcycles and cars. When we reached them, Mr. Torres let out a sigh of relief.

A second later the building exploded. I ducked down instinctively, but I felt hands around me and I was pulled back up to my feet.

I looked at who was holding me and had to blink a few times, wondering if I was seeing things due to a lack of blood or something.

"Detective Swanson?" I asked, confused, before it all became too overwhelming and everything around me went black.

Chapter Six
Olivia

Since I was holding onto Elsie already when her legs buckled from under her, she fell right into my arms. Jorge Torres pulled away from his daughter's embrace and hurried over to us, grabbing onto Elsie's feet so we could carry her to the nearest car.

"We have to get her to the hospital," I said, panicked. The knife that was sticking out of her neck was held in place by the makeshift compression dressing, but it didn't stop the bleeding that was coming from the first cut.

"Not the hospital," Jorge grunted in response. Lu hurried over to our side, tears rolling down her cheeks.

"We have - to go - to Maria's clinic!" Lu yelled between her sobs. We carried Elsie to the nearest car, which was Jorge's.

I had forced my way into his car as he was leaving his home to come to this abandoned factory, just on the outskirts of Sutton.

He didn't want me to come. In fact, he threatened to shoot me if I didn't leave his car, but I wouldn't budge and told him I wasn't going to give up a chance to help my daughter. He must have seen the seriousness in my eyes, because he begrudgingly allowed me to come with him.

Now that I had seen and heard everything he'd just done to get my daughter and Lu out of that factory, I knew things were going to get even more complicated. There was no way he was going to let me leave, as I had witnessed him committing several crimes.

We piled into the back of the car where I sat cradling Elsie's head on my lap. Lu sat down next to me, holding onto Elsie's hand in distress.

"I'm so sorry," she whispered through her tears as she leaned as close as she could to Elsie without hurting her. My heart pined at the sight.

Jorge hurried back around the front of the car and jumped in. It wasn't long until he had the car zooming down the gravel road towards the main road, followed by his gang's many motorcycles.

"What happened?" I asked, running my fingers through Elsie's now-black hair. That in itself made my heart flutter, as it made her look more like her father.

"They wanted to teach me a lesson," Lu sobbed. She looked at me, everything in her eyes telling me she felt responsible.

"They wanted to hurt her because I love her. Because of what happened with Dante," she continued. I moved my other hand and grabbed Lu's empty one. I gave it a reassuring squeeze. She looked at me and her sobs grew louder, which made Jorge look back at her in the rearview mirror. I could tell that he was concerned for his daughter. It wasn't only Lu who had got taught a lesson, as she looked like she had been hurt too.

"I tried to explain what happened, but they wouldn't hear it. They didn't believe me when I told them it was to stop him from assaulting her," she cried. I squeezed her hand again.

I looked down at Elsie, noticing her face was clammy. I moved my hand from her head and pulled a handkerchief from my pocket to wipe away the sweat, being careful not to jostle her.

"Can you go faster?" I snapped at Jorge, who looked at me in the rearview mirror with an annoyed look on his face.

"You've already committed several murders and arson in front of me, what's speeding compared to that?" I pointed out. He narrowed his eyes, but he must have stepped harder on the gas, because as we turned the corner I had to move one hand from Lu's to support Elsie's head while I moved the other one to hold the handle above the car window to stay upright.

"*No me digas qué hacer, chica,*" Jorge spat, as he adjusted the car and sped down the now straight road.

"First of all, I'm not a girl. And I'll tell you what to do if it means getting my daughter to Maria faster," I spat back. I saw his eyes widen slightly, probably surprised that I knew what he was saying, but then he narrowed them again and focused on the road again.

I looked back down at Elsie again, returning to wipe away the sweat that was seeping down her face.

Lu's crying at quieted, but she had brought Elsie's hand to her lips and was whispering an old Spanish prayer about healing. I closed my eyes, saying the words along with her in my mind. I wasn't Spanish myself, by any means, but it was one of the first languages I chose to learn before becoming a cop.

"*Amén*," I said with Lu as she finished the prayer. I opened my eyes and we looked at each other, her eyes searching mine for a moment.

"Why didn't you tell her sooner?" Lu asked, and I let out a small sigh and looked back down at my daughter, who was sweating more. I dabbed the cloth gently on her forehead.

"I was scared," I admitted. Jorge turned another corner and I had to brace myself again.

"I was scared of how she would react, considering everything that was happening in her life," I continued.

"Did you know?" She asked, and I looked up at her.

"Know where she was this whole time? No. I only began to suspect and only found out for sure when she had that gym accident," I replied. Lu looked away from me and back down to Elsie, who was now so cold, sweaty and pale that I started to panic.

"How much further?" I asked, and Jorge looked back through the rearview mirror.

"We're here," he announced, stopping the car so suddenly that I lurched forward, almost knocking into the knife that was sticking out of Elsie. Pain shot through my broken ribs.

"Watch it!" I cried as Lu threw a few swear words towards her father. He glared at me but apologized to his daughter.

He got out of the car, moving to my side, to open the door. He gently grabbed Elsie under her arms and lifted her out. I grabbed onto her legs as I got out and we hurried her towards the front entrance of the clinic. Lu had rushed ahead of us, presumably to get Maria. It wasn't long until they both exited the clinic, along with a stretcher and a few people in scrubs.

When they met us, we gently laid Elsie on the stretcher. Maria gave me a knowing look before she and the medics rushed into the clinic, where I hoped to hell that she could save my daughter.

Sitting in the waiting room of the clinic was torture. Lu couldn't sit still and her hands were getting more raw by the second. I tried to calm her, as did Jorge, but nothing we said seemed to help.

I was worried I was going to lose my daughter, before I had the chance to really get to know her. I also wondered why she seemed to have the most rotten luck.

Jorge had sent his guys away, so it was only the three of us in the waiting room. He had taken my phone from me, smashing it into millions of pieces by stomping his heavy boot on it. I had tried to protest, but he merely put his hand on his gun, which promptly made me shut up. But if he kept doing that, he would see exactly what my hand-to-hand combat was like.

I had paced the room several times myself, watching the time tick by. Elsie had been in surgery for two hours, and we still didn't have any news. I just had to remind myself that no news was good news.

As I was pacing I noticed that there was a phone in the lobby. I hadn't spoken to my mom or dad since I left his office yesterday, so no doubt they were just as worried about me as I was about Elsie.

I made sure no one was looking before I walked to the phone, punched in my dad's number and waited for him to pick up.

"Captain Raymond Swanson here," he answered. I held the phone close to my ear with both hands and closed my eyes and let out a sigh of relief that he had picked up.

"Dad, it's me," I told him. There was a slight shuffling sound in the background.

"Olivia, honey?" came the voice of my mom.

"Where are you? You never came home yesterday and you're not at your apartment," pointed out my dad. His voice sounded firm but I could tell that there was a hint of concern.

"It doesn't matter where I am. Just know that I'm ok," I responded, quickly glancing around to see if there was anyone coming. There wasn't.

"Honey, what's going on?" My mom asked and it almost broke my heart to not be able to tell her.

"I couldn't let her down again. I couldn't let her think she was going through this alone," I whispered, tears filling up my eyes. I quickly wiped them away. I wasn't about to start crying.

"Is this about Elizabeth? Have you found her?" My dad questioned, his voice turning from concern to business-like very quickly.

"Where are you? I'll send units there straight away to

pick her up. Is Lucita Torres with her?" He questioned further.

"I can't tell you. I'm sorry," I said quietly.

"Olivia. Stop this nonsense right now. You are an officer of the law. You have sworn to -," he started, but I let out an irritated sigh.

"I know that. But I have a duty to protect my daughter too. You took that right away from me when I was sixteen. I am not about to abandon her now," I snapped.

Just as my father was going to respond, a finger pressed the hook switch, causing the dial tone to ring in my ear. I lowered the phone down from my ear and looked at who the finger belonged to. Jorge was glaring at me, his face so angry that I had to admit I was a little intimidated.

"Nice chat? Speaking with your cop buddies?" He asked, snatching the phone out of my hand and slamming it back on the hook. I started to shake my head, but he grabbed me roughly by the upper arm and pulled me back into the waiting room.

"I told you already, I am not here as a cop," I snapped, trying to get my arm out of his grip. He pressed his fingers harder into my skin.

"And like I told you, I don't believe you," he bit back.

Lu walked over to us, her arms folded, looking both

concerned and annoyed.

"I am here for my daughter. To make sure she is safe. I've probably broken just as many laws as you have tonight by allowing everything you have done to happen. Do you think I'm going to sabotage the safety of my daughter and risk all of us getting arrested by telling the cops where we are?" I asked, narrowing my eyes, trying to get away one more time, but he wasn't budging.

"Fuck you," I cursed as I stepped forward, moving my arm up and around his. I twisted my body slightly then brought my other elbow down onto his arm so hard that he let go of me with a yelp. The pain in my ribs protested my movements, but I gave him a satisfied smirk.

"*La puta!*" Jorge growled, about to lunge at me, but Lu put herself between us.

"Stop it!" She cried. Jorge stopped moving.

"My girlfriend got stabbed in the throat, and you're fighting about whether or not she called the cops? Like I give a shit about that right now! I will happily go to prison if it means that Elsie doesn't die," Lu yelled. I lowered my gaze, feeling ashamed. Of course she was right.

"Mija, of course, I'm sorry," Jorge started, but Lu just shook her head.

"And what *was* that!? Were you about to hit her for

defending herself? You're against violence against women," she pointed out, glaring at her father.

"She's a cop," Jorge replied, glaring at me again. I glared back.

"She's still a woman!" Lu snapped. "She had every right to get out of your hold. Just because she's a cop doesn't mean her gender is suddenly irrelevant. Sort your shit out, Papi!" she continued and then burst into tears again. I wanted to hug the poor girl, but Jorge had already moved forward and cradled her in his arms.

There was a sound of someone clearing their throat and we all spun around to find Maria standing behind us with a small smile on her face.

"Sorry to interrupt, but I thought you would want to know that Elsie is out of surgery and she's going to be absolutely fine," Maria announced. I let out a large sigh of relief.

"Thank God," I murmured, taking a step forward to hug Maria, but Lu rushed past me and got there first.

"Where is she? Can I go to her? What happened? Why did it take so long?" Lu asked as she took a step back from hugging her. Maria let out a small laugh.

"She's in the recovery area. You can go and see her, but only one at a time. The knife just nicked the artery, so she lost a lot of blood, which we had to replace. We also had to stitch it up, as well as the cut that was made before the actual stab wound," Maria explained.

I tried to take it all in. Her artery was nicked. If the knife had gone in any deeper, or if someone other than medical professionals had pulled out the knife, she would have died. That was hard to process.

"Can I go see her?" Lu asked, looking at me then at her father. I nodded my head. Lu had more right than me to see her first, even if I was desperate to see her.

Lu and Maria hurried to the recovery area, leaving Jorge and I alone. I walked past him to sit down on one of the seats. He walked to the opposite one and sat down. He put his elbows on his knees and his chin in his hands but continued to watch me. I crossed my legs and crossed my arms over my chest.

"If you keep grabbing me and threatening me with a gun, we're going to have problems. And I don't mean legal ones," I stated, turning my head so I wasn't looking directly at him.

"If you keep annoying me, making private phone calls and telling me what to do, that'll be the least of your worries," Jorge retorted. I narrowed my eyes, but I refused to look at him.

"For the sake of our daughters, can we put aside the fact that I am, well I guess, *was* a cop and I'll put aside the fact that you're an egotistical, murdering gangster that sells drugs for a living?" I asked, slowly turning my head to finally look at him. He narrowed his eyes at me, but after a few seconds he nodded his head.

"You do anything that jeopardizes the safety and freedom of my daughter and the girl she loves, then all bets are off," he stated, his voice dark. Considering that I'd gone this far and not turned anyone in, there was no way that was going to happen, so I nodded my head.

"Deal," I replied. He extended his hand towards me, his palm outstretched. I unfolded my arms, placing my hand in his and we shook on it. He then leaned back on his chair, and we spent another half an hour in awkward silence, until Lu came back into the waiting room, with a brighter and happier look on her face.

"She's ok. She's up and talking and probably on heaps of pain killers, but she doesn't want to sleep until she talks with you," Lu nodded her head towards me. "I reckon she's got about ten minutes before the pain killers really kick in and she goes to her normal pain-killer-induced deep sleep ," she said with a grin, which made me breathe easier. If she was grinning, then Elsie really was okay.

"I'm going to take a shower. This blood is beginning to set on my skin and its gross," Lu announced and headed towards an area marked *Medical Personnel Only*. I looked down at myself and realized for the first time that I also had blood all over my clothes. I cringed at the thought that it was mostly my daughter's, and also it was mixed with some dead man's blood too.

"I'll be back," I muttered out loud to no one in particular. I went in the direction that Lu and Maria had gone earlier and followed the signs until I came across a room labeled *Recovery Room*. I knocked gently on the open door, announcing my presence.

"Come in," Elsie spoke in a soft voice, so quiet I almost didn't hear her. I wondered if it had something to do with being stabbed in the throat and if it hurt to talk.

I walked in, tentatively, as I didn't know how she felt about everything. She still looked pale, but at least now she didn't have a knife sticking out of her throat. She just had one of those big white pads with an adhesive dressing on it.

"How are you feeling?" I asked, silently cursing myself at the stupid question as soon as I asked it.

"Like I've been stabbed in the throat and lost a truck load of blood," Elsie replied, though she said it with a smile.

She patted the space next to her on the bed, which got my hopes up since there was a perfectly good chair next to her bed which she could have pointed me to instead. I sat down carefully next to her, putting my hands awkwardly on my lap.

"So, you're my birth mother," she stated, and I nodded as I watched her features carefully.

"That would explain why you were so obsessed with me," she commented with an amused grin. I let out a slight laugh and shook my head.

"I wouldn't call me being concerned about your safety an obsession," I said quietly. Elsie dropped her smile and looked away from me.

"If you were so concerned about my safety, why did you give me away?" Elsie asked. My heart broke. I grabbed her hand, and she looked back at me, her eyes filling with tears.

"I didn't have a choice, my darling girl," I told her, my voice breaking as my own tears welled up. "I wanted you. I wanted you with all my heart and soul, but I was only sixteen years old," I whispered. I turned her hand over so I could put my other hand on top of hers. "When my parents found out I was pregnant, they made me fill out adoption papers. I tried to fight them with every ounce of strength I had, but they wouldn't listen. They found a newly married couple to adopt you and that was that," I explained quietly. Elsie's tears fell down her cheeks.

"I had no idea that it was your father's sister, as it was a closed adoption," I continued. "And I definitely didn't know that she was married to a monster." I felt my own tears falling. I moved my hand and wiped away Elsie's tears then gently cupped her cheek. She closed her eyes and leaned into my hand.

"I'm so sorry that I didn't find you earlier. Even with all my police resources, your adoption files were sealed from me," I stated. Elsie let out a soft sob and my heart clenched.

"You tried looking for me?" She asked, opening her eyes to look at me. I smiled as I nodded.

"Every day. Nothing I did would unseal those files," I admitted. Her eyes widened.

"When I saw you the first time, that day you were arrested for stealing that make up, I couldn't believe my eyes. You look exactly like I did as a teenager," I told her with a small laugh.

"When I got promoted as a detective and the call came in about the car being blown up at your school, I jumped to take the case, knowing I would get to see you again," I confessed. I dropped my hand from Elsie's cheek and put it back on her hand.

"When did you know for certain?" She asked me, her

eyes questioning.

"The day of the gym accident." I looked down at our hands to avoid the look in her eyes. I had known for a while, but I hadn't told her.

"I took the dressings from the school's nurses office, that had your blood on them and got it tested after you were brought to the hospital. I got the results that afternoon," I explained.

"You knew for that long and you didn't tell me?" Elsie asked, moving her hand from between the two of mine.

"I was scared," I admitted shamefully. Elsie let out a scoff, which was followed swiftly by a groan of pain. I looked at her with concern as she lightly touched the spot where she had been stabbed.

"And to be honest, a little bit selfish. If I told you - or anyone, for that matter - that you were my daughter, then I wouldn't have been able to continue investigating *that man* for abusing you. I wanted him to go to prison for the rest of his life for what he did to you, and I wanted to be the one to do it... I wanted to, well, I wanted to kill him," I explained quietly.

Elsie's gaze dropped again, but I saw the look of guilt on her face before she hid it from me. I cupped her cheek again and lifted her head gently to look at me.

"What happened that night was unlawful and to some people a cruel act, but I think what you did was brave," I told her. "I know, coming from someone in law enforcement, saying you're brave for killing someone isn't something you hear every day. But that man took advantage of his position over you. He was meant to keep you safe. Make you feel loved. But instead he hurt you, broke you and made you feel like it was all your fault. He made you second guess yourself, feel worthless and I bet, a little unloved?" Elsie nodded.

"You might not have meant to pull that trigger to kill him, but when you did, you mentally pulled that trigger to become free. You freed yourself from his torment and his abuse and that's why I think you are brave."

I gave Elsie a small smile and she let out a large sob, which resulted in me pulling her into my arms. I hugged her as tight as my ribs would let me, as well as making sure her wound wasn't getting squashed. She rested her head on my chest and cried while I held her close.

"It really was an accident though. I didn't realize I had flicked the safety off when I grabbed it from Lu. But you're right. As soon as that bullet hit him and I realized he wasn't going to make it, I felt relieved," Elsie explained once she had stopped crying so hard. "I think that's why I felt so guilty about it. Not because I actually killed him, but because I was thrilled that all of the abuse was going to stop." She moved away from the hug to look at me.

"That's completely understandable, darling," I said quietly, nodding.

Elsie yawned widely, and I remembered that the last time she was given morphine, she fell asleep as soon as it had kicked in. Obviously the pain killers she was given after her surgery were beginning to take a toll on her.

"You better get some rest," I pointed out, moving off the bed. Elsie shook her head and grabbed my hand to stop me.

"But I want to talk to you more. I want to know everything. About you, about my real father?" She told me, adding a questioning tone at the end of her sentence.

"And I will tell you everything, just not right now. You need rest. I'm not going anywhere, I promise. We're going to go through whatever happens next together. I'm not leaving you again," I promised her as I squeezed her hand. She looked at me for a second before nodding her head and laid back down on her pillow.

"Alright then," she said with a smile. She closed her eyes, and she was out before I could even reply. I smiled down at her, then walked out of the room, deciding that I desperately needed a shower because even Elsie was cleaner than me, and she was the one who was wounded.

Chapter Seven

Lu

I had barely finished my shower when Olivia came back into the waiting room, announcing that Elsie had fallen asleep. She told us she was going to have a shower, noting that she hoped there was spare scrubs for her to wear after seeing me in scrubs that Maria had let me use.

She walked off in the direction of the staff-only area and I went to sit next to my dad, who put his arms around me. I snuggled into him, leaning my head on his shoulder.

"That was too close, Mija," Dad stated as he kissed me on the forehead.

"I thought we were going to die," I admitted. "I would never let that happen." He squeezed my arm as I closed my eyes.

"I know. Thank you for getting to us quickly. Thank you for getting Elsie here fast enough so she could be saved. I honestly thought she was going to die. She lost so much blood." I gulped, trying hard not to start crying.

"What a couple of nights, huh," he said with a soft chuckle. I knew he was trying to soften the mood, but I really couldn't see the funny side. I lifted my head and looked at him, giving him a pointed look.

"Hey, come on, it could have been worse. You girls could have actually gone to jail. You could have actually died," he pointed out, rubbing my shoulder.

"Papi, I have killed two people in the last three weeks, had several guns pointed at my head, not to mention actually getting hit by one," I started, pointing to the large bruise on my forehead. "Elsie got assaulted, stabbed, dislocated her hip, found out her parents weren't actually her parents, shot and killed the man who abused her all her life and found out her real mother was the cop who arrested her for having flour in her bag. It's pretty bad already," I finished, shaking my head before lowering it back down on his shoulder.

Dad sighed and pulled me closer to him and I let my eyes close, hoping I could get some sleep while we waited for Elsie to recover. I had no idea how long we could stay here, but I wasn't going to let the waiting time go to waste. Dad sat in silence, so he must have seen that I was trying to rest.

I don't know how long I had actually rested when I heard Olivia come back into the room. My eyes fluttered open, and I could see she had managed to find a set of scrubs and was now free of blood.

"We're going to have to get more clothes. Our bags

were left at the motel," I pointed out, lifting my head from Dad's shoulder. He cleared his throat.

"Well, actually, the Moretti gang took your bags when they abducted you. Probably didn't want to leave behind any evidence that you were there," he stated.

I looked at him with a slight frown.

"One of the boys found your bags in the backseat of the car they stashed you in," he explained. My mouth formed an "oh" in understanding.

"They've taken the bags to my private jet. Once we leave here, we will get out of America," he finished, which caused Olivia to let out a surprised noise.

"Do you have something to say, *puerco*?" Dad asked as he turned to look at her. I rolled my eyes. We had established Olivia could speak Spanish, so she would have known she was just called a pig. He could have just called her that. Olivia put her hands on her hips in a defiant manner.

"Maybe it's a good time to give up and turn the girls in?" Olivia suggested softly.

My dad stood up quickly, knocking me slightly to the side as he advanced on Olivia. He didn't touch her, but he stood right in front of her face, trying to intimidate her.

"And why would we do that?" he asked, his voice

a low growl. Olivia didn't move from where she was and she glared back at him. I folded my arms across my chest, watching the scene carefully, ready to jump in if they started to get physical.

"Clearly, being on the run hasn't exactly been safe for them," Olivia pointed out. "If they turn themselves in now, maybe we could get the sentences reduced, like I would have tried to do if they hadn't escaped from my custody in the first place," she continued and my heart skipped slightly, feeling guilty.

"What they did was in self-defense. They might have gotten light sentences, if any at all, for those charges. The burglaries and the murder of Keith Miller will get them a heavier sentence, but it could be pleaded down to a lesser charge if they pled guilty. It will get worse for them the longer they evade the police, especially if you leave the country," she continued. My dad stood where he was the whole time, his scowl getting more angrier by the second.

"We. Are. Not. Turning. Them. In," he spat. Olivia had to blink at this point, because I was sure that when he spat, she got some on her face. I was about to step in when the bracelet Techy had given me started to vibrate on my wrist.

"Umm, hate to interrupt this lovely banter, but if

we're getting out of here, we have to leave now," I exclaimed, holding up my arm.

My dad turned to look at me, his eyes wide. He ran in the direction of the recovery room, returning moments later with Elsie in his arms. She was groaning from being forced awake and my heart fluttered at the sight of her.

Maria rushed into the room with a wheelchair and Dad gently lowered Elsie onto it.

"You have to get out of here," Maria stated, as she threw a bottle of pills to my dad who put them in his pocket. They must have been more painkillers for Elsie.

"We know, the police are coming," my dad and I said together. The vibration of my bracelet was getting more intense, as we ran out of the clinic, with my dad pushing Elsie on the wheelchair and Olivia following close on our tails.

When we got to the car, dad quickly transferred Elsie into it and put the wheelchair in the trunk. I'm not sure why he kept it, but I guessed it could be helpful considering Elsie still had a bad hip. I got into the car next to Elsie and Olivia jumped in the front passenger seat next to dad.

It wasn't long until we were speeding away. I turned to look out the back window and could see several police cars coming up the road, sirens wailing and lights flashing.

"Hurry Papi! They're gaining on us," I cried, and I could feel the car move faster.

Elsie was wide awake now and when I looked at her, I could tell that she was scared. I grabbed her hand and squeezed it.

"It's ok, they're not going to get us. My dad is a great driver," I promised her.

I had to move my other hand to hold the handle on the side of the car as Dad sped around the corner.

"For the love of God, don't kill us by crashing," Olivia snapped from the front.

"Shut it," growled my dad in return. I rolled my eyes again. Clearly the longer these two hung together the more fun it was going to get.

Dad turned another corner and then another, which resulted in Elsie having to lie down on my lap so her head wouldn't move.

The vibration of my bracelet was losing its intensity.

"You're losing them, Papi!" I announced with encouragement. He turned another corner and sped down a new road, causing the vibrations to stop completely.

He hit a button on the middle console and a dial tone sounded, following by a ring tone. A second later it was answered.

"Boss," Techy said on the other end.

"Start her up. We'll be there in five," Dad ordered.

"Roger," Techy responded, then the line went dead.

"I really think you should consider what leaving the country is going to mean for the girls. You're going to make it worse for them if they get caught," Olivia stated.

"They won't get caught. You're more than welcome to stay behind and tell them it was all my idea and that I forced them to board the plane," countered my father. I ran my fingers through Elsie's hair as I listened to our parents bicker.

"I'm not leaving Elsie," Olivia declared, and I felt Elsie stiffen slightly.

"That's your choice then. But this is happening whether you like it or not, so shut up, so I can concentrate on the road," he snapped. I could see that Olivia was glaring at him, but she shifted in her seat and remained silent, so I could only assume she had given up on the fight.

I didn't know how to feel about all this. I didn't want to go to prison, but I also didn't want to make things worse. What if they continued to think we were so dangerous and ended up killing us on sight if they caught us? What if we ended up in prison for life, just because we didn't turn ourselves in when we had the chance?

I looked down at Elsie, who looked back at me, her eyes filled with tears. I continued to run my fingers through her hair.

"Whatever happens next, we'll do this together. Whatever happens next, know that I will always love you, E, no matter what," I said quietly. She smiled up at me.

"I love you too, L," she whispered back.

I looked up to see Olivia watching us through the rear-view mirror. She had tears in her own eyes, and I didn't know if she was crying because we weren't handing ourselves in, or if it was because she thought this moment was precious or something.

When she locked eyes with me, she gave me a small smile and then looked away again. I looked back at Elsie, who had closed her eyes and fallen back asleep, despite the car speeding around more corners to get to the small airfield where my dad's private jet was parked.

When we arrived at the airfield, I saw the jet for the first time. I knew dad owned one, but he never let me go on his oversea business trips. It was huge.

Dad slowed down slightly as we drove in and I saw that the back of the plane had a ramp big enough for a car to drive onto the back of the jet. My mouth dropped open as we drove up the ramp. Just as we got into the jet, my bracelet started vibrating and I looked back behind me to see the police cars gaining on us again.

Dad parked and turned off the car, got out and started hooking the car up to the prefixed tie downs to stop it from moving.

The ramp had started to lift up and once the car was secured, the jet started moving forward. Dad got back into the car.

My heart pounded in anticipation as I saw the police get closer, and I hoped the ramp would finish closing and that the jet could get in the air in time before the cop cars created a barricade around us.

The jet picked up speed just as the ramp closed, shutting out the police and I wondered how close they had actually gotten.

My heart pounded wildly, as the jet took off from the runway and I could feel we were no longer on the ground. When the jet bounced as it gained height, I closed my eyes tight and let out a small moan. This was the oddest sensation I had ever felt, and I didn't think I liked it. Dad turned to face me and let out a chuckle.

"I must admit, it does feel weird being in a car as we get in the air. Normally we would be sitting inside the cabin which has normal seats where you can look out and see what's happening. You'll be fine Mija, I have the best pilot," he assured me, leaning over and grabbing the hand that wasn't holding Elsie's. "We'll get a call shortly saying it's safe to get out and we will go into the cabin. We're safe now." He gave my hand a squeeze.

Olivia grunted from the front seat, which made my dad turn to glare at her.

"Please don't start, Papi," I begged, knowing him well enough to know he wasn't going to let that slide. He looked back at me, gave me a slight smile then sat back in his seat. Sure enough as the jet leveled, the car phone rang, and he pushed the button to answer it.

"Come on up," spoke the voice on the other end. It must have been the pilot, because I didn't recognize the voice.

Dad hit the button again and unbuckled his seat belt. He got out of the car and opened the back door on Elsie's side. I gently nudged her awake and she let out a little groan as she sat up.

"Are we there yet?" She asked, in her sleepy tone.

"Yeah, we're in the jet now, already in the sky," I explained with a smile. She let out another groan.

"I missed the take off?" She asked and I nodded.

"Damn. I've never flown before," she told me, and I kissed her cheek.

"It felt like my stomach was dropping out," I explained,

which caused Olivia to let out a laugh as she exited the car. Elsie wrinkled her nose, then looked at my dad.

"I think I can walk, Mr. Torres," she announced, and my dad grinned at her and stepped back, gesturing to the space that was now free for her to get out of the car.

"By all means, but I'll be here if you change your mind," he told Elsie, who grinned back at him.

"Thanks," she said as she moved out of the car. When she stood up, her legs buckled from underneath her, and Dad caught her just before she hit the ground.

"Maybe I was being a bit overly optimistic," she said with a laugh as she leaned back into my dad. Olivia walked around the car to make sure she was okay.

"I'm fine, Olivia," Elsie reassured her.

I unbuckled my seatbelt and got out of the car. I walked over to them just as my dad picked up Elsie, holding her underneath her knees and her shoulders.

"Can you please grab the wheelchair out of the trunk?" He asked me as he started walking towards the flight of stairs that must lead up to the cabin. I grabbed the wheelchair and Olivia walked over to me.

"Do you need a hand?" She asked. I looked down at the wheelchair and saw that it could be folded down.

"Do you know how to fold one of these?" I asked and she nodded. She took the chair from me and within moments it was folded down to an easier shape to carry.

She lifted it and nodded towards the stairs.

"After you," she stated with a smile, and I headed towards them.

"I assume somewhere in one of those bags of yours, you're hiding my gun?" Olivia asked and my heart faltered.

"You're correct in that assumption," I responded as I got to the top.

We walked into the cabin and found it set out with couches, seats, a dining table, a kitchen and even a bed in the far corner.

Elsie was lying on the bed, and Techy and my dad were sitting on either side of the table. Techy was working on his laptop and my dad was already sipping his whiskey. The bags that I thought were still in the hotel room were now placed on the couch.

I walked over to the bags and grabbed the one that had Olivia's gun in it. I opened it and pulled it out, making sure the safety was on, before I walked over to give it to her. She placed the wheelchair on the ground and leaned it against the wall. She took the gun from me and lifted up her scrub shirt where she had an empty holster and slid the gun back in place.

"I'll have you know, that if you try and unholster that

gun, you'll be dead before you move your hand towards it," my dad promised, not once taking his eyes off his whiskey glass.

"How very gentlemanly of you," Olivia replied, rolling her eyes and walking over to him. I thought she was going to do something in retaliation, but she bent over him to grab the whiskey bottle off the table.

"Thank you so much for offering me a drink," she said with a smile. She walked over to the little kitchen to grab a glass and poured herself a drink before walking back to the table. She sat down next to Techy, pushing the bottle back towards my dad. I shook my head at the scene.

I headed over to Elsie and slipped into the bed beside her. She shifted her body towards me, so I could cuddle her from behind. I put my arm over her and rested my hand next to hers. She linked our fingers, and we sat in silence for a moment.

"Have I told you how much I love you lately and how glad I am that you're not dead?" I asked, carefully nuzzling my face into her shoulder, making sure I didn't go anywhere near her wound.

"About fifteen minutes ago and again about an hour before that about me not being dead," Elsie replied with a small laugh. She snuggled back against me.

"I love you too, Lu," she whispered. We didn't speak anymore and soon we fell asleep.

~.~

I woke up to Elsie shouting out in her sleep. She was tossing and turning and pleading with her nightmare.

"No, please don't touch me, stop it please," she begged as she thrashed in the bed beside me. I sat up as fast as I could, and reached out to touch her, but Dad had already gotten up from his seat and was shaking his head to tell me not to.

"If you touch her while she's like this, it will freak her out more," he explained, as he walked over to Elsie's side of the bed.

"You used to do this. I learned the hard way," he told me. Elsie moaned and I could see by her face that she had to be reliving what happened on prom night.

"Elsie?" I said, loudly, seeing if that would help to wake her. Nothing happened other than her fidgeting in her sleep.

"Elsie!?" I tried again, but louder. Again nothing happened.

"ELIZABETH!" I shouted this time and Elsie finally opened her eyes, sweat pouring down her face and soaking her dressing.

"Lu," Elsie breathed, blinking as she refocused on

where she actually was. She turned her head and saw my dad.

"Mr. Torres," she stated. She sat up slightly and moved herself against the pillows.

"What happened?" She asked, seeing the concerned look on our faces.

"You were having a nightmare," I said quietly as I scooted myself over and leaned up against her, sliding my arm behind her so she could lean her head on my shoulder.

"Oh. Yeah. I thought I was back there," she said with a shudder.

"Want a shot of whiskey to calm down?" Dad asked, standing up and walking towards the table again to pick up the almost empty bottle. I heard a noise from over by the couch and saw that Olivia had just awoken.

"I don't think drinking while she is on strong pain killers is a good idea," Olivia stated as she stood up, walked over to the end of the bed and sat down.

Dad shrugged his shoulders and raised the bottle to his mouth and finished it. Olivia rolled her eyes and turned to look at us - well, mainly her daughter.

"Dreaming about what happened is completely normal," Olivia explained, and I had to wonder if she'd had a similar experience.

Why does being a female mean that males can take what they want? Don't they realize that their act in the moment might be over and done for them, but for us, it is a lifetime of torture? A lifetime of painful memories and fear and not to mention the constant second guessing of yourself, wondering what you did to deserve it?

"Do they stop?" Elsie asked in a mere whisper. She looked from Olivia and then to me. I bit my lip and moved my other arm that wasn't around her shoulder and grabbed onto her hand. I linked my fingers in hers and brought it up to my mouth to place a kiss on the back of her hand.

"I don't remember from when I was younger, but I know I hadn't thought or dreamed about what happened to me until I saw him in the cafeteria that day at school," I said quietly, not wanting to say Dante's name in case it triggered her. "Since then, I've been dreaming about it every night. If it wasn't for the joi-," I started, but then stopped, turning bright red as I realized what I was about to say and who I was talking in front of. Olivia merely rolled her eyes and let out a soft chuckle.

"If it wasn't for the joints," she finished for me. "Don't worry; I might just be an old woman cop to you, Lucita, but I know why you had eye drops and perfume in your bag that day. I was a teenager once too, you know," she said with a smile. Then her face turned serious and looked back at Elsie. She leaned forward and put her hand gently on Elsie's knee.

"I don't know about completely stopping, but I promise you they will become less regular and maybe easier to handle after some time. It's natural for it all to be raw right now. Especially with everything that happened afterwards." She looked at the dressing on Elsie's neck, which was saturated in sweat.

"We need to replace your dressing," Olivia stated, patting Elsie's knee slightly. She walked over to Dad, who had grabbed a second bottle.

At least this time he had grabbed another glass and offered one to Techy, who was still typing away at his keyboard and connecting some kind of machine to his laptop. Olivia said something to my dad, and I turned back to look at Elsie.

"How are you now?" I asked and Elsie lifted her head up to look at me.

"Happier now that I'm with you. I'm done with sleeping now anyway," Elsie replied, and I moved my head down lower to kiss her. Olivia returned a moment later, so we pulled apart to look at her.

"Sorry to interrupt," she said, turning slightly pink in the face. She held up a new dressing in one hand, which she must have gotten from my dad and a wet washcloth in the other.

"Why do you always get embarrassed when Elsie and I are kissing or talking about our relationship?" I asked, feeling slightly offended. "Do you not approve of us?" I raised my eyebrow. Olivia reddened even more. Elsie shifted uncomfortably next to me and squeezed my hand, which I could tell was a warning.

"Oh no! Not at all. Please don't think I'm homophobic or anything. If I was, I would be highly hypocritical, considering I'm bisexual myself," she said as she sat back down on the edge of the bed. That was new.

"It's just hard to see the girl I gave birth to fall in love with anybody, when I didn't get to be there for her growing up. Plus it doesn't help that you two remind me of me and her father when we first started dating. Minus the illegal activities, of course," Olivia told me, and I blushed myself for jumping to the wrong conclusion, yet again. Elsie let out a small chuckle.

"Oh good," I said with a slight smile. Elsie sat up from me, so Olivia had access to change her dressing.

"But while we are on the subject…I don't approve of what you two have done. Theft, drugs and everything else," Olivia said as she gently took off Elsie's dressing.

It didn't take a genius to know what she meant by everything else. Elsie looked away from Olivia, but I didn't avert my gaze.

"We didn't mean to do everything else," I pointed out. "Well, I meant to kill *him*, but the store owner was an accident," I clarified.

Elsie let out a soft groan as Olivia gently wiped away the sweat with a wet cloth. I watched with slight alarm as I saw how long the stitched wound was. It started just below Elsie's ear and continued about two and half inches down her throat.

Elsie watched me looking at it and cleared her throat with a slight smirk on her face.

"Do I look badass?" She asked. Olivia let out a half-hearted laugh as she put the new dressing on.

"Yeah, you do," I told her, bringing her hands up to my lips to kiss them again. Elsie moved back against me and put her head back on my shoulder. Olivia gave us a pointed look, which made me think she wasn't going to allow the change in subject.

"Besides the fact that it was an accident, you were still doing something illegal at the time. Now you're both in a world of trouble," she continued as she sat down again.

"Injured and escaping the country…this wasn't the life I thought you would have, Elsie," Olivia said quietly.

I couldn't help but feel like she was blaming me for this predicament. She would be right, though; this was my fault.

"And she would never have had this life if she hadn't met me," I finished the unsaid words for her. Olivia turned red and as I looked at her, I noticed that my dad, behind her, was now watching us closely. Elsie shifted uncomfortably beside me.

"Olivia…this is not Lu's fault," Elsie said quietly as she squeezed my hand. She knew I thought differently. I agreed with Olivia.

"I chose to do everything. Lu didn't force me," she continued.

I wanted to say something to defend myself, but when I saw Dad gesture me over, I knew that this was probably a conversation Elsie should have with her mother alone. I kissed Elsie's hand.

"I think you two need to talk about this without me," I said quietly, my face warming slightly. Before either of them could protest, I got up from the bed and walked over to my father, leaving the two to talk.

Chapter Eight

Elsie

I watched Lu as she walked to her father. I had a feeling that if she stayed she would have argued against what I was trying to tell Olivia. I looked back at her and frowned slightly.

"You made her feel awkward," I accused as I moved back against the wall.

"That wasn't my intention," Olivia said quietly.

"I chose to do everything," I repeated.

"I'm the one who stole the make-up. I was the one who wanted to break into clothes stores, hotels and jewelry stores. If anything, it was *my* idea to start H.E.L.L," I continued.

Olivia shifted uncomfortably on the edge of the bed.

"It made me feel excited. Like I was taking drugs without actually taking them. I *loved* it," I explained. I shifted again and moved my legs over the side of the bed.

"Don't blame Lu for any of this, or you'll find you broke the law by aiding our escape for nothing," I told her, putting my feet down on the ground. Olivia stood up and came to my side.

"I understand. I'm sorry," Olivia said with a small smile.

"Let me help you," she said, and I nodded. Olivia put her arm around my waist and helped me stand. I wobbled slightly and I wondered why I felt so weak. It wasn't like I was stabbed in my leg or anything.

"Is this the first time you've tried to walk since after your surgery?" Olivia asked and I nodded again. "Anesthesia does funny things to the body, it'll come right with time. Where do you want to go? The couch?" She asked.

I looked over to Lu, Mr Torres and Techy over at the table.

"Can we go sit with everybody? I don't want to talk about this anymore. I know what I've done is a disappointment to you, but there is nothing we can do to change it," I stated. Olivia gave me a small smile as she nodded her head.

"Of course," she said, as she started to guide me to the table.

We walked slowly, as she had to keep me upright because I kept swaying. When we got to the table, Lu stood up and moved around to the chair to pull it out for me. I sat down, then Lu took the chair next to mine, and Olivia sat back down next to Mr. Torres, where Lu had been sitting.

Techy tapped something into his keyboard, cleared his throat and turned the screen towards Lu and me.

"Seems your friend Ryleigh is taking advantage of the news coverage about prom night," he announced, which made me roll my eyes at his comment about her being a friend.

When I looked at the screen, I saw that Ryleigh was being interviewed. Techy turned up the volume.

"What can you tell us about that night?" the interviewer asked. Ryleigh puffed her chest out to make herself seem bigger on live television.

"Well, to be honest with you, I always thought that Lucita Torres would crack and murder someone. I just didn't think it would be at a school prom," Ryleigh responded, causing Lu to let out a small growl. I grabbed her hand.

"Care to elaborate?" asked the interviewer. "Well, you see, Lucita is practically psychotic. She carried the murder weapon with her at school, and even threatened numerous times to cut my face!" Ryleigh explained, dramatically putting her hand on her face for emphasis. "She was overprotective of Elsie, like borderline obsessed. We all thought it was weird."

Lu let out another sound and it was the first time that I was actually thankful that we were high in the air, probably thousands of miles away from Ryleigh.

Techy took away the laptop and started typing away,

while the interview was still playing in the background.

"Our viewers are curious to know, what do you think made Elsie shoot her own father?" the interviewer asked.

"Well, as it turned out, not her real father," Ryleigh corrected.

There was a slight pause where all we could hear was the typing of the keyboard. My heart faltered slightly, wondering if Ryleigh was going to tell everyone what he did to me.

"I'm not at all surprised by the fact that she did that… I mean I didn't think she would ever shoot a gun, but Mr. Neilson deserved what he got," Ryleigh said, in the sincerest tone I had ever heard from her since our friendship ended. "I'm not sure if she would want this aired on national television, but I need everyone to understand that what she did was done under duress. Maybe it will help her defense, once she's caught," she continued.

Mr. Torres grunted in response, took a shot of whiskey and slid the bottle to Olivia, who filled up her glass too. She watched me closely as she put the bottle back on the table. Lu squeezed my hand, as she probably could feel my pulse beating rapidly.

"Mr. Neilson abused her. Mentally, physically," Ryleigh stated.

"Sexually?" asked the interviewer, curiously.

"I don't think so, but I wouldn't know. Elsie and I haven't been close for years. Our friendship ended because of what Mr. Neilson did to Elsie when she was twelve. He pushed her into a glass coffee table in a rage and almost killed her," Ryleigh explained.

I groaned, closed my eyes and leaned over so I could rest my forehead on Lu's shoulder.

"I know there were other incidents too, because she was always injured growing up. When Mr. Neilson told Elsie that she wasn't his daughter in front of the whole senior class, it was the last straw. I understand why she did it," Ryleigh finished. I know she was just trying to help me, but why was she trying to be nice to me now?

Techy moved the screen back, just in time for me to see the interviewer pressing something against his ear.

"Thank you for that information, Ryleigh. Now, we have received some information. Rumor is you were the one who brought Dante Moretti to the senior prom. Is that true? The viewers would like to know."

"I did, yes," she said, all sounds of sincerity gone and a tone of embarrassment.

"Even though you were just defending Miss Neilson's actions, wasn't it only a couple of weeks ago that you two were in a public fight, where she broke your nose?" the interviewer asked.

Ryleigh absentmindedly put her hand on her nose but didn't respond straight away.

"What are you? A lawyer or something?" She asked, jokingly after a moment, trying to get the attention away from her. The interviewer merely shrugged his shoulders and continued his questioning.

"Are you aware of what the reports are saying about what Dante Moretti did to Elsie?" the interviewer continued.

Lu squeezed my hand again and everyone was now focused on my reaction. I squeezed Lu's hand back and gave Olivia a small smile, to show that I was alright.

I thought I knew where this line of questioning was going, and I had to know. Was she only defending my actions because she felt bad for setting me up? Ryleigh cleared her throat as she nodded.

"Yeah. They say he raped her," she said quietly. I could see that her eyes were filling up with tears.

"The question being asked by many viewers tonight is, did you set your former friend up to be raped, Miss Atkins?" the interviewer asked her. Ryleigh's eyes went wide and shook her head profusely.

"I didn't know, I swear! He just told me he really wanted to go to prom. He gave me a hundred dollars to let him go as my date and I needed it to finish paying for my dress. I swear I didn't know he was going to hurt Elsie. I didn't know that Lu would kill him," Ryleigh cried.

I cringed at the sight of her crying. She didn't get to cry. This wasn't about her. I reached toward the laptop and moved the curser to close the page.

"I don't want to hear anymore," I stated, and then I leaned back against the chair.

"She's full of shit anyway. She probably paid to get her face on TV," Lu commented, as I leaned my head back on her shoulder.

"Where are we going anyway? How far away are we?" I asked, wanting to change the subject.

"We are going to New Zealand," Mr. Torres said, as he took another swig of his whiskey.

"New Zealand?" Lu repeated.

Even Olivia had looked at Mr. Torres funny. New Zealand was like, on the other side of the world. Did this jet even carry enough fuel to get us there?

"Yes, New Zealand. It's the only country that doesn't know who I am," Mr. Torres explained.

"We've already been traveling for ten hours. We have about eight to go," he finished. I looked back over to the bed and then put my head back down on Lu's shoulder.

"We were asleep for ten hours?" I asked and let out a small laugh. "I guess being on the run, getting stabbed and having surgery really takes a toll on your body," I said, feeling amused, because if I felt anything else, I would cry. Lu squeezed my hand.

"Isn't New Zealand that country that has like three islands?" I asked, thinking of the world map. Mr. Torres nodded.

"We'll be landing on the island they call the South Island. It's the middle one," he continued.

"But won't the police that were chasing us inform other countries?" Lu asked and then looked at Olivia for confirmation.

"Yes, they will. So how are we going to get around that? As soon as you land this thing, they will have the local police surrounding us. All they need is to see the plane ID on the air control tracker," Olivia said, glancing at Techy and then back at Mr. Torres.

"Why do you think I'm here?" Techy responded with a grin. He had taken the laptop back as soon as I had exited out of the interview, so he turned it around to show what he was working on.

"I've made it so they think we are legit. They have no way of knowing we are escaping the country. I have even procured us travel visas and new passports," Techy explained, moving the laptop back and grabbing the box of stuff he had next to it.

Inside were five passports and some papers.

"The only thing I have left to do is take photos of all of you so I can put them in the passport. That's what this machine is for," he added, pointing to the black machine that was attached to his laptop. He reached for the passports opening each one before giving it to the person that it was meant for.

I lifted my head from Lu's shoulder as I took mine.

"Veronica Marie Black?" I questioned. He gave me a wink. Lu opened hers and chuckled.

"Claudia García Lopez," Lu commented, showing me hers.

I noticed that our birth years made us slightly older than we were. According to our new fake passports, we were both already twenty-one.

"Ronnie and Claude," Techy said with a grin. I rolled my eyes as Lu laughed again.

"Do you get it?" Techy asked me and I gave him a pointed look.

"Anything to do with Bonnie and Clyde?" I asked, and he nodded. Olivia shook her head in amusement.

"They killed people for the fun of it, idiot," I snapped, not finding it all funny. Lu stopped laughing immediately and Techy lost his grin.

"I didn't mean it in that way… I just figured it would be a bit of fun, considering you've been referred to as a modern-day lesbian version of Bonnie and Clyde," Techy explained slowly.

"I can change them," he went on and I shook my head.

"It's fine, just leave it," I said, coldly.

I reached over to grab Olivia's drink and took a swig of it before she could protest. I cringed at the taste, but then took another.

"I really don't think you should be drinking that, when you've recently taken painkillers," Olivia started, but I narrowed my eyes at her.

"Just because you gave birth to me, doesn't mean you get to tell me what to do," I said, as I finished the glass off. I shuddered as it went down.

"Should we take the photos now?" Techy asked, grabbing the camera that was lying next to the black machine. I knew he was trying to divert attention.

We all agreed and soon all our photos were taken to be put with our new identities.

I grabbed the bottle of whiskey and gulped down a few mouthfuls. Cheers to Veronica Black.

"E," Lu said quietly. She tried to squeeze my hand,

but I took my hand out of hers before she could.

"I'm fine," I replied, pushing the chair back. I stood up, feeling the alcohol rush to my head and swayed slightly. Lu stood up next to me, to catch me, but I put my hand out to stop her.

"It's just my hip."

I walked over slowly to the small kitchen and opened up all the cupboards until I found the rest of the alcohol. I knew that there had to be other options, considering I knew Mr. Torres liked his spirits. I pulled out a vodka bottle, two glasses and a bottle of lemon-lime soda from the fridge.

"Elsie," Lu said again as she walked over to me. I looked at her and put down the bottle of soda slightly too hard.

"What?" I asked as I looked back to look at her.

"He didn't mean to upset you. He just wanted to make light of the situation," she explained, as she put her hand on the small of my back. I jumped slightly when her hand made contact. She frowned at me, but I gave her a small smile, trying to pretend it didn't happen.

"I know," I said quietly. I turned myself around so I could put my arms around her waist.

"I just can't stop thinking about everything," I explained. Lu put her arms around me and pulled me into a hug.

"I know what you mean," she responded, kissing me on my forehead.

"Other than Mr. Miller, you know we had to do what we did," Lu continued. I took a deep breath as scenes from the past few days flashed across my mind; Dante's face as he had his fingers in me, then Lu stabbing him in the throat. Flash to the bullet striking my so-called father. I blinked to try to clear the images but instead saw the men that had captured us falling to the ground as their blood sprayed all over me. I let my breath out. I pulled away from Lu and returned to making my drink.

"Do you want one?" I asked, shifting the second glass slightly closer to Lu.

"Olivia's right you know; it will make you sick," Lu said quietly. I looked at her and narrowed my eyes slightly.

"I don't really care, as long as it makes me forget," I replied, mixing the soda and the vodka together.

I grabbed my finished drink and walked back over to the table, ignoring the look of concern that Olivia was giving me.

"So what name did you get?" I asked her, taking a sip. Lu walked back over, with the bottle of vodka, soda and empty glass. She sat down and started pouring her own, much to Mr. Torres's amusement.

Olivia had already refilled her glass with whiskey, and she was nursing it when I asked her. She put the drink back down on the table and opened her passport.

"Amanda García," Olivia choked and then she looked at Techy with a frown, then grabbed Mr. Torres's passport and opened it.

"José García Ortiz," Olivia read out loud.

She dropped the passport down on the table and looked at Techy pointedly. Mr. Torres laughed. I took another swig of my drink as I watched with slight amusement. Now this was funny.

"What is this?" Olivia asked, looking from Techy to Mr. Torres.

"Well, we had to come up with a cover story as to why we're in New Zealand. You two have recently married and chosen to take his son, daughter, and daughter's girlfriend on the honeymoon with you," Techy explained, his chest puffing slightly as he said the word 'son.'

Again, I had to wonder if there was a story that Lu wasn't being told there.

"Nope," Olivia said, moving herself away from Mr. Torres.

"It's done, wife," Mr. Torres stated in amusement. His

eyes were twinkling with humor as he took another swig of his whiskey.

"Change it then. I did not agree to this," Olivia pointed out, folding her arms defiantly across her chest. I saw Lu grinning as she took a drink out of her glass.

"Just like I didn't exactly agree to bring you along on this excursion," Mr. Torres pointed out, the twinkle in his eyes disappearing. Olivia shifted uncomfortably in her seat.

"I'm not pretending to be your wife. I'm not that good of an actress; they would know it was a lie within seconds," Olivia pointed out.

I couldn't help but agree with that statement, considering how Olivia was glaring at Mr. Torres. I could tell that he would have been glaring back if it wasn't for the many whiskeys he had consumed on this journey. It probably mellowed out his obvious dislike for Olivia.

"You have no choice," Mr. Torres snapped. "It's too late to make changes now. Techy took every day since the girls fled to make our passports and because you invited yourself along, he used all this time to make yours and come up with a cover story. Since you were too busy catching up on your beauty sleep, there wasn't many options to choose from. So it's done," he stated, the hint of finality clear in his voice.

Olivia glared at him a few more moments then sighed as she gave in and grabbed her drink.

"Fine, but I'm not happy about it," Olivia muttered. I couldn't help it - I laughed.

"Well, that's obvious," I pointed out, and took a gulp of my own.

"Be glad it's only on a fake passport. It would be weird for my birth mother to marry my girlfriend's father. Pretty sure it's illegal," I stated, as I finished my drink.

I grabbed the vodka bottle and tipped it into the glass, this time adding a bit more vodka. Lu put her hand on my knee and I jumped again, so I started jiggling my leg to try and hide the fact I kept doing that when she touched me unexpectedly. I looked at her for a moment, then continued to mix my drink by grabbing the soda bottle.

"Don't worry, that will never happen," Olivia Promised as she watched me closely over her glass of whiskey.

"I know I don't have the right to tell you what to do, Elsie, but please, can you ease up on the drinking? You could seriously do yourself harm," she stated quietly.

I knew she was only looking out for my health and

well-being, but I couldn't help but feel just as defiant as she had just been moments earlier. I didn't care that I would risk harm to myself. I already dislocated my hip, been stabbed and violated, and had a body covered in scars. I was already harmed and if the drinking meant I could forget what had happened to me, then it would be worth it. Since I was still seeing flashes in my head, it was clearly not working.

I picked up the vodka bottle, uncapped it and took a gulp straight out of the bottle. I continued to chug the vodka until Lu let out a choked noise herself and pulled the bottle from my hands. Some of the vodka fell down my front, soaking the front of my shirt.

"Fuck it, Lu," I swore, as I grabbed a napkin that was in front of Mr. Torres and tried to dry myself. My head was now feeling lighter, the visions disappearing from my mind. I picked up my glass instead and went to drink that, but Lu took that from me as well.

"Don't," I warned, grabbing it back from her. "Don't start dictating what I can and can't do now, just because you feel guilty about what happened. If I want to drink, then I will drink," I pointed out and then I threw my drink back till it was finished.

I stood up, wobbling on my feet again, only this time I couldn't blame it on my hip. I drunkenly walked over to the bed. I laid myself down, where the alcohol in my system lulled me into a dreamless sleep for the first time in three nights.

Chapter Nine

Olivia

Things got a bit awkward after Elsie's outburst. Lu awkwardly followed her and laid down on the bed next to her, but not close enough to actually touch her.

With both chairs now free, I stood and moved to the opposite side of the table, keen to get away from Jorge. We sat in silence for a few minutes until I couldn't take it anymore.

"When we arrive in New Zealand, what's the plan?" I asked, and Jorge leaned back in his chair, pushing his now empty glass away from him.

"We will go to a hotel and get over the jet lag," he said with a smile. "After that, there is no plan other than staying out of the local police's radar."

"Well, I need clothes for a start," I pointed out and Techy looked up from his laptop.

"That's already taken care of," Techy announced. I frowned slightly as I waited for him to elaborate.

"Well, since you forced your way in to help rescue the girls, I had a feeling you wouldn't let us leave the country without you," Jorge explained. "I got the guys to get you some clothes, while Techy started working on your passport." He turned around on his seat and pointed to the black suitcase that was tucked between two seats facing the front of the cabin.

I frowned even more when I recognized it.

"That's my suitcase!" I exclaimed. "That was in my apartment! How? When?" I asked, trying to wrap my head around the idea that people had been in my home.

"When Elsie was in surgery," Jorge explained. "They made it look as if you were taken. That way, if you return, you can say I forced you to come with us," Jorge said softly. I looked at him curiously. That was actually a generous thing to do, considering I had broken the law as well as forcing myself upon them.

"I may be an egotistical, murdering, drug seller gangster, but I'm a thoughtful one," Jorge added with a grin. I shook my head, but I gave him a small smile in return.

"Thank you," I said, finishing my drink.

"Well I guess I'm going to catch more of that 'beauty sleep,'" I announced, standing up.

I grabbed the girls glasses as well as my own and took them to the sink. I then walked back over to the couch, where I had set up a little bed with a pillow and a blanket. I took off my gun belt and put it down next to the girl's bags.

Jorge got up himself and walked to the door at the end

of the cabin.

"What's in there?" I asked, curiosity getting the better of me.

"My private bedroom," Jorge answered, grinning as he went through the door, shutting it behind him.

I laid down and pulled the blanket up over myself. I looked over at Techy, who was still typing away at his keyboard.

"Are you going to get some rest, Techy?" I asked, wondering when the last time the young man had actually slept.

"Can't. There is too much to do. I'll get some rest later," he stated, not even taking his eyes off the screen.

"What are you doing anyway?" I asked. He continued to type away, but at least this time he looked up from the screen and at me.

"The FBI is still trying to hack into the jet's system. I'm trying to make it look like we are going to China instead of New Zealand, but their tech guys are top notch," Techy explained, then he looked back down at the screen.

I figured it was best to leave him to it, so I turned myself around, closed my eyes and drifted into a deep sleep.

~.~

Hours later, I woke up to turbulence. The jet bounced so violently that I fell off my makeshift bed. I landed on the ground, shock and pain radiating through my body as I hit my ribs.

A cry sounded out from over where Elsie and Lu were and I looked up to find them huddled in each other's arms. Techy looked over his laptop, with dark rings under his eyes.

"We're coming into New Zealand now – it's known for its windy conditions, nothing to be frightened of," he declared and then continued with what he was doing.

I had no idea how he was still awake, especially if he hadn't had a drop of sleep during our eighteen hours of flying.

I sat up and gathered the blanket around myself, as I breathed through the pain. I reached for the little bottle of painkillers I was given at the hospital and grabbed two codeines out. Since I never had an issue about dry swallowing pills, I popped them in my mouth and swallowed.

I watched Elsie and Lu let go of each other as the turbulence eased and the plane became more settled. Jorge opened his door, fully awake, showered, and with a new change of clothes.

"That's one way to hurry you up out of the shower,"

he announced with a chuckle. He walked over to Lu and kissed her on her forehead.

"Morning, Mija," he said as he then walked over to the kitchen and started cleaning up the glasses and putting away the alcohol bottles.

`"I've been informed that we will touch down in about half an hour. I suggest if you want to get out of those scrubs and hospital gowns, you do it now, cause we'll soon have to fasten our seat belts for landing," Jorge stated, as he finished washing the glasses and putting them away.

I forced myself to stand up and folded the blanket, putting it beside the pillow. Jorge had gotten it out for me, so I wasn't sure where it went. I walked over to my suitcase, pausing slightly as I wondered where I could get dressed.

"You can use my bedroom," Jorge offered, as he watched me with an amused look on his face.

"Thanks," I said, wondering why it was so funny. I pulled out the handle and rolled it behind me as I walked to the bedroom door.

As I walked past Elsie and Lu, I looked over at Elsie cautiously and saw her looking at me with a small smile. She also looked as if she was regretting her drinking choices, in that she looked like she was going to hurl the next time the jet bounced.

"You alright, hon?" I asked and she nodded. "Yeah," she replied, but her pale face said otherwise. I gave her a small reassuring smile and then I walked into the bedroom.

It was quite big, considering it was on a plane. It had a queen size bed, two bedside tables, a closet and a bathroom to the side. I shut the door behind me and rolled the suitcase over to the bed, cursing at the pain as I lifted it onto the bed.

I was glad that I had already taken a shower at the clinic because I didn't think half an hour was enough time to have another one. I would have to wait until we got to the hotel.

It didn't take me long to get changed into a pair of pants and a t-shirt. As Techy had mentioned that New Zealand was known for its windy conditions, I hunted around the suitcase until I found a sweater, just in case it was cold when we landed.

I rezipped the case, pulled it to the ground, and walked back out into the cabin. Lu had moved from the bed and was standing by their bags. She had already gotten out clothes for her and Elsie and had a makeup bag in her hands. When she saw me come out of the room she walked back over to Elsie to help her out of the bed. I put my suitcase next to the others.

"Bet you wished you listened to reason now, don't you, Elsie?" Jorge asked, as he stepped away from the sink as Elsie rushed over and vomited into it. I grimaced as she emptied the contents of her stomach.

I walked over to her and grabbed a new glass out and filled it with water from the faucet. I left the water running to get rid of the mess.

Lu stood behind Elsie, rubbing her upper back. Elsie looked at me, with contentment in her eyes as she took the glass and slowly sipped it.

"This is better than having the nightmares," Elsie said quietly, then put the glass down and walked to the bedroom with Lu. I watched them for a moment, feeling almost like I was going to vomit myself.

How could I fix this for Elsie? How could I make this better? I knew only time would fix it and even then it didn't always completely get rid of the pain and memories. But seeing her like this broke my heart and there wasn't a thing I could do about it.

I turned back to the sink and cleaned everything up again, putting the glass away. When I opened the cupboard I saw an empty water bottle, so I grabbed that and filled it up.

The girls came out moments later, Elsie dressed with

a scarf around her neck to hide the dressing covering her wound. Lu's bruises were covered by make-up.

I walked over to Elsie and handed her the bottle of water.

"Thank you," she said, bringing it to her mouth. She sipped it slowly.

"Best to leave the bag of cannabis here, Mija. I don't think it will get past customs," Jorge commented, gesturing his head to a small cupboard in the kitchenette that I hadn't even noticed. Lu gave me a worried look, before she pulled out the bag and shoved it quickly into the cupboard. I already knew they smoked it, so I merely shrugged my shoulders.

Lu then helped Elsie over to the seats where we were to sit and buckle up for landing. Elsie looked weak and struggled as she walked, so I couldn't help but wonder if, in addition to the hangover, the pain of her hip was getting to her.

I sat down in the seat beside Elsie and buckled myself in. Jorge sat in the seat in front of me and Techy had finally shut down his laptop and chosen the seat in front of Lu, who was sitting on the other side of Elsie. When we were all buckled up, I felt the jet shudder underneath us.

"The wheels have come out for landing," Jorge

explained, probably hearing the squeak from Elsie.

"Nothing to worry about," I added, leaning over to grab onto Elsie's hand. I gave it a small squeeze and she looked up at me with a smile.

"Have you ever flown before?" She asked and I nodded.

"When I was 25, I went to Chicago with some of my police academy friends," I told her. I heard a grunt come from Jorge. I narrowed my eyes slightly but ignored him.

"I was pretty focused on the job, so I didn't really have time for holidays. But it was the first time I had left New Haven and I had a blast," I explained, and Elsie smiled at me.

"I want to hear more about your life," Elsie said quietly and I squeezed her hand again.

"And you will," I promised.

I felt the jet tip forward as it started to descend. Elsie's grip on my hand tightened and I gave her a reassuring smile.

"It's ok. It'll be a bump when we land, but it'll be fine," I stated. I noticed that Elsie had also grabbed onto Lu's hand and Lu's face looked just as frightened. Elsie's face paled further, so I took my hand out of her grip.

"Have some water," I urged and she did, slowly

sipping away as she continued to hold Lu's hand.

After what seemed like an eternity, the jet finally touched down, causing that bump that I had told Elsie we would feel. The jet gradually slowed, until we were gently rolling forwards. We turned to the right and eventually came to a stop. A green light flicked on at the front of the cabin and Jorge unbuckled himself from his seat.

"Well, we're here. Grab your things and wait by the door," Jorge told us, pointing out to the exit door on the right of the cabin.

"Someone will knock on it shortly, when they're ready with a ramp for us to get down," he explained.

I nodded as I unbuckled the seat belt, then I stood and walked over to my suitcase. As I walked past the folded-up wheelchair, I looked back at Elsie, who was slowly following me with Lu.

"Do you need the chair?" I asked, nodding my head towards it. Elsie looked at it for a moment before turning to consult with Lu.

As they spoke amongst themselves, I put my gun belt, along with my gun into my bag.

"I think it will be easier for me to use the chair," Elsie said to me, as she walked – well, hobbled - over to one of the bags. I nodded my head in agreement and grabbed the chair, unfolding it and locking it into place so she could sit down on it. Once she was settled and the bags were sitting on her lap, Lu unlocked the wheels and started to push her towards the door.

I grabbed the handle of my suitcase and rolled it behind me. Jorge had grabbed his suitcase, which I was sure had been packed and ready to go since the moment he heard his child was on the run.

Techy had his laptop bag over his shoulder and had a duffle bag on the floor next to him. In his hands, he had the passports and several pieces of paper. He handed out the passports and I cringed as I remembered that I had to pretend to be Jorge's wife.

Techy then handed out the papers.

"Your travel visas. Also, Olivia, you have a copy of your permit to carry the gun. I already sorted out the declarations the country needs, so they should have it in their database, but just in case. Jorge, you obviously have one as well," Techy explained, just as the knock sounded on the other side of the door.

Jorge opened the door, swinging it back and hooking it to the wall. He walked out of the jet first, with his suitcase rolling behind him. Techy grabbed his bag and followed after him. Lu carefully started pushing Elsie out the door and down the small ramp to the ground.

Noting the sudden change in weather, I was glad I had chosen to grab my sweater. I quickly put it on, before following everyone out. I looked back at the door.

"The pilot will get that, honey," called out Jorge.

I cringed at the unwelcome nickname before turning back around and walking down the ramp, pulling my suitcase. When I reached the bottom, Jorge put his arm around my waist and kissed my cheek. I wanted to vomit.

"Time to put on a good show," he whispered in my ear and I swear to God I wanted to knee him where it would hurt.

Chapter Ten

Lu

Going through customs at the airport in Christchurch, New Zealand was the most nerve-racking thing I had ever experienced. Even though we had declared everything that we had with us, including the guns, the cash, and the medication for Elsie and Olivia, we were still questioned and had our bags searched. Even my dad was strip searched by one of the officers.

Elsie was sweating due to the anticipation that we could get caught, so to avoid suspicion we blamed it on her recent surgery.

When the custom officers weren't looking, she had pointed out a picture of the two of us with my pink and her blond hair posted on the wall of the interview room. That was when I actually got scared that we might not get out of this without being caught, but luck was on our side, because they didn't even look at us twice.

Techy had organized with someone to get my dad's car from the jet. He had to have more paperwork for that, so all that Techy had to do to get us into this country became apparent. I had to remember to thank him.

When we were finally allowed to leave the customs area, we walked out of the airport and waited along the front of the building for one of the employees to bring the car around. It wasn't long before we were on our way to the hotel.

The first thing I noticed was that New Zealanders drove on the other side of the road! I thought that was pretty strange and I was glad I wasn't driving.

When we arrived, Techy paid for our rooms, with a card I assumed came from an offshore bank account.

We were led to our rooms; Elsie and I had a room to ourselves. Techy had managed to get a single room across from ours. But, the funniest thing was that Dad and Olivia had to share a room and we heard Olivia yelling that they had only one bed.

Techy had explained that he did that on purpose to keep up the pretense of them being a newly married couple. Their room was adjoined to ours.

Our room had a queen bed, a set of dressers, a small kitchenette and a table with two chairs. Now that Elsie and I were alone in our room, I started unpacking our bags into the dressers. Elsie chose to use the time to sleep off her hangover.

Once I had finished unpacking, I climbed into the bed next to Elsie, careful not to touch her. I had come to realize that whenever I touched her unannounced, she would start and look frightened and I didn't want to upset her.

However, my movement next to her awakened her slightly, and she shifted herself backwards so she could cuddle into me.

"I'm sorry for biting your head off earlier," she said, as she adjusted herself, so her bottom was tight against my front. I moved my arm carefully over her and she moved her hand to link her fingers with mine.

"I'm not angry at you. In fact, I understand why you want to drink. I felt the same way, when it happened to me," I said quietly, gently nuzzling my head against her shoulder. I was careful not to touch her anywhere near her dressing, to avoid accidently hurting her.

"I just wanted to stop the visions," Elsie explained in a whisper.

"I know. Really, I do. You don't have to explain it to me. But you have to understand that Olivia and I are both concerned about your health. Mixing painkillers and alcohol could make you very sick," I whispered back. Elsie squeezed my hand but didn't respond.

"Speaking of which, when was the last time you had your painkillers?" I asked, after a moment.

"Not since the hospital. I'm not in any pain. Well besides my head," Elsie replied, with a half-hearted laugh. She then moved herself away from me and sat up against the pillows. I moved myself as well so I could sit up next to her.

"Perhaps the pounding in your head is masking the pain to your throat? You just had surgery less than twenty-four hours ago; you should be in some sort of pain," I pointed out.

Elsie let out a sigh. "Maybe," she replied.

Elsie moved her body, so her face was next to my own throat. My breath hitched as she put her lips on my skin and placed a kiss on the same area where she was stabbed.

"Maybe I could make it so you're in pain too," she said quietly, her lips brushing my skin as she spoke.

"Oh? And how are you going to do that?" I asked, closing my eyes. She pulled at skin between her lips and gently began to suck on it. I let out a moan as my pulse started to quicken and the area between my legs began to awaken.

"Elsie," I moaned and she let go of my skin, but not before she gently bit me. I gasped and she moved herself up and kissed me hard on the lips.

"That's not my name anymore," she reminded me.

"I'm not calling you Veronica," I stated. She moved herself carefully, so she was straddling me. I raised my eyebrow slightly and she smirked at me.

"Fine, but you better come up with another name, because if anyone hears you, we could get caught," she reminded me. She moved back down to my throat, trailing kisses down it. When she got to the top of my shirt, she started to unbutton it, not stopping the trail of kisses.

"Babe," I groaned, as she pulled apart my top, revealing my bra. She paused her kisses when she got to the top of my breast. I watched as she gulped.

"You don't have to do this," I whispered, as I grabbed onto her hands and brought them to my lips. I kissed her knuckles gently. Elsie moved her forehead to rest it on mine.

"But I want too, *mi amor*," Elsie responded and my heart skipped.

"You learned Spanish," I said, with a grin. I moved my head so I could kiss her. When we parted, I could see that she was blushing.

"I had to ask Olivia what 'my love' translated to," she admitted and I let out a small laugh.

"Well, don't worry. Since we have a whole lot of time in front of us, I will teach you more Spanish," I promised.

"And self-defense?" she asked and I nodded.

"Once I know your stitches won't split open, of

course I will," I responded.

Elsie grinned at me, then leaned forward to start placing kisses on my right breast. She pulled my skin with her lips and began to suck gently, just like she had done on my throat. I leaned my head back and closed my eyes. She moved her hands around my back, not pausing as she unhooked my bra and moved it down my arms, moving it off my body along with my shirt. She threw them on the ground and then looked at my half naked body.

"These are what breast bruises should look like," Elsie declared, which made me move my head back up and look at her.

"Babe," I said quietly, unsure what to say. She gave me a small smile and shook her head.

"Forget I said anything," she said and then moved her hands down my belly, towards the top of my pants.

I lifted my hips so she could push them, along with my panties, down my legs. She threw them on the floor next to my shirt and bra.

She moved herself so she was kneeling between my thighs, pushing them apart. She leaned forward, one hand on my breast while the other moved down slowly past my belly button towards my increasingly wet pussy.

I let out another moan as she continued her fingers

right down to my awaiting clit. I let out a gasp as her fingers hit the sweet spot. Elsie leaned herself down so she could rest her head in the crook of my neck, as she continued to rub me so passionately that brought forward the sweet oblivion that I knew was coming shortly.

"Elsie," I groaned, my hands moving on top of hers, urging her to continue.

Something wet fell against my skin, something I knew I shouldn't be feeling. I moved Elsie's hand away from my sensitive nub and I moved myself so I could look at her.

"Babe, are you crying?" I asked, horrified that I had made her do that. She let out a sob as she fell gently to my side. I gently put my hands on the side of her face, urging her to look at me.

"I'm sorry, I thought I could do this. I thought I could pleasure you, but all I can think about is him," she sobbed.

"Hey, it's ok," I whispered as I gently stroked through her hair with my hand.

"You have nothing to apologize for," I said as she let out another sob. Elsie wrapped her arms around me and we sat holding each other.

"We don't have to do anything until you feel comfortable doing it," I pointed out. "Besides, I love you for you, not the sex," I added, kissing her on top of her head. Elsie let out a light laugh and moved her head to look at me.

"I'm really sorry for getting you so close…I could tell you loved it in that moment," she said, her face reddening. I merely shrugged my shoulders.

"I can take care of it," I said with a small smile. Elsie moved away from me, lay down on the bed and patted the space beside her on her right.

"Do it beside me. Maybe it will help," Elsie requested. I looked down at her and smiled.

"Do I get to kiss you while doing it?" I asked and Elsie nodded.

I grinned and wiped away the wetness from her eyes before lying down next to her, on my side. She turned to face me and I moved my head forward to start kissing her.

Elsie put her hand on my cheek, bringing my face even closer as we kissed, causing the intensity to heighten. I moved my right hand down between my legs, finding that sweet spot that was abandoned moments ago and started rubbing myself as I continued to kiss Elsie.

Our tongues started a war in each other's mouths, twisting and molding against each other's as I continued to bring myself to my peak. My breathing became hurried as I rubbed my fingers eagerly against my clit.

Elsie pressed her body against mine and I could feel her nipples piercing through her shirt as she leaned against me. This helped immensely and I felt my orgasm shatter through my body, causing me to pause the kissing and instead moan into Elsie's mouth.

She put her hand on my ass as I continued to rub myself through my orgasm and rested her forehead on mine as I struggled to breathe through it. When it was over, I removed my fingers from between my legs and gently put them on Elsie's hip.

"Never apologize for not wanting to have sex. I will never pressure you into doing anything you don't want to do and please don't force yourself to do anything, just because you think I would want it," I stated, looking into her beautiful blue eyes. They started tearing up again, but she smiled all the same.

"Keep getting yourself off while you moan in my mouth like that, then maybe I'll be ready sooner than you think," Elsie responded with a slight laugh.

I chuckled as I moved myself away from her to stand up from the bed. I grabbed my clothes and put them back on, then slide back down next to her, though this time I was on the other side of her so I could spoon with her.

"How's your headache?" I asked.

"Almost gone," she responded, grabbing my arm from behind her and bringing it over her so we could link our fingers together again.

"I think an afternoon nap with *mi amor*, would cure me completely," she stated and I chuckled.

"Also known in Spanish as a *siesta*," I clarified, as I nuzzled my head into her shoulder again and we both drifted off to sleep.

~.~

The afternoon nap turned into overnight. It seemed that the jet lag and time zone differences really took a toll on our bodies. Elsie and I were awoken by a single knock on the hallway door, which burst open before we could respond to the knock.

"Hope you're decent," Techy announced as he walked in. I groaned as I rolled myself to face him.

"Too bad if we weren't. Give us a minute to answer would you? You could have gotten an eyeful," I snapped as I stretched myself out. Elsie sat herself up and put her legs over the edge of the bed.

"Then it would have been a good start to the day," Techy replied, with a wink. I rolled my eyes and he walked over to the table with his laptop.

"What do you want, Kyle?" I asked him, standing up and walking over to the small kitchenette to get myself a glass of water. I looked over at Elsie and gestured to a glass and she nodded with a smile of thanks.

"I'm really regretting telling you that," Techy replied, shaking his head.

"It's been almost thirty hours since you've eaten anything, so I thought we would order room service," he continued, as he opened his laptop.

I hadn't really thought about eating. With everything that was going on, food was the last thing on my mind, but now that he had mentioned it, I realized how hungry I actually was.

"Oh, well, thanks," I responded, handing Elsie over her glass of water.

"I also came with news for Elsie," Techy added and Elsie lifted her head up to look at him.

"What news is that?" Elsie asked, standing up from the bed and walking over to Techy to sit down next to him on the other chair. I made my way over to the table as well, willing to stand to listen to the news. However, Elsie had other plans and pulled me down to sit on her lap. She wrapped her arms around my waist and lightly rested her chin on my shoulder. Luckily I was light, as I would hate to think how her hip was handling my weight.

"How cute," Techy commented with a smirk. I rolled

my eyes as I put down my glass on the table.

"The news?"

"Right. So, I managed to get the messages and photos off your old phones before they were permanently deleted. I wanted to show you these earlier, Elsie, but you were otherwise engaged," Techy pointed out.

He turned his laptop around and a picture of Mrs. Taylor and her newborn baby.

"Congratulations, big sis," he announced and I felt Elsie tense behind me. I put my hand on top of hers and patted it gently.

"Did she say what his name is?" Elsie asked quietly.

"Noah Elisha Taylor," Techy replied, with a slight smirk. Elsie let out a small sigh behind me and I turned my head to look at her.

"Elisha," she whispered the name as tears filled her eyes.

"She named him after you," I pointed out the obvious. I turned my body slightly so I could put my thumb on her cheek to wipe away a falling tear.

"She doesn't hold it against you, E. She didn't give the baby, his name. She's on your side," I continued with a smile. Elsie struggled to smile back at me and let out a small gasp as she tried not to cry.

"Can we send her a message?" I asked as I looked

back over at Techy.

"I think you should be fine to send her a text message. I have obtained some New Zealand SIM cards that allow international messaging. I hacked Mrs. Taylor's phone and I saw no signs of anyone else trying to track it," he declared. He pulled a small SIM card from his pocket and handed it to me.

I had left the phone Techy had given me on top of the dresser, so I stood up from Elsie's lap and walked over to get it. Elsie followed me and we sat down on the edge of the bed. She watched me eagerly as I transferred the SIM over. Once I was ready, Techy read out Mrs. Taylor's number and then I handed the phone to Elsie.

Elsie: Hi. It's your former favorite homeroom student here. Congratulations for the start of your new NET. It's gorgeous.

Elsie paused and looked up at me.

"It's not too obvious right? I mean, she'll get it but if someone else was to read it they wouldn't know what I was talking about?" She asked me and I read it over a few times.

"It's very cryptic," I assured her and Elsie pressed the send button.

"I hope she doesn't get offended by me calling him an 'it,'" Elsie exclaimed, as she looked down at the phone.

"What's the time over there?" She asked, looking over at Techy. It was 9:20am local time.

"5:20pm," Techy responded almost immediately. I raised my eyebrow slightly, wondering if he had that already up on his laptop, or if he knew the time difference between the two countries.

Several minutes passed by, but eventually the three blinking dots appeared at the bottom of the screen.

Mrs. Taylor: I'm glad you reached out. NET is everything I hoped it could be and more. I wish you could see it in person. Are you ok?

Elsie: As ok as I can be right now.

Mrs. Taylor: Stay safe

Elsie: Send more NET updates when you can.

Mrs. Taylor sent a picture of Noah sleeping, while sucking on his hand. I wasn't one for babies, but when I saw Elsie's face as she looked at the boy she once thought was going to be her brother, my heart broke. It was full of disappointment and love.

"He's still your brother," I reminded her in a whisper. Techy started typing away on his laptop.

"Just ordering us food," he announced and I gave him a small smile of thanks before turning to Elsie.

"Just because he isn't your blood doesn't mean that he isn't your family," I explained and grabbed her hand.

"I killed his father; once he learns of that, he won't want to be part of my family," Elsie retorted, and I gave her hand a squeeze.

"Once he learns of that, he will also learn the circumstances of why you did what you did."

Elsie hung her head and I lifted my other hand and gently put it on her cheek to lift her head up to look at me.

"You saved him from potential harm, babe," I pointed out. She looked in my eyes for a moment and then gave me a small smile.

"At least he looks like Mrs. Taylor," she noted and I laughed as I nodded my head in agreement.

"Imagine if he had his nose," I replied and she laughed along with me. When Elsie suddenly stopped laughing, I did too because she looked serious.

"What if I never get to meet him? What if we're caught and thrown in prison, or worse what if we're killed?" Elsie asked me, and I could see that she was fighting the tears again.

I took the phone out of her hand and threw it on the

bed before pulling her into a tight hug.

"If we're caught and we go to prison, then at least we will be together. Mrs. Taylor is on your side, remember. I don't think prison will stop her from coming to see you, or letting you meet her son," I told her. "And we won't get killed, because no one is out there to harm us anymore. They're gone E, and besides, we're in a whole different country. I doubt the Morettis had any of their remaining people follow us across the world," I pointed out.

I put my hands on her shoulders and leaned back to look at her. I searched her eyes and I could tell by the look in them that she was still doubtful.

"And if it's the police you're worried about, then they can only harm us if they think we're a threat. And we're not. If it comes to it, then we will surrender. We won't give them a reason to shoot," I told her, thinking maybe that was what she meant.

"Like that stops the police," Elsie said with a small sigh. She then moved her hand to grab mine and pointed to my skin, trying to make her point.

"The police are a lot different here," I said quietly. I heard Techy scoff in the background and I turned to glare at him. He wasn't helping the situation.

"What I mean is, there are far fewer police-involved

shootings in this country," I corrected myself as I looked back at Elsie.

"New Zealand has a multicultural population with people who have browner skin than me. Perhaps they might think I'm one of them. Besides, I only look dark because you're whiter than a sheet of paper," I teased and Elsie let out a half-hearted laugh.

"Alright then, you've convinced me," Elsie responded, leaning forward and kissing me. I grinned into the kiss as I kissed her back, pulling her closer towards me.

There was another knock on the door and I heard Techy let out a sigh of frustration, which made my cheeks warm as I had almost forgotten he was there. Elsie and I pulled apart as Techy got up from the table and opened the door. There stood a young man, dressed in the hotel's uniform, beside a cart with our food.

Techy stepped aside with an amused smirk on his face as the employee walked in, avoiding Techy's gaze, pushing the trolley of food. When the trolley was next to the table, the employee cleared his throat.

"Please leave the trolley outside your room when you have finished with it," he stated. He looked at Techy, turned even redder then hurried out of the room. I raised my eyebrow as Techy's look changed to a satisfied smile as he shut the door behind the young man.

"What was all that about?" I asked, as I walked over to the trolley and grabbed two plates from it. I handed one to Elsie who moved to stand beside me.

"I don't think he expected to see me so soon after *servicing* my room last night," Techy responded in a risqué tone. I almost dropped my plate.

"Wait – you're – wait what? Are you bi?? You never told me," I pointed out, feeling slightly put out that he hadn't confided that in me, considering how close we were. I started to put food on my plate.

"Oh no, Cita. I'm pan. I love everybody," Techy responded with a grin. I picked up a bun and took a bite.

"How'd you think I met your father?" Techy asked, raising his eyebrow suggestively. I choked on my bun. Elsie put down her plate and rushed over to me and slapped my back until the piece of bun I had choked on came out and landed in front of Techy's feet. He was laughing so hard he was doubling over.

"I was joking, Cita. Fear not, your father is only into women," he clarified. I narrowed my eyes at him.

"You're a jerk," I told him and then walked over to the table and sat down.

Elsie sat down on the other chair and we ate the food that our stomachs desperately needed.

Chapter Eleven

Elsie

The food tasted a million times better than anything I had ever tasted in my life. I guess that is what happens when you haven't eaten in nearly two days.

Techy had left Lu and I to finish eating in peace. He must have realized that his joke didn't come across as funny as he thought, so he got out of there before Lu could yell at him again. He left us with our passports, explaining it would be our only form of identification.

When we finished eating, Lu gathered our plates, put them on the trolley and put it outside the hotel room.

When she came back into the room, she walked over to me and took my hands.

"What do you want to do today, babe?" She asked me, lifting me to my feet.

I didn't feel like doing anything. All I wanted to do was lie in bed, under the covers, to hide from my thoughts and my feelings. I wanted to numb the pain and go back to that oblivion that I had felt the night before. I knew we were in a new country and we had lots to explore, but even the thought of leaving this hotel room was almost too much to bear.

"Do we have to do anything?" I said with a slight pout

of my lip. Lu gave me a once over and then nodded her head.

"It'll be good to get outside and enjoy the fresh air. Explore a new country. Take your mind off things," Lu responded. I bit my lip, wanting to argue against it but I sighed instead and nodded.

"Fine," I agreed and Lu grinned. We had a shower and got ourselves changed into new clothes. Since it was quite windy still, I decided to wear my scarf again. I felt it was a better idea than having people stare at the dressing and ask questions.

Just as we were about to leave the room, somebody knocked on the adjoining door. I thought about Techy, thinking the door was about to open without us answering, but when it didn't, Lu walked over to it and opened it to reveal Olivia. She was holding the front page of a newspaper, her face slightly pale.

"What is it?" I asked. I walked over to her and stood behind Lu who took my hand. We stepped aside so Olivia could walk into the room. She went straight to the table and laid out the newspaper.

We walked over to her and saw immediately why she looked sick. On the cover was a picture of Lu and me, with a headline that made me suck in my breath and forget to breathe.

FBI's MOST WANTED: Fugitive Teen Couple Kidnap Local Detective and Flee The Country.

"They're blaming that on us?" I asked, letting my breath out after a few moments.

"Like anyone would believe that we could overpower a detective who has experience taking down criminals," Lu scoffed, reaching forward to grab the paper. Olivia stopped her.

"They mention my injuries, said you were able to take me because I was in too much pain to fight back," Olivia explained, pointing back to the text. I continued reading the article and my heart plummeted.
"Someone told them that you're my birthmother…" I pointed out and I looked at her. "They made it out to sound as if I had gone crazy due to shooting him, then finding out the truth about who you were to me and I held you at gun point." I felt my heart clinch in my chest.

"What a load of shit," Lu responded and then finally grabbed the paper and crumbled it up.

"The media are always finding false truths and publishing them," she added, giving my hand a gentle squeeze.

"I noticed they didn't mention anything about Dad

or Techy. They obviously don't know that they fled with us. Which is good, considering people will be keeping an eye out for the three of us, not five," Lu pointed out. Olivia nodded with agreement.

"At least there is that," Olivia stated, grabbing the crumbled newspaper and walking it over to the bin near the kitchenette. She turned to look at us.

"I never meant for me coming with you to put another strike against your names. I just wanted to make sure you were safe…I never expected this," Olivia said quietly and she walked over to me and took my other hand.

"I didn't think it would come to this either…being in another country, I mean. This has gotten out of hand," she continued.

I gave her a small smile. "I don't think any of us, other than Mr. Torres and Techy, had any idea what he had planned," I pointed out, and then gave her hand a squeeze. "I'm glad you're here though and glad you're not here trying to arrest me. Glad you're here as someone who cares about me," I added, my smile growing slightly more genuine.

Despite everything, finding out that Olivia was my mother and that she truly cared was probably the best thing that had happened besides Lu.

"Of course I care," Olivia responded, putting her hand

gently on my cheek. I felt Lu move her hand away from mine to leave me and Olivia to talk alone.

"When you decide you've had enough of the running and want to turn yourself in, I will make sure I get the best lawyer for you," Olivia said in a mere whisper.

I knew she didn't want to talk too loudly, because Mr. Torres was bound to be next door. I heard Lu let out a small noise, but I concentrated on Olivia.

"I don't want to go to prison," I responded just as quietly. I felt tears well up as I thought about everything I had done, from stealing to killing and how my life would be if I was behind bars. Sure, according to the TV shows I had watched, it was more like a terribly behaved boarding school, without the teachers and lessons and more fighting and orange.

But I wanted a life. I just turned eighteen and I didn't want to give it up just yet. I would rather die than be behind locked doors knowing there was a world out there.

Perhaps it was a good thing that Lu had convinced me to leave the room, because the more I thought about it, the more I knew that moping in this room was like being stuck behind those locked bars.

"Of course you don't," Olivia agreed and gently stroked my face. Lu cleared her throat again and walked back over to us.

"Sorry to cut this short Olivia, but Elsie and I were about to leave for the day. We're going to explore the city," she stated and I could tell by the tone of her voice that there was no invitation for her to join us. That's when Olivia looked at what I was wearing and noted the scarf around my neck.

"Oh right! Well, be careful out there. Make sure you don't do anything to grab anyone's attention," she warned. Lu just grinned at her and took my hand, pulling me towards the door.

"Of course not," she called over her shoulder.

"Have you got your passports? Money?" Olivia called after us.

"Yes, mom!" Lu responded in her teasing voice. I couldn't help but grin at that and turned to look at the satisfied look on Olivia's face.

"We'll be back later," I promised. Olivia grinned back as she watched us leave the hotel room.

~.~

It turned out that Christchurch had experienced a major earthquake in 2011. Even though many buildings that were damaged in that earthquake had been repaired, Lu and I walked past many sites that were cordoned off or had once held a building but were now vacant land.

Walking past these sites made me realize how lucky we were back in Sutton, as I had never felt an earthquake before. Lu had found out how many people had died and other facts that she shared.

We walked about the city for the rest of the afternoon in a bit of a somber mood. Christchurch was about the same size as Sutton and we had practically known everyone who lived there. If Sutton lost 185 people, chances were that we would have known most of them. That's what Christchurch would have felt at the time and probably still did.

That made me sad and I could tell it hit Lu hard too, considering we had been walking for half an hour, not saying much to each other.

We soon came across a section of the city where almost all of the buildings were made from storage containers. We walked around a few of the shops for about an hour, then we settled down at one of the cafés. Lu and I ordered our drinks, then sat outside at one of the tables.

We watched the people walking and shopping as we waited. I looked around the café shop and noticed a newspaper stand, holding the paper that had us on the cover. I reread the headline. FBI's Most Wanted. That meant they wouldn't stop looking for us until they found us.

"Do you think they will catch us here?" I asked, whispering so no one else could hear me. Lu followed my line of sight before responding. "I'd like to hope not."

I glanced around, looking at the people who were also in the café, wondering if they recognized us from the newspaper. I had hoped that when Lu had ordered our coffees her accent wasn't too strong, considering that was one hell of a giveaway that we didn't belong here.

Lu's fake name was called and I went to respond, but a waitress came over with our two drinks, placing them in front of us.

"Thank you," I said, as she left and she gave me a look before nodding her head.

"Enjoy," she responded, then turned to walk back to the counter.

I couldn't help but notice that her head turned to the newspaper stand as she walked past it.

"She recognized us," I said, with a grimace, taking my hand away from the handle of the mug I was about to pick up. Lu looked behind her towards the counter, then back at me.

"Elsie, you're just being paranoid. It'll be fine," Lu promised, picking up her mug and bringing it to her mouth.

I watched the lady behind the counter, but she had gone back to making more drinks and wasn't paying us any attention at all. Maybe I was paranoid.

I picked up my mug and took a sip of my coffee. It was the first one I had had for a while and it tasted as good as the first day I ever tried coffee. We sat in silence again as we drank our coffees, taking in the scenery.

As I drank the last drop of my coffee, Lu suddenly looked at me in surprise, almost dropping her mug on the table.

"What is it?" I asked, my eyes flying wide.

"The bracelet," she stated, putting her hand around it.

"It's vibrating," she added, then looked around, to see if she could spot any police.

"They're not here for us, are they?" I asked, my eyes flickering over to the counter again, and saw the lady avert her eyes as I caught her staring.

"I knew it!" I exclaimed and grabbed Lu's hand in mine and pulled her up.

"She recognized our faces," I moaned and we hurried out into the shopping complex courtyard, just in time to see two uniformed police officers heading directly towards us.

"Fuck," Lu groaned, just as one of the officers picked

up their two-way radio and the other put his hand on something yellow at his side.

Lu and I turned around and started to run in the opposite direction. My hip protested to this sudden change, but I tried to ignore it as we ran towards the nearest street. We didn't know where we were going, but it looked like the street we had walked down to get here, so we decided that was the best direction to take. I looked behind us and I could see that the police were pursuing us on foot as well and they seemed to be a lot faster than us, as they had nearly caught up.

"Stop running!" One of them called out, but we ignored them and I tried to ignore the increasing pain in my hip and my haggard breath as I struggled to breathe and ran faster. I knew I was slowing Lu down – she was hardly panting, whereas I felt like I was about to pass out from not being able to breathe. At times like these, I cursed my half a lung.

"You can do it, E," Lu said as she tugged me along behind her. We turned down an alleyway, which led us to another small suburban street. We dashed up a long driveway and hid behind the house and I almost collapsed on the ground outside a small window.

Lu helped me sit up against the house, before walking quickly around it and peeking into the windows. She came back and dropped down beside me, peering out around the corner of the house to watch the driveway.

"No one is home," she told me, and even though I struggled to get my breath back, I couldn't help but let out a sigh of relief. At least that was one less thing to worry about. Lu pulled her phone out of her pocket and handed it to me.

"Send Techy our location with an SOS," Lu told me. I took the phone and did that. I could hear the police sirens in the background getting closer. I hoped that Techy could track our location, because I doubted we were going to be staying put for much longer.

I handed the phone back to Lu, who shoved it in her pocket and then turned to help me stand up.

My hip didn't want to cooperate; the pain was almost unbearable. I groaned as I forced myself to move and Lu squeezed my hand.

"I promise you can lie in bed for days after this. We just have to get out of their search area and back to the hotel," Lu stated, as she moved her hand around my waist so she could help me move.

Luckily, we found a gate at the back of the house that went onto a back neighbor's property. Lu unlocked it and we went through it. It looked like children lived at this house, because there were toys and bikes all over the lawn.

Lu's eyes lit up when it landed on a bike that seemed to be the right height and size for us. She let go of me and hurried over to it. She transferred her phone from her back pocket to her front, then picked up the bike.

"Ever rode on the handlebars before?" She asked, as she walked the bike over to me, then mounted it to hold it up right. I shook my head, scared of the thought of falling off.

"I've got you, E," Lu stated, holding out her hand for me. I gulped, but as the sirens were getting louder, I knew I had to move.

I grabbed her hand and she pulled me to the bike. I turned myself around and put my hands on either side of the handlebars and lifted myself up, so I was sitting on them. It was very uncomfortable, but I knew it was the best way for us to get out of here quickly because I was sure my hip was going to seize up soon.

Lu moved the bike forward and I closed my eyes tight as she started to peddle. Once I was sure I wasn't going to fall, and realized Lu was good at riding a bike with someone on the front, I opened my eyes to find that we were already biking down the street. The police sirens sounded near, but they still had to be looking on that other street.

"Do you know where you're going?" I shouted, not sure if she would be able to hear me over the noise of the wind.

"Not a clue. I was planning to just keep biking until we see something familiar," Lu responded.

The sirens faded out, and I wanted to turn back to look around, but I was too scared that would cause me to fall, so I gripped the handlebars tighter and kept looking forward instead. Soon we came to a busy street, which actually did seem familiar. I remembered that we had walked down it to get to the container shopping complex. I felt Lu let out a sigh of relief.

A car beeped their horn behind us, causing Lu to swerve slightly. I felt the bike hit the curb, making it start to fall to the side. I screamed slightly as I jumped from the bike, landing on my stomach. I let out a cry, thinking I had landed on the road, but as I felt wet softness under me, I realized I had fallen on the grass.

I moved my legs, wondering if I had broken anything, and sighed with relief that it was only my hip that was sore. I turned myself over and looked for Lu. She had landed on the grass and the bike had fallen on top of her.

"Lu!" I cried, as I hurried over to her.

The car that had beeped at us had stopped meters

behind us, and I let out another sigh of relief when I realized it was Mr. Torres. He had gotten out of the car and had hurried over to Lu as well. Fortunately, she was laughing.

"Get this thing off me," she said in between laughs. Once Mr. Torres had gotten the bike off her and thrown it to the side, she pulled me into a fierce hug.

"I never thought I would see you fly," she commented, and I grinned as I hugged her back.

"Get in the car," Mr. Torres said in an urgent tone.

Lu let go of me and I helped her stand and we hurried into the car. Mr. Torres was soon back in it, and zoomed away from the side of the road, taking us back to the hotel.

"*Idiotas*," Mr. Torres hissed, as he looked at the rearview mirror at us.

"Second day in a new country and you already have the police chasing you!" He stated, angrily turning a corner. The tires screeched.

"It was the café waitress. She recognized us from the newspapers. She must have called the police," I explained, my voice shaking slightly. That really was a close call. I didn't know what I would have done if we hadn't found that bike. I didn't know how long my lungs or hips would have let me go on.

"The two of you were meant to keep a low profile. Not go parading around the city!" Mr. Torres stated. He turned another corner. Again the tires screeched. Lu grabbed my hand to squeeze it. I looked at her and she gave me a look that told me to let Mr. Torres rant.

"Olivia told me that you two had left, so I got Techy to patch into the police radio signal. I knew exactly when they spotted you," he explained.

"The café waitress had her suspicions as soon as you asked for your order. You have strong American accents! You could have at least put on a fake one!" he spat. I sat back in my seat and leaned my body against Lu, who put her arm around my shoulder.

"She told the police she had seen the article when she put out the papers and she took the picture of you, Lu, and cut off the pink hair. Didn't you think a wig would have been a good precaution?" Mr. Torres asked, looking in his rearview. I felt Lu tense beside me and I knew that it hadn't even occurred to her.

Mr. Torres shook his head and turned his attention back to the road. It wasn't long until we pulled into the hotel's parking lot. We got out and Mr. Torres slammed his door.

"You're not to leave the hotel until the heat dies down. They have a pool and stuff, so go enjoy that. Best to stay in your room for the rest of today though," he said before walking through the hotel's entrance without looking back at us.

"He'll get over it," Lu said quietly, as she put her arm around my waist again to help me walk.

After what seemed like an hour later, we finally got back to our hotel room. I found it painful to walk so we were walking very slowly. I was lucky to have someone as patient as Lu by my side. As soon as we walked into the room, Olivia ran to the door and threw her arms around me.

"Thank goodness," she exclaimed, pulling me close to her. I let out a small chuckle as I hugged her back.

"I'm fine," I promised, trying to get her to loosen her grip.

"I should have gone with you. I shouldn't have let you go at all," she said in a rush and Lu merely laughed as she walked past us.

"Like you could have stopped us from going," Lu responded.

I gave Olivia a small smile and hobbled fully into the room. I walked over to the kitchenette and opened a few cupboards before I came across the one with the mini drinks in them. I picked out the vodka bottle, uncapped it, and drank it all at once before putting it down on the counter.

"Elsie?" Olivia asked, gingerly, putting her hand on my back as I grabbed another bottle.

"It's been a long, tiring, eventful day, Olivia. I just need to take the edge off," I explained, before uncapping the second bottle.

I could tell that she wanted to say more, but she took her hand off my back and moved towards the table and sat down.

Lu walked over to me instead, holding a pill bottle in her hand.

"Guess you won't need this then?" Lu stated. I could hear a hint of disapproval in her tone, but I ignored it as I brought the bottle to my mouth and downed it again. I shuddered slightly as it went down my throat.

"This works just as well," I responded. I grabbed another bottle and walked over to the bed, thinking it would be better than sitting on a hard chair.

This time when I brought the bottle to my lips, I only took small sips. But the pain in my hip was fading as I continued to drink and the ever-increasing visions were starting to disappear.

Chapter Twelve

Olivia

Over the next few weeks we all laid low, staying in the hotel. Because it was fully equipped with an indoor pool, gym and restaurant, there wasn't any reason to leave.

Thankfully, a couple of days after we arrived, Techy managed to get another room for me so I didn't have to share with Jorge. When I realized that we were put in the same room, with one bed, I had refused to go along with it. I ended up sleeping on the floor on a spare mattress that one of the hotel staff found for me, until they put me in my own room which adjoined Techy's.

There had been a few more newspaper articles about the girls, and they had featured a few times on the news confirming that they had been sighted in New Zealand, though no new leads on their current whereabouts. Other than that, there wasn't too much trouble. None that involved the police anyway.

The biggest thing I noticed was the amount of alcohol Elsie was consuming. She wouldn't listen to any of us when we asked her to slow down, to stop. She had even gotten to the point where she would sneak a drink when she thought we weren't looking.

It got even worse when she realized she could order a whole bottle with room service instead of consuming all of the mini bottles that were restocked each day when the rooms were cleaned.

I was really worried that she was becoming addicted. She swore she could stop if she wanted too, but it was the only thing that she could do to stop the memories.

Jorge had offered to buy her cannabis from a local biker gang, but she turned it down, which I was secretly, glad about, considering it was illegal in New Zealand. I didn't want her to be in legal trouble in this country too.

Luckily, the pain in her hip was easing and she found it easier to move around. She had even started self-defense lessons with Lu in the gym now that the stitches in her neck were also gone. She was left with a terrible looking scar.

I had found myself watching and giving some pointers during the self-defense lessons, much to Lu's annoyance. I felt as if I was a burden being there, but I didn't really have anywhere else to go. I hated being alone with Jorge and Techy because I could tell they still held the fact that I was a cop against me. I could feel the mood change the moment I stepped into a room. It does wonders to a woman's ego, knowing she's hated for what she does for a living.

Elsie, Lu and I were in their room, sitting around the table. I had moved a chair in from my room, so there was enough seats for all of us.

After hearing how good she was at art, I had gotten Elsie some supplies. I took pride in the fact that she took after her father in that respect. She still hadn't asked me much about him, but I think she was still trying to get over the fact that the man she grew up thinking was her dad was really just her abusive uncle.

Elsie had been sketching something new every day, which, thankfully, kept her mind off everything which in turn meant she didn't need to drink. She had drawn me, in such a realistic way that I was amazed. She had drawn several pictures of Lu as well, ones that she showed me and others where she refused to pass over the sketch pad, much to Lu's embarrassment. Today she was drawing an outline of three roses.

"What's this for?" I asked, with a small smile as I leaned across the table to get a better look.

Elsie looked up from her drawing, her hand absentmindedly going straight to her throat.

"I was thinking of covering up my scar," Elsie said, her eyes going slightly wider as she waited for my response. My heart skipped a beat, realizing that she wanted to cover her skin with ink. I had never gotten a tattoo and I didn't think I was ever going to.

"If that's what you want to do, then I'm all for it," I responded and Lu got up from the table, letting out a small chuckle. She kissed the top of Elsie's head.

"I told you she wouldn't have a problem with it!" Lu exclaimed and gave me a smile before turning to go to the bathroom, leaving Elsie and me alone for a moment.

"Did you think I would object?" I asked curiously. Elsie averted her eyes and nodded her head. She continued to draw her rose.

"It's your body… I only gave birth to it," I said with slight amusement in my voice.

"Do you have any?" Elsie asked me as she started shading.

"Tattoos? No…I thought about getting one after your father died, but then I found out I was pregnant with you and didn't want to risk anything…I haven't really thought about it since," I admitted.

Elsie finished one of the roses, then looked at me, putting her pencil down.

"What was he like?" she asked quietly.
I grinned at her, glad that she had finally asked me. I didn't want to pressure her by telling her anything until she was ready. "The biggest gentleman," I said, smiling.

Lu came out of the bathroom and sat down in the

empty chair. Elsie turned to grab her hand then looked back at me.

"Olivia was just going to tell me about my birth father," Elsie explained and Lu smiled as she looked at me to go on.

"We met when I was fifteen and he was in his last year at high school," I stated, quietly. Most people got turned off by the age difference, thinking I was too young. My dad would have agreed with them. "Quite cliché, but I was a cheerleader and he was on the football team. We traveled together to the football championships and things, so we got to know each other quite well.

"We didn't do anything officially until I turned sixteen, and even then, my dad, was quite against it."

Elsie took my hand.

"Because he was older than you?" she asked me and I nodded my head.

"Even though I was of age to consent, he threatened to charge him with statutory rape, if he ever went near me again," I told her.

I heard Lu make a noise and I looked at her.

"Clearly that threat didn't stop you," Lu commented with a smirk. I gave her a small smile.

"No. In fact, it made us closer. I didn't want to go

home, because I was afraid that my dad would find out and arrest him, so I hardly ever went home. I always said I was at a friend's place, studying or having a sleep over, but I was always with him," I replied.

"What was his name?" Elsie asked me and I turned to look at her.

"Elias Blackmore," I answered. My heart fluttered as I said it.

"My mom, I mean, Rosemary, she named me after him?" Elsie asked.

I squeezed her hand, my heart pounding faster.

"She's still your mom," I said quietly. "Yes, I suppose she did. I didn't know she had adopted you, but I guess it was kind of fitting that she adopted her brother's daughter and named her after him," I explained quietly.

"He died in a fire, right?" Elsie asked.

I gulped as I nodded. I could feel tears welling up in my eyes.

"Because I wasn't sixteen until after he graduated, and I still had two years left of high school, he wanted to stay around so we could go to college together," I explained.

"He joined the fire department, going to the academy while I was at school and then started as a rookie. It was his third day officially working as a firefighter," I said, gulping slightly as I felt my eyes burn and my throat swell up as I tried not to cry.

"There was an explosion in the building where he and his crew were trying to fight a fire. It killed him and two other firefighters," I choked out.

Elsie squeezed my hand again and I couldn't help starting to cry. Lu got up and hurried to the bathroom, bringing back some tissues for me to wipe my tears.

"Thank you," I said, laughing slightly as I wiped my eyes.

"I found out I was pregnant with you on the day of his funeral," I continued.

Elsie's eyes started to tear up as well.

"So he didn't even know about me?" she asked and I shook my head regretfully.

"He would have been over the moon about it though. He told me once he wanted enough children to start his own football team," I said laughing.

Elsie's smile grew.

"I would have disappointed him then, considering how terrible I am at any sport," Elsie retorted and I shook my head.

"You would have never disappointed him, in any way, shape, or form," I promised.

"Even though I'm a lesbian?" Elsie questioned and I smiled.

"He would have painted the house so we would have lived in rainbow colors," I told her.

"He was pretty special then," Elsie concluded, and I nodded.

"Just like his daughter," I responded.

Elsie grinned.

"And just like his daughter, he was a pretty good artist too. But I feel you would have given him a run for his money," I noted, nodding down to her unfinished work.

"My mom didn't ever talk about him. But she did have an album full of drawings. I asked her about them once, but she said her friend had drawn them for her. They could have been his right?" Elsie asked.

Knowing Elias, he definitely would have filled up an album with his drawings to give as a birthday or Christmas present. I had one sitting in my apartment, which I hoped hadn't been destroyed when they had staged my abduction. I nodded my head with a grin.

"More than likely," I replied and Elsie grinned back.

"He was amazing! The detail he put in his work! I used one of his paintings once to see if I could replicate it. I don't think I did it justice. But to think that he had drawn that!" Elsie said in a rush of excitement.

My heart faltered again as I thought about how much Elias and I missed out on Elsie's childhood. If only he had gone to college without me. If only I had found out I was pregnant a week earlier. There was a lot of 'if onlys' and I knew I couldn't change any of them. I took my hand out of Elsie's and stood up.

"I have a picture of him in my room. I'll be right back."

I usually kept the photo in my purse, but when I had gone to Jorge's house the day we rescued the girls from the factory, I had taken it out and put it straight in my pocket, thinking there was no point in bringing the purse along. Now I kept it in the room, so I didn't wreck it.

I hurried out of the girls room and walked over to mine. It didn't take me long to grab it before returning to the room, where I handed the picture of Elias to Elsie.

"You have his nose," I pointed out, with a grin on my face. "And his ears. His chin."

Elsie grinned down at the photo.

"You must have found him handsome," she stated and I laughed.

"Without a doubt. He grew more handsome every day," I noted and Elsie actually wrinkled her nose.

"Gross," she declared and I laughed again. Lu walked around the back of Elsie and looked down at the picture.

"Well, all I can say is thank god you two couldn't wait to get in each other's pants, because if you waited any longer, I wouldn't be with your beautiful creation," Lu stated, grinning as she kissed the top of Elsie's head.

Elsie looked up at her and they proceeded to kiss on the lips.

I grinned at the two of them.

"She was actually conceived our first time together," I commented and Elsie's nose wrinkled again as she looked back at me.

"Wow. If he had lived, he might have gotten that football team!" Lu exclaimed and I blushed slightly. "We will never know," I responded, disappointment edging my voice.

"Have you ever…you know, loved anyone again?" Elsie asked me, her tone clear about what she was actually asking.

"I've had sex. With both men and women. But no. I've never loved anyone since your father. I don't think I could ever love a person as much as I loved him," I stated, sadly.

"Wouldn't he want you to find love though, to move on?" Elsie asked quietly.

I sat back down on the seat and Elsie passed me the photo. I looked down at him, stroking my thumb gently down his face.

"Probably. But I haven't felt the need to have anyone

in my life like that. I've been too busy with work to even think about getting into a relationship," I admitted.

"You're only thirty-four. You still have time," Elsie commented and I tilted my head a bit.

"It's slightly difficult at the moment, considering we're in a foreign country, trying to keep a low profile," I said with a small smile.

Elsie turned red.

"Oh yeah. Sorry about that," she stammered, and I laughed.

"Well you're already married to my dad, Amanda," Lu pointed out, and I glared at her.

"Not going to happen," I responded, at the same time that Elsie shouted, "No!"

We all started laughing, which was the first time in a while that I had actually seen Elsie genuinely happy. When the laughter died down, I stood up again. It was nearing dinner time and I still had to get ready.

"I'll meet you two down at the restaurant," I told them, grabbing Elsie's hand and giving it a small squeeze before I headed towards the door.

"Thank you for telling me about Elias," Elsie called out. I turned and gave her a small smile.

"You can ask me anything, any time, Elsie. It's good to talk about him to someone again," I admitted, then I left the room and headed to mine.

Chapter Thirteen

Lu

Time seems to drag when you have to spend every day in the same place. Elsie and I spent most days doing something, but it got boring doing the same thing three times a week.

I had started Spanish lessons with her. She could now effectively say who she was, where she lived, count to one hundred, and say how much she loved me.

We also started self-defense lessons, as she could now move her hip with no limitations. Her throat had also healed, so I didn't have to worry about reopening her wound.

We had been in New Zealand and on the run for two months.

One Wednesday, Elsie and I had just woken up and had our breakfast brought up with room service. There was a newspaper sitting on top of the tray, and even though it was folded I could tell that it held yet another article about Elsie and me; I could see Elsie's eyes and I knew her blue eyes like the back of my hand. I picked up the newspaper and opened it.

Fugitive's Blood Found At Burnt-Down Factory Along With Several Bodies

Elizabeth Neilson's blood was found at an abandoned factory in Sutton, New Haven, USA. The factory was being investigated after a large fire revealed burnt remains of several people. Sources say it was members of the Moretti family. Police sources say the deceased were killed by gunshot wounds to the head and that the fire was postmortem. Another source has confirmed that the fugitives are in possession of abducted detective Olivia Swanson's service weapon. Forensics are still needed to confirm whether or not the bullets came from that gun.

Lucita Torres Alvarez's father, Jorge 'Bomber' Torres, well known for his bomb rigging skills, currently can't be located. Employees of the Torres estate refuse to comment on his whereabouts, but one source has stated that he was the owner of the private jet that the fugitives may have used to flee the country.

Evidence indicates that Torres may have been involved in the factory mass murder, possibly in an attempt to cover up a crime committed by his daughter. He is suspected of having done so in the past. Police have issued a warrant for his arrest related to these crimes.

Francesca Moretti, mother of Dante Moretti who was killed during the events of prom night at Neilson High School, expressed her wishes to have her family's murderers brought to justice.

"Please, I beg of you, please turn yourself in and face justice for killing my last remaining son. Face justice for killing the remaining members of my family. You've taken everything from me. Don't make this any harder for me or yourselves," she stated in a desperate plea to fugitives Neilson and Torres Alvarez.

I refused to read anymore. I crumpled up the newspaper and threw it against the door.

"Hey, I was reading that," Elsie exclaimed, her mouth full of toast. I looked at her and gave her a slight smirk as I turned to pick up a piece of my own.

"They're only trying to blame us for more deaths," I pointed out, taking a bite.

"By the end of this, we're going to have a body count that passes Elizabeth Báthony," I commented, rolling my eyes.

"How many did she kill?" Elsie asked, putting her feet up on the chair. She brought her knees to her chin so she could rest it on them.

"Six hundred," I told her and her eyes widened as she tried not to choke on her piece of toast.

"They couldn't possibly think we would kill that many people."

I shrugged my shoulders.

"They're already pinning another five bodies on us. We're up to eight," I replied. I finished off my toast and grabbed a bowl of cereal, which I handed to Elsie, before grabbing one for myself. She took it, balanced the bowl on her knees and began eating it slowly.

"They're only guessing it was us. They'll know it wasn't from the gun we stole soon, won't they? Then they'll have to look to other suspects," she asked, after taking another mouthful.

"Yeah and the next person they're going to blame is my father," I said, after taking a mouthful of mine. "No matter what we do, E, until we set the story straight, we're going to be blamed for a number of things. It's easier to pin it on us and make up the evidence than actually solve it properly." I put my spoon in my half-finished bowl and pushed it away from me. I had lost my appetite.

"And if it's not us, then it'll be my father. What we did has ruined everyone's lives," I said quietly.

Elsie put the bowl from her now-finished cereal on

the table and put her feet back on the ground. She reached forwards, grabbed both my hands and pulled me up from the chair. She drew me towards her, so I was sitting on her lap.

I gave her a curious look as she looked at me, her eyes resting on my lips for a second before flicking back up to my eyes. My heartbeat grew stronger at the thought of her kissing me while I was in this position.

"I know our choices have brought many people into our mess, but we didn't force your dad to kill those people or fly his jet to New Zealand. Nor did we force Olivia to go against her oath and come with us. They made those choices, just like we made ours," Elsie pointed out and then proceeded to lean forward to kiss me on my lips.

As the kiss became more passionate, I put my arms around Elsie and pulled her body closer to mine. I could feel her heart pounding against my chest.

It reminded me of the way we used to be, before everything had happened. Elsie moaned in my mouth then pulled away, putting her forehead on mine. Our bodies remained close and I could feel Elsie's breath struggle to keep up.

"*Lo siento, mi amor*," Elsie whispered and my heart broke for her again.

"Stop apologizing," I told her and I lifted my head to look at her properly.

"I'm just so frustrated with myself!" She exclaimed and I got off her as I felt her body shift, because I didn't want to be thrown to the ground when she stood. She moved across the room.

I watched her carefully, secretly hoping she wasn't going towards the alcohol cupboard. I knew it was only a matter of time before she started day drinking.

"Why? I'm not frustrated with you," I pointed out, frowning slightly.

"Because, Lu, I want to make love to you so badly," Elsie responded. I felt my cheeks warm. She turned to look at me.

"I want to hold you close to my body. I want to make you moan, scream and come as I fuck you so hard, you won't be able to see straight," she continued. My cheeks got hotter, as did the area between my legs.

"But I can't. I can't because all I can fucking see is *him*," she finished, picking up the pillow from the bed, and throwing it across the room.

"He's ruined everything, Lu," she sighed.

I walked over to her and pulled her into a hug. I felt her body tense slightly and I knew it was just because she was remembering what happened to her, so I didn't take it personally. I had gotten used to her jumpiness at my touch. She often wasn't even aware that she was doing it.

I felt her shoulders drop and then her arms around my waist as she hugged me back.

"You know how I feel about waiting for you to be one hundred percent ready before we do anything more than kissing," I stated, dropping my head on her shoulder, nuzzling my nose into her neck. I don't know why I kept doing this. Maybe it was like a comfort thing.

"If you're ready tomorrow, then great, I'm all for it, obviously. But if you aren't ready until next year, or even ten years from now, then I'll wait," I stated and Elsie let out a small laugh.

"I'm glad you're confident that we will still be together in ten years," she said quietly. I lifted my head and gave her a serious look.

"You're my soulmate, Elizabeth Rose, and I love you with every fiber of my being. I will be with you until we're either old and gray, or dead," I vowed. Elsie's eyes searched mine for a second, before she pulled me close again.

"I love you so much," she declared and I grinned as I hugged her back. When she let go of me I let my arms fall to my side and took her hand in mine.

"What's the mission today? Have you almost finished your drawing for your tattoo design? Maybe I could ask Dad to let us out of this fancy prison on furlough for the day," I suggested, my grin still strong.

Elsie chuckled and pulled me over to the kitchenette bench to open the drawer. She pulled out her almost finished drawing of three roses, handed it to me so she didn't have to let go of my hand to reach back for her colored pencils.

We walked over to the table and sat down, finally letting go of each other so she could work on her drawing. The drawing was similar to the one she had drawn in art class, but this time there was an extra rose. This one sat behind the orange rose and she was yet to color it in.

She still hadn't told me who it represented, but I had a feeling it was meant to be for Olivia.

My suspicions were proven correct when she picked up a yellow pencil and started shading it in.

"Olivia?" I asked, watching her in awe as she worked. It was amazing how realistic it looked already. Elsie nodded her head and continued to work.
"The three most important women in my life," she stated. "It's in this order, because it's the order they were in my life. Yellow for Olivia, because she gave birth to me.

Orange for Mom, because she adopted me and loved me as her own. And pink for you, because you are the love of my life," Elsie explained, pointing to the roses from the back to the front. I grinned at her as she looked up at me.

"I thought that having the pink rose closest to my heart was fitting," she added, and I chuckled.

"I love it when you're corny," I responded and leaned over to kiss her on her cheek. Elsie's cheek turned pink.

"Trying to make up for not being horny," Elsie stated, her face serious for a moment before we both burst out laughing.

"I love you," I stated once again, when our laughter had died down.

"I love you too," Elsie replied, kissing me, then returned to her work.

"You never said if you wanted a tattoo as well," she pointed out as she added in a different shade of yellow. I leaned back on the chair as I watched her.

"I never really thought about getting one. I haven't had a reason to, until now," I admitted. "I mean, Dad has so many that they cover up half his body and I remember Mom had one on her wrist. It was my name." I thought about the tattoo my mom had gotten. It was my name in my handwriting, written in a birthday card for her when I was five. It was the messiest handwriting I had ever seen, but she loved it to pieces.

"What's your reason now then?" Elsie asked, looking at me as she grabbed a darker pencil.

"You," I stated and she blushed even more.

"You don't want to get my name tattooed on you, do you?" Elsie asked with a small laugh. I grinned at her.

"Not exactly," I replied. Elsie paused her drawing to look at me again.

"Are you going to keep me in suspense?" she asked, and I smirked as I nodded.

"It's a surprise," I told her, and she pouted slightly before turning back to her drawing.

"Who did you get to design it?" She asked. I'm sure she was trying to trick me into giving up my secret, but I wasn't going to.

"I'm not saying a word. You'll just have to wait and see," I told her, grinning. Elsie let out a defeated sigh.

"Fine. I'll wait," she said, looking up at me with a grin.

The truth was that there was no design at all. I wasn't in any way artistic, so I couldn't think of anything that I would want on my body permanently.

All I had in mind was the letter E with a red heart around it, tattooed right above my heart. I told her the truth when I said it wasn't exactly her name.

She went back to her drawing and I watched her silently for the next hour as she finished off her roses and colored in the leaves.

~.~

Three hours later, we found ourselves sitting in a tattoo parlor, waiting for it to be Elsie's turn to get her tattoo. She was currently holding my hand and jiggling her leg as she tried to fight her nervousness.

"Come on E, you've had worse pain than this. This will be nothing," I whispered, trying to make my words more tangy to fake an accent.

It wasn't like I had any clue what getting a tattoo felt like. My dad had come along with us and was talking to the owner of the parlor, who had moved around all his bookings and closed the parlor for the afternoon after seeing how much he was going to be paid to do our two tattoos.

Dad had agreed to let us go and get them the moment I asked, telling me that his only condition is that he'd go with us.

Olivia had tried to come along too, but Dad had told her to stay because he didn't want any chances of any of us getting recognized now that people knew that all four of us were New Zealand. He had made me wear a red wig and had even gone so far as to get us colored contacts so people couldn't recognize our eyes.

Dad was the best at putting on a fake accent, so he pretended he was Australian when he spoke to the owner. Now we had to pretend we were Australian too, so Elsie and I were sitting at the waiting area, whispering to each other, practicing our fake accents.

"I know, I know," Elsie replied, her voice sounding more Australian than mine. "It's just that this is permanent. I can't take it back."
I gave her hand a squeeze.

"Your roses are amazing, E. You're not going to regret it," I promised, then I nodded my head towards the pictures on the wall of the tattoos the artist had done.

"His work is just as amazing as yours; you have nothing to worry about," I added. She let out a sigh and nodded.

"I know," she said, just as Jay, the tattoo artist, came over, grinning as he held the drawing of the roses in his hand, which my dad had given to him.

"My dear, your work is wonderful! If you ever decide to move here on a permanent basis and need a job, you've got one here," Jay declared and Elsie actually turned her worried look into a grin.

"I never thought of being a tattoo artist," Elsie

commented and I couldn't help but picture Elsie tattooing her initial and heart on my chest. Maybe I could ask Dad to pay him extra to let her do it.

"Well, let's get started," he declared and gestured Elsie over to a tattoo bed.

Elsie gave me a concerned look, but I gently shooed her away, with a smile. She followed him and soon she was positioned on her side on the tattoo bed, with a roll under her neck, so her scarred throat area was exposed and in the best position for the artist. Dad must have mentioned to him not to ask about the scar, because he got to work without commenting on it, though I knew by the look on Jay's face that he was conflicted about going over it so soon. I guess the money helped persuade him.

Dad walked over to me and sat down on the chair that Elsie had just vacated.

"You want Elsie to tattoo you, don't you?" He asked me and I turned to look at him with a grin.

"You know me too well, Papi," I said, nodding. He chuckled.

"You bet I do, Mija. We'll see that it happens," he promised.

Elsie's tattoo took about four hours. In that time, she actually fell asleep, which made me laugh. I guess this was the type of pain she could tolerate. The tattoo was beautifully done. It was an exact replica of Elsie's drawing, with no changes.

She was passed a mirror by the tattoo artist, then Dad asked if he could have a word with him and pulled him to the other side of the parlor.

I walked over to Elsie.

"What do you think?" I asked her quietly. She didn't answer me for a while, as she moved her head around to look at it in different angles.

"I love it," she whispered. I grinned at her.

"It really is beautiful," I told her. Elsie put the mirror on the bed and stood up.

"Do I look badass?" She asked, and I chuckled as I stepped forward to hold her up as the blood rushed to her head and she swayed a little.

"Definitely," I responded. I walked her over to the water dispenser and poured her a cup of water. She drank it down quickly, so I took the cup from her and refilled it just as Jay came over to talk to us. He looked happy, so I guess Dad got what he wanted.

"Perhaps you can be a tattoo artist sooner than you thought," he said to Elsie, who lowered her drink from her mouth with a confused look on her face.

"What?" She asked, looking from him to me and to Dad who had walked behind the man.

"I just need to put cream on your tattoo, put some wrap on to cover it, and clean the station, but after that, you can tattoo your girlfriend!" The man explained with a grin.

Elsie gulped down the rest of her water then shoved the cup into my hand, causing it to crumple.

"Was that your idea?" Elsie asked, biting her lip. I threw the cup in the garbage bin and then looked at her with a smirk.

"I wouldn't have anyone else mark my skin," I responded, then looked at the tattoo artist.

"No offense," I added, quickly. He held his hands up in the air.

"None taken," he replied and I looked back at Elsie. I put my hand on my chest, over my heart.

"It'll be really simple. Just your initial in black, with a red heart around it, like the one we've drawn before," I told her, giving her a knowing look. She looked at me for another moment before shaking her head.

"I can't do it, Lu. I've never tattooed anybody before. What if I mess it up?" She asked.

"Then, I will take over and fix it," the man promised.

Elsie bit her lip as she looked between me and the tattoo artist. I pouted my lips and gave her my best puppy dog look and she sighed, defeated.

"Fine," she agreed

I clapped my hands with joy.

"Great," I declared and she shook her head as she turned and walked back to the tattoo bed to get her aftercare completed.

It wasn't long before the station was sterilized and it was my turn. I took off my shirt, not caring that I was now wearing only my bra in front of my dad and a stranger.

All I cared about was the girl who was looking at me like I was crazy for thinking this was a good idea. I laughed at her as I laid down on the tattoo bed.

"I trust you, E," I told her and then she began.

The man instructed her step by step. When the tattoo needle first touched my skin, I was surprised that it didn't hurt as much as I thought it would.

I watched Elsie's face as she concentrated on her work and listened to everything Jay was saying. She must have been a natural because Jay was still smiling by the time she had finished the E. I looked down at my chest and grinned because she had done it the exact way we did the E in H.E.L.L.

"Are you sure you want me to continue?" Elsie asked, her cheeks slightly pink.

"You're a natural!" the man explained and I nodded

with agreement.

"Absolutely," I declared, so Elsie grinned as she was shown how to swap colors. It wasn't long until she was putting the needle into my skin again to start on the heart.

When she was done and had put down the tattoo machine, I sat up and kissed her hard on the mouth.

"Thank you, babe," I said as I pulled away. I looked down at my chest and grinned.

"It's exactly how I pictured it," I announced.

"Really?" She asked, blushing. I nodded and kissed her again. The man cleared his throat, apologized, then handed Elsie the cream to put on my tattoo. She rubbed it in gently and my heart pounded against her touch. She raised her eyebrow slightly at me and gave me a smirk.

"I wouldn't mind doing this for a living," Elsie declared and I chuckled slightly.

"You can practice on me," I stated, which Elsie grinned at.

"I'm not buying you a tattoo kit," Dad said as he walked over to us to have a look at Elsie's handiwork.

"Even if it is your birthday in two days," he added. I looked up at him, my heart pounding for a different reason. I had forgotten about my own birthday. I guess after being stuck in a hotel for weeks at a time, things like eighteenth birthdays were blips in the memories.

"Maybe when we're less locked down?" I asked, my voice hopeful. Dad looked at me for a moment.

"Maybe when things die down. We will talk about it later," he told me and I nodded, knowing now wasn't really the time.

Jay cleared his throat again and handed Elsie a clear bit of wrap to put over my creamed tattoo and tape to hold it down. He then handed us two tubs of cream and a sheet on how to take care of our tattoos. I put my shirt back on and then grabbed onto Elsie's hand.

"Thank you," I said to her and she leaned forward to kiss me.

"You're welcome. Though it feels like I branded you. Does that mean I own you now?" Elsie asked and I laughed and pulled her into a hug.

"You owned me the moment you looked at me," I pointed out. Dad let out a scoff, which made me look at him. He grinned as he shook his head.

"You two are hopeless," he commented and I grinned back, agreeing.

"Come on," he gestured to the door for us to leave. "Thank you!" Elsie and I both said to the tattoo artist. He shook hands with my dad, who said a few words to him.

We then waved our goodbyes and headed back to the
hotel.

Chapter Fourteen

Elsie

Life with a tattoo on your throat and part of your neck was a whole lot better than a scar. Instead of the looks of disgust that I had gotten from people who glimpsed my scar when my scarf fell, I was getting looks of wonder and questions about who had done the design.

The sudden attention I got from the other hotel guests was quite concerning to Olivia, but I was overjoyed. One of the guests even paid me to draw them something that they could get tattooed. Lu was pleased because it gave me something to focus on.

I knew she and Olivia were worried about my drinking, but it was hard to find something else that could black out the memories. I didn't want to start smoking joints because I knew I would want something stronger. I didn't want to go down that road, for fear I would end up like Lu and almost overdose.

I only drank enough now to help me go to sleep. That way I knew I wouldn't have any nightmares.

Things were getting slightly easier, but every time I kissed Lu, I remembered how he forced his lips on mine. Every time Lu touched me, I remembered his touch on my skin. I tried to stop it and it was getting less frequent, but I jumped every time she touched me. I could tell by the look in her eyes that I was breaking her heart.

The Spanish and self-defense lessons with Lu also helped get my mind off things. We often walked around the hotel as she pointed to random objects and taught me the words for them. Then she tested me later by pointing at the same objects again. We had also spent a lot of time in the gym, where Lu taught me how to get out of choke holds and arm grabs.

We were in the gym one afternoon. It was Lu's birthday, but I was pretending that I hadn't remembered because we were throwing her a surprise birthday dinner at the hotel restaurant that night. No one had said "happy birthday" to her, and although she didn't mention it I could tell she was a little sad because she wasn't holding me as hard as usual. I could easily get out of her grasp when normally she would make me struggle.

"Come on, Lucita, you're making this too easy for me," I pointed out, as I lightly, but still hard enough to make it hurt, stomped on her foot and elbowed her in the stomach as she put her arm loosely around my throat.

"Hmph!" came the sound out of Lu's mouth as her arms fell away and she stepped back.

"Maybe I don't want to hurt you," Lu retorted, putting her hands on her hips.

"I'm never going to learn properly if you keep doing that. I don't want to be a damsel in distress, and I don't want you always being my knight in shining armor. That's why you're showing me how to do this," I exclaimed, putting my own hands on my hips.

Lu tilted her head slightly.

"Fine, but maybe I can show you a few punching techniques before we go back to the choke hold," Lu suggested and I nodded in agreement.

"Show me how you would punch someone," Lu commanded, and I pulled my fingers in a fist.

"Is that how you punched Ryleigh?" she asked, her eyebrow raising slightly.

"Yeah," I responded, my cheeks warming slightly.

"I'm surprised you didn't break your thumb," she told me. She stepped a bit closer to me and put her hand over my fist.

"First, your thumb needs to be on the outside of your knuckles," she informed me and pulled my thumb from under my fingers and rested it against my knuckles.

"Punching with your thumb in like that increases the risk of breaking it," she stressed.

"Now you want to make sure your wrist is straight, or you could break that too," she pointed out, moving my hand so it made my wrist straight. "Your point of impact should be these two knuckles."

She pointed to the knuckles on my pointer and middle fingers. I nodded, taking it in.

"Now, hold up your other fist," she instructed and I lifted up my other fist, making sure I had my thumb on the outside and my wrist straight. She nodded.

"Stand as if you're going to fight me," she said next. I moved my body, so I had one foot in front of the other my elbows down, and one fist in front of the other.

Lu moved around me and put her hands on my hips to adjust me slightly. I had expected my normal reaction of jumping at her touch, but instead the only thing that jumped was my heart. It pounded quickly in my chest and I looked at my girlfriend as she looked over my body and moved me around into the correct stance.

"Pay attention to where your feet and arms are supposed to be," Lu scowled as she caught me watching her instead. I blushed and looked down at my feet position.

"Sorry," I murmured. Lu lifted my right hand so it was closer to my chin and moved my left out further and slightly higher.

"Bend your knees slightly," Lu directed and I did just that.

"When you throw a punch, you need to pivot your

back foot and lift your back heel. Both your foot and knee should be pointed towards your target," Lu told me.

I nodded.

"You then want to twist your hip and chest towards them, like this," Lu instructed, putting her hands on my hips again. I took in a deep breath. She twisted my hips gently and then moved her hands up to make me move my chest as well. I let out my breath as she let go, only to slide her hand up my right arm. I shivered slightly as I felt her body press against mine, but it wasn't from an unwanted touch. It was more from arousal, something I hadn't felt for a long time.

"Concentrate," Lu whispered in my ear. I bet she could feel my heart beating fast.

"I am," I whispered back.

Lu smirked as she put her hand gently over my right wrist.

"Now you're going to want to extend your elbow and move your arm so your fist is pointing down, but remember to keep the wrist straight," she said as she helped me move my arm. "You want to try and hit your target with mainly the middle knuckle. When your fist connects, you want to continue extending your elbow, so it's completely stretched out," she told me. I nodded and she took a step back away from me.

"Ok," I gulped.

"Go back to the original stance I showed you," she ordered. I brought my right fist back under my chin and moved my feet back in position. She looked me over once more and smiled.

"Good," she noted and then stepped in front of me. "Now, punch me," she instructed. I almost dropped out of my position, but Lu shook her head and merely pointed to her left cheek.

"I doubt your first punch would even hurt," Lu said with a chuckle. I narrowed my eyes slightly, but then bent my legs and started bouncing slightly as I weighed her up. I then pivoted my back foot and raised the heel, moving my knee to the front like she told me. I then struck forward, aiming for Lu's face as I extended my elbow and aimed my fist downward.

Before I could land the punch, Lu stepped forward and grabbed my fist in her hand, pulled it down quite roughly, which caused my knee to buckle slightly. She moved quickly as she twisted my arm with so much force that suddenly she and my arm were behind my back and she had brought me down to my knees.

I let out a slight cry as I felt her drop down behind me and suddenly her other arm was around my throat, pulling me into a choke hold. It wasn't tight, but it was definitely a lot firmer than it was before.

"Now what are you going to do? I have your dominant arm pinned and you're on your knees, which only leaves you with your weak arm and your upper body strength," Lu whispered against my ear, her breath tickling me in ways that set my libido on fire and made my heart race even faster.

I brought my left hand to her forearm around my throat and I tried to pull it away from me, but she only tensed up harder, so it was more difficult to move. I then tried moving her arm down from my throat and at the same time, with all the force I could, I pushed back on her.

When I had enough room to move my legs from under me, I swung my right leg around until I felt hers. I hooked it under her and moved my leg back towards me, causing Lu to have to move herself so she didn't break her knee.

Now that her leg was beside me, I twisted myself to the right, until I had fully turned myself around and was now lying on Lu, with both my arms free. She still had one leg tucked under her, but by the look on her face it didn't bother her.

"Well done," she commented and she shifted her leg so now both legs were on either side of me.

I knew if anyone was to walk into the gym at this precise moment, they would think they had caught us in a compromising position. But as I found myself on top of Lu, our bodies pinned together with my pelvis resting on hers, everything around me faded and I could only see the girl I loved more than life itself. Today was her birthday and for the first time in ages I felt like I was ready to let go of what had happened to me. I had just thought of the perfect present.

"We should -," Lu started, but I stopped her from talking by putting my lips on hers. She moved her hand from my right wrist and moved it up my arm, stopping when she reached my shoulder and gently pushed me back from her.

"If you're not ready…" she said slowly. I used my right hand to prop myself up slightly, moving my left hand to grab hers and guide it to my heart.

"This isn't from being scared, or not ready," I stated, smiling. I then moved her hand down lower to brush my hardened nipple. Lu bit her lip.

"And this is definitely not from not wanting to do this," I whispered. I opened Lu's hand for her and placed it fully on my breast, my hand on the back of hers. I squeezed my hand, which meant that she was squeezing my breast and we both let out a slight moan.

"Babe," she whispered. I took my hand off hers, letting her fingers linger where they were and moved my hand so it was between us. I gently ran my fingers along the elastic of her gym pants, my knuckles running along her lower belly.

"*Mi amor*," I responded, lowering myself down again to kiss her. This time she kissed me back with so much passion that I forgot where we were.

I slipped my hand down her pants and found her readily awaiting clit and started rubbing it gently, as her tongue slipped into my mouth. Her hand massaged my breast and we both moaned as the movement of my hand became more frantic.

Because we were so close together, I could feel my own movements against my own aroused clit.

Lu moved her hand from my breast and I was almost disappointed, but suddenly both her hands were under my workout top and pushing away my sports bra. Her hands returned to my breasts and she squeezed my nipples between her fingers, playing with them as I continued to play with her nub.

Our kissing became less passionate, as it was replaced with sounds of pleasure. I moved myself back and forward against my fingers as I quickened the pace. Lu's moans got more frequent and her twisting of my nipples got more painful, but surprisingly not in a bad way.

I kissed her mouth, along her chin and down to the spot on her throat where I had once left a love mark. I started sucking on her skin again and soon I could feel her body tense up and her legs shudder under me as she let out a large moan of satisfaction. I soon came with her as my body filled with the ecstasy of my orgasm.

I had forgotten how wonderful the feeling was. I couldn't believe I had let the demons in my head make me forget how great it was to share this moment with my soulmate. My one true love.

Once our orgasms finished, I removed my fingers from her pants, lifted my mouth from her throat and looked at her, a grin spread wide on her face.

"Welcome back, E," she whispered as she took out her hands from under my shirt. I laughed slightly as I leaned forward to kiss her.

"I'm sorry it took me so long," I replied and I raised myself up again, to look at the woman I loved.

"Happy birthday," I whispered and Lu's grin grew.

"I thought you had forgotten."

I shook my head.

"Never. How could I forget the first birthday of yours that we've shared together?" I replied.

"Well you didn't mention it earlier," Lu pointed out.

"And she wasn't meant to mention it now," said a voice from behind us.

I jumped out of my skin, suddenly remembering that we were in a very public place where anyone could walk in at any time.

I rolled off Lu and I sat up, adjusting my shirt as my face reddened. Lu sat up, pulling down her own top. We both glared at Techy who walked closer to us now that we were apart.

"How long have you been standing there?" Lu demanded, her face just as red as mine.

"Oh, just long enough to catch the end of the show," Techy responded with a smirk and my face went hot. I cowered slightly behind Lu to try and hide my face.

"You fucking perv," Lu replied, picking up a 5kg dumbbell that had been lying near-by and moving it into a position that looked like she was going to throw it at him.

"Hey!" Techy exclaimed, holding out his hands in front of him. "You two were the ones who thought it was a clever idea to have sex in a public use gym."

"You could have announced yourself!" I responded, my voice hitching slightly. Lu lowered the weight.

"And ruin your fun? You would have been angry that I stopped it, considering how long it's been. Damned if I do, damned if I don't," he stated with a shrug of his shoulders.

Lu let out an annoyed sigh and stood up. She turned and held out her hand so she could help me up.

"Why weren't you supposed to mention my birthday?" Lu asked, looking from Techy to me, trying to change the subject.

I turned red again. So much for that surprise.

"We weren't supposed to acknowledge it to make you think we had all forgotten. We booked the restaurant tonight, so it will just be us and we were going to surprise you with all your favorite foods and drinks and actually have fun without having to worry about what's happening," I told her. Techy clucked his tongue and I shot him a glare. He chuckled.

"Party pooper," he commented and I shrugged my own shoulders this time.
"I hate lying to her anyway," I pointed out and Lu wrapped her arm around my waist and pulled me close, kissing me on the cheek.

"I know how to act surprised," Lu commented, looking back at Techy. "It will be like she never told me."

I smiled at her, kissing her back on her cheek. Techy rolled his eyes.

"What are you doing here anyway?" Lu asked him. "I was going to lie and say I could smell you two from out in the hallway and that you needed a shower, but I guess now I can point out that you need to get ready," Techy replied.

I rolled my eyes this time.

"Great. Well, we'll see you at the restaurant," I replied and he nodded and turned to walk out of the gym. I turned to look at Lu and then we both burst out laughing.

"At least it wasn't Olivia or your father," I pointed out after our laughter died down.

"No. Getting caught having sex by your parents isn't the best thing to happen," Lu agreed. "I'm just glad it wasn't a kid."

I cringed slightly at the thought.
"Come on," Lu stated and moved her hand to mine, and started to pull me out of the gym. We went back to our hotel room to get ourselves ready for the evening. It took a lot longer than usual to shower as Lu and I got reacquainted with each other multiple times. Two hours later, we headed towards the door to go to the restaurant where everyone was waiting.

Chapter Fifteen

Olivia

When Jorge, Techy and I entered the restaurant to set up party decorations for Lu's birthday dinner, the last thing we expected was for the room to be filled with police.

As soon as we opened the doors, guns were pointed at us and we were forced onto our knees by officers who had snuck up behind us. Jorge didn't have any time to draw his gun as a police officer pushed him to the ground and forced his arms behind his back, shouting at him to stay down.

I raised my hands up into the air the minute I saw the first gun. An officer took my hands, surprisingly gently, and handcuffed them behind my back. I felt hands on my side as my own gun was unholstered and I turned to see that it was getting handed to an FBI special agent.

"Olivia Swanson. I'm surprised to find someone who is believed to be an abducted member of the Sutton Police Department to be armed," the agent taunted. He then looked at the gun closely before putting it in an evidence bag.

"Even more surprising that the gun is the one that was supposedly taken from you," he added. I said nothing. I had the right to remain silent. I wasn't sure if that was true in New Zealand, but since he was an American FBI agent, I was not willing to risk it.

"She *was* taken," Jorge snapped, struggling slightly under the officer that still had him pinned, while another officer took his gun from him. Techy was silent. I looked at him and could see that he was actually scared and confused. He kept looking at a hotel employee who was watching with the other staff; his face was full of guilt.

"But if you knew how stubborn this woman was, you would give the gun back too, just to shut her up," Jorge continued and I turned to look at him.

The officers were now forcing him to his feet and had turned him, so he was now facing me. He looked furious.

"Right," the FBI agent commented, sounding not at all convinced. I gulped as he looked at me. It just so happened that I had dressed up especially for the occasion. I knew it didn't look at all like I was an abducted person. He knew I was a willing participant in the crime of getting my daughter out of the country.

"Olivia Swanson, Jorge Torres Rodriquez and Kyle Smith, you are all under arrest for aiding and abetting, accessory after the fact, first degree murder, criminal impersonation and computer fraud," the agent stated and I almost broke my own rule about staying silent.

I tensed up and tried to pull away from the officer who was holding me, but he tightened his grip and I realized that if I continued to do that, resisting arrest would be added to the list.

"Olivia had nothing to do with any of those things," Jorge pointed out for me, his eyes resting on mine. I looked at him, raising my eyebrow slightly as I wondered why he was defending me. He had spent the last two months trying to either ignore my presence or irritate me to the point that I wanted to smack him. There wasn't any in-between.

The agent ignored Jorge again and continued to read us our rights. He explained to us that we would be extradited back to America as soon as Elsie and Lu were captured.

I secretly hoped that they had caught wind of what was happening and had fled already, but at the same time I knew their eventual capture was only inevitable. Perhaps this was the time for all of it to end and for everyone to face the consequences, including me.

The agent then turned to the young male employee that Techy had been watching.

"Thank you again for coming forward. You have done your country a great service by reporting the fugitives' whereabouts," he commented, causing the young man to look at Techy immediately. Techy swore loudly.

"I had to! It was eating me alive, not telling anyone that the most wanted fugitives were right under our noses the whole time," the young man explained, looking only at Techy. I didn't know what their connection was, but Techy looked beyond crestfallen.

"You fucking bastard," Techy responded trying to get out of the hold of the officer. He was so angry that he almost did get free, but several officers forced him to the ground, pinning him so he couldn't move.

"You're fucking dead, Justin!" Techy called out, still fighting the hold on him. The young man, Justin, whimpered and hurried out of the room, clearly not keen to find out if their hold on Techy was strong enough. The agent nodded his head towards the officers holding each of us. I was pushed gently, which made me start walking. I was escorted out of the restaurant, followed by a surprisingly silent Jorge and a foul-mouthed Techy who wouldn't stop swearing.

Soon I was put in the back of one of the police cars and was on the way to the station. My only hope was that the girls would be alright, whatever they chose to do from here on out.

Chapter Sixteen

Lu

As soon as I reached for our room door to open it for Elsie, I knew something was wrong. Just before my hand touched the door handle, my bracelet started to vibrate. I froze and looked at Elsie. The vibration was getting stronger by the second, which meant that the police were getting closer.

Elsie's eyes got wide. I grabbed her arms and started pulling her towards the bed, where I had stored the two duffle bags under the mattress. I pulled them out and threw her one and nodded my head at the dresser.

"Fill it up and hurry!" I instructed her, as I grabbed the other bag and moved toward the adjoining room where I knew my father had hidden weapons and money.

When I got into the room, I headed straight to the dresser and opened the second drawer and threw out his clothes until I reached the bottom. He had installed a false bottom, so I put my finger in the corner and lifted it up. I threw it to the side. As I had hoped, there were a couple of guns, bullets and lots of cash.

I put the cash and bullets into my bag, then checked each gun to make sure the safety was on before putting one in my back pocket and the other in the bag. I looked around the room, seeing if there was anything else I needed, but the vibrations of my bracelet was getting stronger.

I hurried back into the other room to find Elsie dropping the little bottles of alcohol into the bag.

"Seriously, E?" I asked, as I grabbed her arm to pull her away.

"I need them, Lu!" She pulled her arm away from me to finish grabbing them.

"The police are going to be here any second! We have to go!" I pointed out, putting the bracelet against her arm, so she could feel how intense it was. She picked up the whole tray that the bottles were stored in and stuffed it into the bag.

"Let's go," she said, zipping it up. I grabbed her hand and ran back through the adjoining room and straight to the other side where there was a window that led to a fire escape.

The window was one of those slide-up ones, so I unlocked it and slid it up, allowing Elsie to go through first. When she was on the fire escape landing, I followed suit and then shut the window.

I looked over the edge of the railing and saw that there were several ladders, each landing at a platform one level down. I looked around the alley at the bottom of the column of ladders and saw that there was no police in the area.

"I hope you're not afraid of heights," I commented. I swung the bag over my shoulder and walked to the ladder and started to descend.

"I'm more afraid of falling than the actual height," Elsie responded, her face a little pale.

"Just hold on tight and make sure your foot is on something solid before you move onto the next rung down," I offered as I continued my way down.

Soon Elsie was following my lead and we hit the first landing that had been below us. We continued to do this for four other ladders and I quickly made it to ground level.

When Elsie was standing next me, I grabbed her hand again and we ran down the alleyway towards the road. I stopped her just before we got to the end and we hid against the wall. I looked carefully around the corner and I saw my dad, Olivia, and Techy being escorted towards three police cars, all handcuffed. I let out a small groan.

"What is it?" Elsie asked, her hand squeezing mine. "They've been arrested. Someone must have told them that we were here, because I can see about ten police cars," I informed her, after counting the cars. I moved back behind the wall, leaning against it as I looked back at Elsie.

"We've really only got two options here. Either we give up now and turn ourselves in, or we run," I stated and Elsie gulped. "If we turn ourselves in, we would likely be sent back to America to face prison time. If we run, then we are on our own. This time we won't have Techy to make sure no one is tracking us, or my dad to save us from awful men. It would just be you, me and this," I explained, pulling the gun from my back pocket. Elsie looked at it, her eyes going wide. I put it back in my pocket.

"I have one for you too," I added, unzipping the bag and handing her the gun that was at the top. Elsie took it, her hand shaking.

"That is the safety," I pointed to the lever at the back of the gun.

"If it's down and you pull the trigger, it will shoot," I instructed. I knew she was well aware why I was telling her that. If she had known that before she had pointed a gun at her abuser, then maybe she wouldn't be known as a murderer right now.

"Alright," she replied, gulping again.

"What do you want to do?" I asked her, zipping the bag back up.

"I want to run," she said quietly. I looked up at her

and nodded.

"You know that this is going to be even more difficult because we're in a foreign country, right?" I asked, and she nodded again. I gave her a weak smile, then turned to look back around the corner.

The three cars our folks had been loaded into were gone, leaving seven. I could see three officers lined up near the entrance of the hotel with their backs turned to us, but I couldn't see anyone else. Everyone must have been inside, searching for us.

When I heard noise from above us, I knew we had to go now or be caught. There was no way we could outrun those three officers if they knew where we were.

I pulled on Elsie's hand and we hurried out of the alleyway, running in the opposite direction. We ran until we hit the end of the street and turned the corner. I could hear Elsie panting already and I knew it wouldn't be long until her lung stopped her from running anymore. I looked around and noticed a parked pickup truck not far away from us.

"Come on," I urged Elsie and I pulled her towards it. When we got to it, I noticed that there was a *For Sale* sign. I just hoped that this time there was no GPS tracker on it.

"What the heck is a *Ute*?" Elsie asked, as she read the

sign.

"It's the New Zealand word for a pickup truck," I pointed out, trying to hold back a chuckle.

I pulled out my set of lock picks from my other back pocket and quickly unlocked the door. I still found it weird that the driver's seat was on the opposite side.

"Climb in," I told Elsie. She took off her duffle bag and climbed into the truck, over the driver's seat and gear stick.

The only saving grace we had was that it was getting darker. If anyone was to look outside right now, hopefully they wouldn't see anything. All we needed was someone to start shouting and the cops would be on our tail, just like that.

Once Elsie was on her side, I got in the driver's seat. I pulled a flat head screwdriver from my kit and put it in the ignition to turn it on. I pulled back the plastic cover of the steering column and started hot wiring the car.

I could feel Elsie jiggling her leg and I could tell that she was anxious. It didn't surprise me when she grabbed her bag and unzipped it, pulling out a bottle of vodka.

The truck started and I felt relief when I saw that the gas tank was full. I pulled it into gear and put my foot down on the pedal, speeding away from the area as fast as I could. I had no idea where I was going, but at every intersection I turned left.

A few cars beeped at me as I drove towards them and it wasn't until the last second I had realized that I had drifted to the right side of the road, forgetting that they drove on the left here in New Zealand. It didn't help that Elsie kept letting out screams every time this happened.

"Sorry!" I blurted out when I had done it for the third time. Elsie was on her fourth bottle.

"We're going to be killed in a car accident before we get anywhere," she murmured, her voice a little sluggish.

"I said I was sorry," I said again, feeling my cheeks warm.

When we got to the middle of the city, we had to stop at traffic lights. Unfortunately, even if I wanted to run a red light, I couldn't. There was just too much traffic to risk it. I followed the green signs on the side of the road, which had arrows pointing in the direction to a town called Picton. I figured this was a good place to go, because it led us out of the city.

It wasn't long until we got out of the busy section and the traffic died down. We had entered a highway that led to a long stretch of straight road.

Even though it was dark, the scenery was amazing. Hills, farms, animals and even the ocean came into view. Unfortunately for Elsie, she had fallen asleep, so she missed out on it.

After a few hours of driving, I was feeling tired. I knew I had to pull over soon, or I would fall asleep at the wheel. When I turned into a small town called Kaikoura, I turned off at the first place with a sign advertising accommodation.

I knew it was risky, but I needed a good night's sleep, because it was likely that we would be on the road for who knows how long.

I parked up outside the office of a roadside motel, leaving the truck idling. I quickly pulled a red wig out of Elsie's bag and put it on, making sure my brown hair wasn't visible anywhere. I let Elsie stay asleep as I grabbed some cash and then headed into the office, where a gray-haired lady was sitting behind the counter.

"Can I get a room with one double bed please? Nothing fancy, just stopping for the night," I added, putting on a best fake accent I could muster up.

"Of course. That will be a hundred dollars," the lady told me. I pulled out a few green notes with the Queen of England on them and handed them over to her.

"Just sign here," she said, pointing to a clipboard with a sheet of paper on it.

I signed it as Claudia Lopez and she handed me the key to unit 10, which was around the corner.

"There is parking all around the building, including in front of the unit," she explained and I smiled at her.

"Thank you," I said as I walked back out to the truck where Elsie had finally awoken. I got into the pickup and I looked over at her as she blinked trying to awaken to her surroundings.

"I need to sleep and you're too drunk to drive, so we're at a hotel," I responded, hoping there wasn't any bitterness in my tone.

I knew why she chose to drink and I got it, but did she really have to do it when we were fleeing for our lives? Now we had to risk getting caught to avoid my falling asleep at the wheel.

"Hmph," was all Elsie replied and she went to go open the door to get out. I reached across her, putting my hand on the door handle just beside her hand and pulled it shut again.

"I'm moving the truck around the corner. It'll be right outside the unit and it will at least hide the truck from view, in case it's been reported stolen," I explained to her. Elsie grinned at me and flicked me gently on the nose.

"You're a clever girl," she retorted and I rolled my eyes at her as I leaned back towards the steering wheel, putting the truck in reverse. I slowly headed around the corner of the building until I saw unit 10 and pulled into the allocated parking space.

I turned the screwdriver towards me to turn the ignition off and I untied the wires. I banged the plastic cover back on, just in case someone looked through the window. At least it wouldn't look like it had been tampered with.

With the truck now off and parked, Elsie went to open the door again, looking at me cautiously to see if I would stop her. I nodded my head with a small smile and she grinned at me again and stepped out of the truck, pulling the bag she had been holding close to her chest, like it was holding all her worldly treasures.

I grabbed the bag of money and bullets and also got out the truck. I walked over to the unit and Elsie quickly followed me, keeping close to me as I unlocked the door.

The hotel room wasn't overly big, but at least it was a lot nicer than the one we had first stayed in back home. I let Elsie walk in first, shutting and locking the door behind me. I slid the chain lock into place and double checked that it was secure before I walked further into the room. There was a double bed in the center.

It took me a moment to realize that a very naked Elsie was already sitting on top of it, with her body spread across it, waiting for me. I put the bag of cash on a small bench on the side of the room and raised my eyebrow slightly at Elsie, who was beckoning me over with her finger.

"It's not midnight yet. It's still your birthday," Elsie pointed out. I sighed, walked over to the bed and sat down on the edge of it. I looked away from the very naked Elsie, trying to distract myself from her beauty.

"I'm not having sex with you while you're drunk," I stated, my tone clearly showing how disappointed I was to say it.

"You've had sex with me when I've been stoned," Elsie pointed out, moving herself so she was on her knees and kneeling behind me. She put her arms around my waist and put her chin on my shoulder. I could feel her pressing against me and I had to close my eyes and think of disgusting things like a toilet brush to distract myself.

"That's different. I was stoned too," I responded, my breath hitching slightly as she kissed my neck.

"I've only had a little bit to drink," Elsie murmured, her breath almost against my ear. She nipped my earlobe and then ran her fingers up my back to my head, where I was still wearing my wig. She pulled it off me and then threw it on the floor, returning her fingers to my hair, brushing it softly.

"You've had enough that I can smell it on your breath," I responded, trying to move my head away from her. She tightened her grip on my hair, causing me to moan. She knew how much I liked it when she played rough with my hair. Damn it.

"I don't want to take advantage of you in this condition, Elsie," I stated and she responded by pulling my head back hard and putting her mouth on my throat. I felt her teeth scrap my skin and if I didn't know any better, I swear she was trying to bite me.

"I'm pretty sure I'm the one taking advantage of you right now," Elsie retorted, her breath hot against my skin.

"Elsie," I pleaded, as she started sucking, once again marking me. I swear she loved doing this, now that she was permanently marked in that same area.

"Luuu," Elsie taunted, moving her mouth along my throat, trailing kisses as she made her way up to my mouth. She cut off any more protesting by kissing me so hard that I was sure my lips were going to burst.

She slipped her tongue in my mouth and I had no choice but to obey and kiss her back. She moved to the side of me, without letting our lips part, and she gently pushed me down. She mounted me. I could taste the vodka on her breath, which made me remember why I didn't want to do this with her.

I turned my head so we stopped kissing and I put my hands gently on either side of her face to make her look at me.

"You've just come back to me, Elsie," I whispered, my heart pounding in my chest. "You've just got over a major fear of yours and I feel like if we have sex right now, you're going to regret it in the morning."

Elsie screwed up her nose and ripped my fingers from her face. She went to get up, her hand pressing hard on my stomach as she pushed away from me. I let out a groan of pain, but she didn't seem to know what she had just done. She grabbed her clothes angrily from the floor.

"Not everything is about that!" she snapped, pulling her shirt over her and stomping back into her pants.

"If you don't want to have sex with me, then that's fine! I'll just get off on my own," she stated and headed to the bathroom that was in the far corner of the room. She didn't bother shutting the door, so soon enough I heard her moaning as she pleasured herself.

I sighed, lifting my top up to inspect the red patch where Elsie had used my stomach as leverage. I hoped it wouldn't leave a bruise. That was a conversation that I knew would be hard for both me and Elsie.

The noises got louder from inside the bathroom, but I tried to ignore it as I walked over to the bag that Elsie had been holding. I opened it, pulled out the remaining bottles, and walked to the small kitchenette.

One by one, I opened the caps of the bottles and I tipped them down the drain.

Elsie had to stop this behavior. I had to make her stop. I had to help her find another way to cope. She was going to be mad when she came out of the bathroom, but she would thank me eventually.

I was tipping out the last bottle when Elsie, who had apparently successfully given herself an orgasm, came back into the room. I knew she was back because she snatched the bottle out of my hand with a cry that sounded like she was in pain.

"What the fuck, Lu!?" She screamed, picking up the empty bottles, acting like I just burnt all our money and clothes.

"You're getting addicted. It's too much Elsie. It has to stop now," I replied, trying to get the last bottle that wasn't quite empty out of her other hand. She pulled her arm back, causing the empty bottles to fall from her hands and smash all over the floor. I took a step back, trying to get away from the broken glass. Elsie, however, took a step forward, clearly immune to the pain as her bare feet crunched on the broken glass. I cringed slightly as I put my hands on Elsie's shoulders to try to keep her away from the glass, but she slapped my hands away.

"You are not the boss of me, Lucita. If I want to drink, I will drink. You had no right to do this!" she snapped, shoving the remaining bottle in my face. I took another step back.

"It's not healthy, E! You're going to hurt your liver. There are other ways of coping," I pointed out.

Elsie let out a mock laugh, downing the remaining bottle, before throwing it at my feet. The glass shattered and I felt one pierce the top of my foot. My heart plummeted, but I didn't look away as she advanced on me again, walking right over the glass like it was nothing.

"Maybe I should go out and find some cocaine. Get high. Snort enough that I almost die, huh? Maybe that's more healthy," Elsie sneered.

I looked at her, hurt. I had told her that in confidence. I never thought she would use it against me. My anger rose.

"Exactly, Elizabeth! I almost *died* because I used a drug to cope. Alcohol is a drug!" I snapped back, my voice getting almost as loud as hers.

"That drug is the only thing that keeps the memories away!" Elsie yelled back. "The memories of those boys holding me as he forced his fingers into me, his cock being shoved into my face. That drug is the only thing keeping the memory of his blood spraying everywhere, away. That *drug* is the only thing keeping out the memory of me putting a bullet in the chest of the man who raised me." Elsie took a step closer to me each time she listed a memory.

Like a twisted dance, I kept taking steps backwards, until a wall at my back stopped me. She continued to advance on me, closing the distance between us. This time it was anger that fueled the situation, not sexual desire.

"There are other ways to forget, Elsie," I whispered, warily putting my hand on her shoulder. She growled at me before gripping my wrist, pulling it off her shoulder and slamming it against the wall. I cried out in pain.

"Elsie, you're hurting me," I cried and she let go of my hand.

"You hurt me by throwing away the one thing that helped me," Elsie responded, though her voice wasn't as mad as it was before. Perhaps she was realizing what she had done.

"We will talk about this tomorrow," I stated firmly, moving my body from the wall and squeezing past her. She didn't stop me.

I walked to the bathroom and opened all the

cupboards hoping to find a first-aid kit. When I found one, I grabbed it and walked back out, shoving it into Elsie's chest. She took it with a raised eyebrow and I pointed out her feet, which were leaving trails of blood behind. I then grabbed the bag of cash and headed towards the door.

"Where are you going?" Elsie asked, though it sounded far away, so she obviously hadn't followed me.

"We need a night apart. I'm getting another room," I stated without looking back as I unlocked the door. I went back to the office, which was thankfully still open, and paid for another double room for the night. It happened to be the one next door, unit 11.

When I got inside I turned on the light and triple checked that the door was locked. When I was satisfied, I went to the bathroom and grabbed the first-aid kit.

I pulled it open and searched through it until I found an instant ice pack. I activated it by squeezing it and soon it was cold. I grabbed a washcloth and wrapped it around it, then put it on my wrist. The pain was dull and I was sure it was just bruised, but it was better to be safe than sorry.

I yawned as I walked back out of the bathroom, turning off the light as I did. I walked over to the bedside table, turned on the lamp and then went to the front of the room to turn off the main lights. I climbed under the covers of the bed, fully clothed. My pajamas were still in the room with Elsie.

I then reached over to turn off the lamp and settled back down into bed, holding the icepack securely to my wrist and drifted off to sleep.

It was the first night in eight months that I hadn't been in the same room as Elsie and I was heartbroken that it was because we had our first major fight.

Chapter Seventeen

Elsie

When I woke up the next morning, I knew something was wrong. It wasn't because my head was pounding or my mouth was dry as hell or that my feet felt like I had been stabbed with a million tiny knives. It was because Lu wasn't next to me. It wasn't like she had just gotten up to go to the bathroom either – her side of the bed wasn't warm at all.

I groaned as I sat up, holding my head as I cursed myself inwardly for drinking enough to cause a headache. Lately I had mastered the fine art of being drunk just enough to keep the memories away, but not drunk enough to have a hangover the next day.

I blinked as I adjusted to the light of the room and frowned when I saw an open first-aid kit on the edge of the bed. There were bloodied dressings and empty band-aid packets scattered next to it.

I pulled the blanket off me, revealing feet and the puddle of blood where they rested. I groaned as I pulled my feet up to look at the bottom of them and saw a half-assed job of someone trying to cover tiny cuts. I pulled the band-aids off since they were half falling off anyway and noticed that there were shards of glass stuck in the cuts.

I frowned as I leaned forward to get the first-aid kit and looked for a pair of tweezers. I found some and started pulling the shards of glass out one by one. I put them on top of a bloodied dressing so I didn't get them on the sheets.

Once I was done and there was no further blood, I gathered all the garbage and stood up, wincing as I walked towards the trash can. When I got closer to the kitchenette I noticed all the broken bottles all over the floor. I saw a trail of blood that led to the far wall.

My hand flew to my mouth as it fell open. I was staring at a small hole in the wall, which made me immediately remember what had happened the night before. I had hit Lu's hand so hard against it, that the plaster had broken. All because she was trying to stop me from drinking. What the fuck had I done?

Tears fell from my eyes as I hurried over to the door. I ignored the pain in my feet – it was nothing, compared to what I had done to Lu. I unlocked the door and hurried outside, frantically looking around at the different units. I had no idea where she went. All I knew was that she had to get away from me. *Because I had hurt her.*

"LU!" I screamed, not caring if anyone else heard me. "Lu! Lucita where are you!?" I cried, hurrying to the door to the right of our unit and banged on the door. The banging made my head pound, but I needed Lu. I needed to see her. To apologize, to make sure she was okay, to make sure that I hadn't done what my father had done to me and broken her wrist.

"Lu!" I called again, but no one answered that door. I went to the next one, but someone came up behind me, pulling me around to face them, and putting their hand over my mouth. It was Lu. Her eyes were wide and I looked at her, my eyes just as big.

"I'm so sorry," I muffled into her hand. She frowned at me and then lowered her hand.

"I'm so sorry," I repeated, my tears falling desperately from my eyes. I sounded like my father every time he apologized after hurting me.

Lu didn't say anything. She just picked up her bag from the ground where she must have dropped it and pulled me back into the unit I had just come from. When the door shut and she had relocked it, she finally let go of my shoulder, putting her hand protectively on her other wrist. The wrist that I had hurt.

"You could have gotten us caught!" Lu pointed out, looking back behind her, then back at me.

"I'm sorry," I said again, hanging my head slightly. "I didn't know where you were and I thought maybe you had left me," I admitted, looking back at her.

"Elsie, I love you; I wouldn't leave you," Lu responded, letting go of her wrist and taking a carefully placed step in front of me. I could tell she was reluctant to get any closer, and I couldn't blame her.

"But I hurt you," I exclaimed and I broke into tears and pulled her close to me. Lu wrapped her arms around me immediately and we held each other close.

"You didn't mean to," Lu whispered.

I cried into her shoulder.

"I don't know what came over me. I am so sorry. You're right, the alcohol is becoming a problem. I just didn't see it," I sobbed.

"I'm sorry I didn't talk to you first about it before getting rid of the drinks," Lu replied, rubbing my back.

"You did the right thing," I whispered. I then pulled myself away from Lu and gently picked up her wrist to inspect the damage that I had done. It was darker than her normal skin, so she was bruised. My heart stopped. I lifted her other hand to compare. It wasn't swollen.

"It's not broken," Lu said quietly, moving her wrist back and forth to show me. "Just bruised. It will fade."

I looked at her, and I leaned forward to kiss her.

"I'm so sorry," I said again.

"I know," Lu responded. I then lifted her hand up and

kissed her gently on her bruises.

"There. Better already," she stated, as I looked back at her.

"We better clean up," Lu pointed out.

I gently let go of her wrist and nodded in agreement.

"Right," I agreed. I walked over to a little cupboard and opened it to find a broom, a brush, and dustpan. Lu took the broom out of my hand and started to sweep the broken glass towards the dustpan I was holding. I scooped the glass shards up, putting them in the trash can with the bloodied dressings.

When we were done with the glass, Lu wet a washcloth with warm water. She cleaned up the blood on the floor while I stripped the bed.

When everything was done, we grabbed our bags and headed out to the truck. We got in and Lu did her thing to start the car and soon we were off again.

I felt bad for leaving the room in such a state, but if we stayed any longer, there was a greater chance that we would get caught.

As Lu was driving, I gently took her left hand off the steering wheel and held it in mine. She looked at me, smiling, but I could tell that something had changed between us since last night. I had a lot to make up for. My behavior and what I did to her were unacceptable

and I didn't know how to make it better. I was as bad as
my so-called father.

"E, I know you. You're overthinking it. It was an
accident," Lu said slowly, looking back at the road as she
drove. I noticed now she wasn't drifting across the center
line to the right lane anymore.

"I hurt you, L. I physically assaulted you like he used
to do to me," I whispered and Lu squeezed my hand
gently.

"First of all, you are nothing like him," Lu started,
moving her thumb across the back of my hand.

"Secondly, I would prefer it if we agreed that it wasn't
you who hurt me, because you would never, if you were
in the right frame of mind. Let's agree to say it was your
'friend'. Your friend who is not welcome to come back,
mind you." She glanced at me and I smiled grimly as I
nodded in agreement.

"Ex-friend," I corrected. "I don't want her in our life
anymore." My heart pounded as I talked about myself in
third person.

Lu looked back towards the road, her smile widening.
I smiled back at her then looked out the window myself,
our hands still holding on to each other, as if we were
scared that it would become too painful if we let go.

The scenery was breathtaking. The sea, the rock formations. I even saw a couple of seals which made me jump in surprise and point them out to Lu, who reminded me she couldn't look because she was driving. She laughed hearing me getting excited at every animal we passed after that. There were sheep. Lots of sheep. And cows. I swear I had seen them before, but never this many.

The hills were so green and bright with life. It brought me joy- something I hadn't felt in a long time other than the few moments of pleasure Lu could give me with her tongue.

"What are we going to do once we hit the top of the South Island?" I asked Lu when a sign for a town called Blenheim came up.

"I hadn't thought that far," Lu admitted. She glanced at me for a moment before looking back at the road.

"If we try and catch the ferry to the other island, do you think they will be looking for us there? Will the wigs be enough?" I asked, my voice sounding worried.

"They will definitely have ferry crossings on their radar. The airports too," Lu responded, squeezing my hand supportively.

"I read about the Marlborough Sounds on Techy's laptop," Lu said quietly. I looked at her as she continued to watch the road.

"There are hundreds of properties that people don't live in during the winter months," Lu explained.

"When is winter here?" I asked, though I thought about how cold it had been lately, so I kind of knew the answer already.

"Now actually. The first day of winter was yesterday," Lu told me.

"It's probably a good thing – you could wear a scarf and not look funny wearing it, as you'll have to cover your tattoo," she added and my hand went automatically to my throat. I hadn't thought about that.

"It's kind of a dead giveaway," I agreed, reaching for the bag and pulling out a scarf. It was starting to get chilly and if we had to stop, at least I would already have it on.

"Do you think we should find an empty house?" I asked, going back to the conversation.

"One that's secluded from the others. We can probably get some camping gear, so we don't have to use power, get canned food from the grocery store so it's easier to cook. But if it gets too cold, we will have to use a fire…if we're secluded, then there shouldn't be any risk of anyone catching us if they happen to be living in a house nearby," Lu mused out loud.

"Seems like you have thought ahead," I chuckled and Lu grinned at me.

"Not really. I just thought about it when I saw that sign back there saying we're near Picton," Lu told me, as we passed *Welcome to Blenheim* signs.

Lu stopped at some shops along the way, and we bought camping gear and groceries. While she was inside a grocery store, I grabbed my bag and rummaged through it until I found a wrapped-up package that I had almost forgotten about until I felt it when I grabbed my scarf.

It was the present that I had bought Lu for her birthday. I was going to give it to her last night at the dinner party, but with everything that happened, I had forgotten.

I had gotten Olivia to buy it for me, as I wasn't allowed to leave the hotel without Lu and Mr. Torres. Since that put a damper on getting her a surprise present, it hadn't left me with much of a choice. Luckily Techy let me borrow his laptop one night when Lu went to bed early and I found the perfect gift.

I wasn't sure if I wanted to give it to her, considering I nearly died because of one. I knew how much she loved her old one, so at the time I knew I had to get it.

I looked down at the pink wrapping paper, wondering if my present was even worth having now, that we had two guns to keep us safe. I knew Lu was carrying one now, so hopefully she had hidden it enough that no one would notice it. If anyone saw her with it, they would probably freak out and call the cops.

The door opened before I realized that Lu had returned, so I hurriedly put the gift behind my back before she had the door completely open. She got in the truck and soon we were on the road again, heading out of town.

As I grabbed hold of Lu's hand again, I noticed that the fuel gauge was on empty.

"Don't worry, we're going to ditch this truck soon," Lu stated as she looked at me and gave a small grin. I grinned back at her, then I leaned back on the seat and looked out the window, watching the scenery as we drove past it.

We sat in silence for a while, until Lu pulled over in front of a car with a *For Sale* sign on its windshield. It was quiet on the road, so if anyone drove past right now, it would just look like we pulled over to have a look.

"I'm going to unlock it and I will nod to you when you can come with some stuff," Lu told me and I nodded as she got out. I wondered why she left it running, but I knew she would have a plan.

She walked over to the white sedan and stood behind

the driver's door. I grabbed her gift from behind my back and put it back in my bag, then waited for Lu's signal.

After a few minutes she looked up at me and nodded her head. There were no cars in sight. I opened the door and grabbed as many bags as possible and hurried over to the unlocked and open trunk and put all the bags inside it.

Lu had run to the truck to grab the other bags, so I climbed into the passenger seat. It didn't take Lu long to get into the driver's seat and start the car.

"We're going to have to get rid of the truck. Are you okay to follow me, so we can find a side road to ditch it?" Lu asked me. I nodded, reaching for the door to open it. I got out, hurried over to the truck and quickly got in, putting on my seat belt. The road was still quiet, so at least we didn't have any witnesses.

Lu pulled out onto the road and I put the truck in gear and followed her.

After ten minutes of driving, Lu turned right, down a side street that had gravel. We continued until we went over a bridge. She pulled over to the side of the road, but I continued past her, seeing an area near a group of trees that would be perfect to hide the truck.

I put the truck in park and turned the screwdriver Lu had been using as a key to turn off the vehicle. I got out and hurried back to Lu, panting as I got in the passenger seat. Lu gave me a small smile, before handing me over her phone.

"We're going to have to use GPS now. There is a place called Whatamango Bay, but I don't know how to get there. I think that would be a good place to find a secluded house," Lu stated. I searched the word first to get the correct spelling.

Once it was all set up in maps and the app was telling us the directions, Lu got back out onto the main road and we drove in silence.

Just like every time we were driving a long distance, I started to nod off just as we drove through the town called Picton. My face rested against the cold window and I drifted off to sleep.

~.~

I woke up to a gentle shake of my shoulder. I opened my eyes, frowning for a moment, as I had forgotten where we were. I looked around before looking at Lu, remembering that we were trying to find an empty house to squat in.

"Are we here?" I asked, instantly feeling silly for asking considering we were parked, the car was off and Lu was waking me up.

"Yes we are. Come on, sleepy head. Let's get our

stuff so you can get to apologizing to me for the rest of the day," Lu stated and I blushed, remembering the last time I had to apologize.

"Your wish is my command," I responded and Lu grinned as she popped the trunk.

We got out of the car, grabbed our stuff and walked up to the small house Lu had chosen. When we were on the porch, I looked back and noticed that we were down a long driveway and I couldn't see the road. The car was parked in a way that even if someone did come down the driveway, they wouldn't see it.

I turned back around to find Lu watching me with a grin as she held the bags of groceries in her hands. It kind of looked like we were returning home after a day of shopping, rather than about to break into a house and hide out in it for who knows how long. The thought of us being domesticated set my heart pounding and suddenly I couldn't wait to get rid of the bags that I was holding.

"Did I pick a good place?" Lu asked me and I nodded my head with a grin.

"The perfect place," I answered and Lu grinned at me again before putting her bags down and grabbing her lock pick set out of her back pocket. She got to work, only taking a few seconds to unlock the door. She opened it and I half expected to hear a beeping of an alarm, but there was nothing.

"Techy made an app that shows houses with alarms and cameras on a map," Lu explained. She must have seen the look of anticipation on my face.

"That's how I chose this one, really. It was the only house that didn't have any," she added, picking up her bags again and walking through the door.

We walked through the house until we found the kitchen, putting the bags on the counter. We unpacked the grocery bags and Lu set up the little gas cooker that we were going to use.

Once we were done, we found the bedroom and put the rest of our bags on top of the dresser. Lu walked over to the bedside table and pulled out the gun from her back pocket and put it down. I opened the bag of our clothes and grabbed the gift while her back was turned, hiding it behind mine as I walked over to her.

"I never got a chance to give you this yesterday and I know I ruined it, but happy birthday," I said as I took it from behind my back and handed it to Lu. She looked at me then down at the gift as she took it from me.

"You didn't ruin it, E. Stop beating yourself up over it," she commented, looking back up at me. She lifted the gift slightly as she grinned. "Thank you."

She sat on the edge of the bed and started unwrapping

it. When she had finished, she stared at her new pink switchblade in silence. I gulped, wondering if I had made a mistake in getting her a new one. I sat down tentatively next her.

"Is it ok?" I asked, putting my hand gently on her knee. Lu didn't say anything, but a tear dropped on my hand which made me move it to her face to make her look at me.

"I fucking love you," Lu whispered as she pulled the switchblade from its box and clutched it tightly in her hand. I grinned at her and wiped my thumb across her cheek to get rid of the tears.

"These are happy tears then?" I clarified, to which Lu grinned and nodded as she put the knife down next to her gun and pulled me into a fierce hug.

"You have no idea what this means to me," Lu stated and I pulled back to look at her.

"Then tell me," I replied, grabbing onto her hands. Lu let out a little laugh but nodded.

"Well, until the other one was taken from me, I had always carried my switchblade with me," Lu started and I nodded, because I knew that.
"Knowing it was within arm's reach made it easier to get on with my life," she continued. "Losing the other one, made it seem like I wasn't safe anymore…not to mention

that it was like a piece of my mom was missing."

I scueezed her hand softly as her eyes teared up again.

"I know it will never replace the one your mom gave you, but I hope this one can make you feel safe again," I said quietly.

"The funny thing is, I feel a hundred times safer just looking at it, and we have two guns now." Lu let out a small laugh.

"Maybe we won't even need the guns anymore," I suggested, slightly hopeful that she would agree. Guns scared me and I still had the visions of me using one to kill somebody. Lu squeezed my hand, like she knew exactly what I was thinking.

"We'll only use them if we have to, E. But they'll definitely be Plan B," she stated.

Lu squeezed my hand again, then laid back on the bed. She tugged me down and turned me, so I was on top of her.

"Am I doing my apologizing now?" I asked, my heart pounding. Lu grinned at me and nodded. I grinned back and closed the space between us by placing my lips on hers, slipping my tongue in her mouth as I kissed her.

We both shuffled back so we were further up on the bed, without breaking apart. I reached down between us, gripped the top of her button-down shirt and ripped it open. I pushed the fabric aside and grasped her breasts, causing her to let out a moan of pleasure.

I broke our kiss just so I could sit her up to get rid of the shirt and unhook her bra. I threw them to the ground, then pushed her back down on the bed.

Another moan came from Lu as I replaced my hands with my mouth and sucked hard on her breast. I moved my tongue over her nipple, lightly biting it just because I knew it turned her on. She didn't disappoint as she bucked her hips underneath me and let out a small whimper of pleasure.

"Elsie," Lu begged and I knew she wanted me to further stoke her arousal. Since I was the one apologizing, I obeyed and moved my tongue down her belly, stopping when I got to the waistband of her pants.

I moved my hands down her body, sliding my hands inside the top of her pants and underwear, pulling them down her body quickly and throwing them to the floor.

I moved my mouth back to her nipple and used one of my hands to pinch the other. Then I gripped her whole breast in my hand, massaging it, as I moved my tongue around the other one. She let out continuous moans as she bucked her hips again, urging me to get on with it.

I bit her nipple again, and I moved my other hand through her folds, my fingers finding her wet clit. I started rubbing her as I continued playing with her breasts and nipples. The noises coming from her, turned me on so much that I felt like I was going to orgasm just hearing her. I wasn't even sure if that was possible.

I quickened my pace with my fingers and her hips started trembling. I continued to play with her nipple with my other hand, but I wanted to feel her moan in my mouth, so I put my lips on hers and made her part her mouth. I felt her juices run through my fingers as her legs clenched together and her moaning turned into a satisfied scream.

Her orgasm ripped through her and I felt her hand grab my ass tightly as she reached her peak. When the tightness of her grip lessened, I slowed down my rubbing and we began kissing passionately again.

"Get. Naked," Lu ordered between our kisses.

I obeyed and got rid of my clothes as quickly as I could. Immediately, Lu pulled me back down on top of her, but then turned us so I was on my back.

"Hey, I'm meant to be apologizing to you," I pointed out, but Lu ignored me as she moved her pelvis over mine so that our clits were touching.

"You're done apologizing. I've forgiven you. I love you. Now let's make love," Lu responded as she leaned down and started kissing me. She began to rock against me, the sensations immediately causing me to moan.

As she continued to move her hips back and forth our clits rubbed together, causing me to tip over the edge after only a few moments. I was so turned on by making Lu orgasm earlier that it really didn't surprise me that it didn't take much. Lu came a second time only a few seconds after me, rekindling my arousal with her moaning in my mouth again.

"I love you too," I replied after Lu moved off me, allowing me to roll us over so she had her back on the bed again.

"Which is why I am making up for everything. For making you wait. For my behavior and for loving me even though I bruised your beautiful body," I continued, placing kisses down her throat and all the way to her breast again.

"You've put plenty of other bruises on my body before," Lu pointed out just as I started sucking on her breast.

"Case in point," she added with a chuckle. My heart fluttered as her chest raised with her laugh and I could feel her heartbeat in anticipation of what I was going to do next. I stopped sucking on her breast, glancing up at her for a moment.

"At least these ones are good ones," I murmured

before putting my lips back on her skin and trailing kisses down all the way to her mound. I paused the kisses as I spread her legs apart, putting one leg over my shoulder so I could get better access to her.

With my fingers, I pushed aside her folds and I continued my kisses until I found her clit and started licking it. Lu let out a moan of satisfaction and snatched my hair, pulling me forward more, which encouraged me to move my tongue faster in her. I licked up and down her pussy, inserting my tongue into her vagina, causing her to buck against me.

Her moans became more intense, which made me move my tongue in and out of her even more quickly. I licked my way back up to her clit, moving my tongue over it, gently sucking on it a few times as I pushed her closer to her third orgasm.

I paused just for a moment to run my fingers through her juices so I could insert them into her awaiting pussy. I slid two fingers in and out of her as I moved my tongue continuously over her nub, working it harder and faster as her moans became louder and longer.

When they turned into a scream of pleasure I knew her next orgasm was washing over her and it was confirmed when her pussy clenched tightly around my fingers and her hips quaked against me.

"Elsie!" She screamed as she peaked, her legs falling flat against me when it was over. I grinned as I removed my mouth from her clit and slowly pulled my fingers out of her.

She reached down and gently cupped my face, bringing me towards her. She kissed me, tasting her own arousal on my mouth, which made my heart pound. Her heart was pounding too, but for a different reason, so I knew we had to rest. I could feel her exhaustion as she kissed me.

"We are nowhere near finished, but I need a break," Lu admitted, confirming my thoughts as she pulled away from the kiss. I grinned at her and moved so I was lying against her. I put my head on her chest to listen to her quick heartbeat.

"When we've had a good rest, it's your turn," Lu warned and I laughed.

"Deal," I agreed, not that I would have said no.

Since we were both hot from our love making, we lay completely naked. Because it was silent, apart from our heavy breathing, it didn't take us long to fall asleep. The nap allowed us to recuperate so we could enjoy the rest of our sex-filled afternoon and, admittedly, most of the evening

Chapter Eighteen

"I want my phone call!" I called out as I banged on the windowpane, craning my head as I looked around for anyone. The station was empty of cops – they had left the three of us alone, cold in a cell, with absolutely no clue as to what was going to happen. There must have been people in the other cells, because I was sure we should have been separated.

No one spoke to us while we were getting fingerprinted and had our photos taken. No one batted an eye when Jorge kept yelling out that he needed to talk to his lawyer.

The only thing that gave me any hope was the look of pity I kept getting from the uniformed police who looked conflicted about processing me.

I hoped that they believed the story that I was brought here against my will, because if they did, then a jury might also. I was so scared about the prospect of going to prison because as soon as someone found out I was a cop, I would be eaten alive.

Jorge and Techy had been speaking to each other in Spanish, probably forgetting that I was fluent in the language. They were talking about how they were going to get the best representation once they were back in New Haven. They already planned for someone named

'Fingers' to continue running the gang, even though currently there wasn't much to run because everything but the homes they lived in had been burnt down in retaliation for the murder of Dante Moretti.

I purposefully zoned out because the less I knew about anything, the more I could deny I was involved.

I kept banging on the windowpane of the cell door, trying to make more noise so someone could hear me. I wanted my phone call to try to reach the girls. I knew there was a chance that they had gotten rid of the phone, but I was hoping that, like last time, it was the last thing on their mind. It wasn't like the cops had any idea about the phone anyway, so they couldn't be tracking it.

If it was our precinct, we would track the suspect's phone call, hoping they would get hold of the people we were after. Chances were they did that here too, but I was willing to keep the conversation under thirty seconds if it meant that I could find out if Elsie was alright.

The FBI agent came around the corner and headed for our cell with a smirk on his face.

"You don't get to make the demands here, Swanson," he reminded me, as he opened the slot just below the window that was used for giving us food.

"I have a right to one phone call. Surely that is the same in every country?"

The FBI agent shrugged his shoulders but proceeded to pull a set of keys out of his pocket. I stood back as he put the keys in the lock and swung open the door.

I looked back at Jorge, who had stood up and gave me a look that told me he knew I was going to try to get hold of the girls. I could tell by his face that he was telling me to be careful, as he knew just as well as me that they were probably going to track my call. I gave him a small nod just as the FBI agent gently pulled my hands behind my back and handcuffed me.

I wanted to protest, to say I wasn't going to be a problem, but somehow I didn't think it was going to work. It was like this man had taken offense to the fact that I was willing to break the law to help my own child. When he tightened the cuff on my wrist, I winced and looked back at him.

"It's a little tight," I pointed out, but he ignored me and pulled me out of the cell. He locked it up again while holding onto my upper arm. He then led me down the hall and around the corner until we came to a small office with a chair and a desk with a phone sitting on it.

The agent uncuffed one of my hands then cuffed me again with both of them to the font. I raised my hands up.

"Are these really necessary?" I asked, my voice sounding annoyed.

"You fled the country with wanted criminals. Of course they are," he responded. I glared at the man who hadn't even introduced himself, so I couldn't even curse his name.

"Is your name Richard? Because you're sure being a dick," I mumbled under my breath. He must have heard me because he grabbed my arm roughly and forced me to sit down.

"Do you want to make your phone call or not? I can just as easily take you back to your cell and then I really would be a dick, wouldn't I?" He asked and I narrowed my eyes further. I put my hand on the receiver and looked at him pointedly, wondering if he was going to leave the room. He looked back at me with his arms folded.

"I'm entitled to a *private* phone call," I reminded him, even though I knew there would be a team nearby listening to every word while they tracked the line.

"Fine," the agent grunted, turning to leave. He stopped at the door and looked back at me.

"It's Special Agent Lewis, by the way. Robert Lewis," he added, before leaving the room and shutting the door behind him.

"You're Special Agent Dick to me," I muttered as I turned back to the phone.

I picked up the receiver and punched in the numbers that I had memorized a long time ago, just in case something like this happened. After a couple of rings, it was answered.

"Papi?" Lu answered and my heart sank with disappointment for her. Jorge had already used his phone call to contact his second to explain the situation. I didn't know who Techy had called but it wasn't the girls.

That was my job and they had made me wait.

"It's Olivia," I corrected and I heard a disappointed 'oh' come from Lu before a rustle of noise.

"You're on speaker," she announced and my heart fluttered against my chest again. I knew I only had about twenty seconds left, so I had to be quick.

"Are you two safe?" I asked, crossing my other fingers with hope.

"Yes, we are," Elsie replied this time and I smiled at her voice.

"I think we're getting sent back to America. I don't know if they are going to wait till they find you or just make us go," I explained, quickly. Ten seconds.

"Lu, do you still have it?" I asked quickly.

"Yes," she replied. I closed my eyes with relief.

"You know what to do," I stated then hung up the receiver, wishing I had more time to talk.

I'm sure Elsie was sitting next to Lu in confusion.

About a month ago, Lu had come to me to ask me for my opinion and help. I was delighted by her request because it was not only romantic, but it was probably the best thing for them to do. I had helped her pick everything out for it. I had even gone to Techy for help to find someone who would do it. It cost us $500K, but it was the only way it was going to happen. We had only paid half, so I was hoping that Techy's phone call was to someone who could help us pay the rest once it was done.

The door opened and Special Agent Dick walked back into the room, clearly not amused by the fact that I didn't talk long enough for them to track the girls. I raised my eyebrow slightly.

"Why so disappointed?" I asked, tilting my head slightly. He couldn't answer me, of course – what he did was admissible in court if it had worked, so he couldn't even use the fact that I had spoken to the girls against me. Instead he ignored me and grabbed my upper arm, harder than he had done earlier. I tried to pull my arm away from his grip, but he held on tighter.

"You're hurting me," I complained, moving my arm again. I guess due to my tone he finally snapped out of whatever he was thinking and lessened his grip.

"Shut up," was all he replied as he pulled me out of the room. He led me back to the cell, unlocked the door and pushed me inside without bothering to take off the cuffs.

"Oi! Special Agent Dick!" I shouted as he walked away. I banged the cuffs against the bars, which created loud clunking sounds

"It's *Lewis*," he shouted back, but he continued walking away. Jorge chuckled behind me and I turned to glare at him.

"It seems you know how to make friends with everybody," he pointed out and I rolled my eyes.

I walked over to him and Techy and sat down, huffing slightly as my cuffed hands fell into my lap.

"That's because I keep coming across such lovely gentleman," I remarked and he chuckled more.

"How are the girls?" He asked, his voice turning serious.

"Safe," I replied as I leaned back against the cold brick wall.

"Does she still have it?" he asked and I knew he was referring to what I had asked Lu about. I nodded.

"She knows what to do. It'll be her priority other than keeping them both safe," I replied, knowing that Lu wouldn't let anything like what happened with the

Moretti gang happen to Elsie again. She knew what hesitation cost her the last time and she had assured me she wouldn't make that mistake again. I also knew that she would have her birthday gift by now. I hated to admit it, but that girl was very talented with a knife.

"Good," Jorge responded.

I turned my head to look at him. "Once it's done, I guess I will have to get used to the idea that we're going to be family."

"Oh but, Liv, we are already family," he retorted.

My small smile turned into a frown.

"It doesn't take a signed paper to declare who is family. The moment those girls fell in love, it brought our two families together. I'm just glad it's you and not that *maldito abusador*," he spit the last two words, clearly still full of hate towards that 'fucking abuser.' I didn't blame him. I was close to pulling the trigger on him myself the more I found out what he did to my daughter, but alas, Elsie got there first.

"Right," I said with a soft laugh as I closed my eyes. For some reason I had expected him to declare that the fake marriage certificate was actually real or something and the only thing fake about it was the names. Thank god that wasn't the case. We sat in silence and with my eyes still closed, I gently drifted off to sleep, since there was nothing else I could do but wait.

Chapter Nineteen

Lu

"What was Olivia talking about?" Elsie asked as she moved across the bed and sat behind me, her body pressed against me, her chin resting on my shoulder.

The phone call had woken us up from an after-sex nap, so we were both still completely naked. We had to stop falling asleep with no clothes on, because it was getting colder and colder as the days went on. This was the second day in the house and we had been naked for most of it.

I put the phone down on the bedside table and moved myself so I could face Elsie and wrapped my arms around her to bring her body close to mine. Her body heat was the only thing warming me up, so I used my feet to kick up the blankets, only letting go of her long enough to pull them over us. Once we settled under them, I put my arms back around her and pulled her closer still.

"She was just talking about the wigs," I lied, as I kissed her forehead.

The truth was Olivia was talking about the ring I had gotten Elsie, with which I planned to ask her to marry me. I had asked Olivia about a month ago, if she was okay with me marrying her daughter. She was honored that I asked, but said she had no right to say yes or no, but of course she gave me her blessing. She helped me buy the most beautiful ring that I knew Elsie would absolutely love. It was in my pants pocket next to my lock picks.

I wanted to marry her so much. Olivia had seen how much I loved her, but she also pointed out that it was actually a really good idea; if we were married, we couldn't be forced to testify against each other. I just didn't think this was the time to get down on one knee and ask her, considering we had spent the last day and a half making up for lost time and I knew she was still feeling guilty about how she had been the other night.

"Unlikely story," Elsie responded, but she laughed, which told me she wasn't going to keep questioning me about it.

Elsie's stomach rumbled with hunger and I realized that we hadn't eaten since yesterday. Well, we hadn't eaten food!

I pushed the blanket off of us and stood up, grabbing Elsie's clothes from the floor and handing them to her. She shuffled herself out of bed as she grabbed them and she put on her shirt, which had me pouting slightly because her breasts were now put away.

I turned around and grabbed my shirt off the floor and saw that most of the buttons had been ripped off. I put my hands on my hips and showed Elsie, with a pointed look, and she laughed. Her laugh sounded like a flock of angels singing. I don't know what it was about it, but I couldn't look angry at her even if I tried.

I grinned and threw the shirt across the room. I walked over to the bag of clothes that was sitting on the dresser. I searched around until I found one of my shirts and put it on. There was no point worrying about bras - chances were that they would come off soon anyway.

I pulled a pair of underwear out of the bag and put them on too. I then went to grab my pants from the ground, only to find that Elsie had picked them up and was now sitting on the bed, half naked with the ring box in her other hand, staring at it.

"I was hoping you would find out about that another way," I noted quietly.

Elsie looked up from the box.

"I swear I didn't mean to look. I was just grabbing them for you and it fell out," she said hurriedly, standing up so fast that her pants fell to the ground. She was only wearing a shirt and holding the ring box.

I laughed slightly and walked up to her. I picked up my pants and put them on, then grabbed Elsie's. I helped her step into them and pulled them up for her, buttoning them back up.

I took the ring box out of her hand and then knelt on one knee. Elsie's hands went over her mouth as she looked down at me, her eyes glistening with tears. I reached up and grabbed her left arm, so I could hold her hand in mine. I hadn't even said anything yet, but I could feel my throat closing up and tears beginning to form in my own eyes.

"Elizabeth Rose Neilson," I began and flicked open the ring box with my fingers. Elsie let out a gasp and her eyes widened at the sight of the ring made of silver and a gold band that crossed each other, with diamonds lining the cross and it had one large diamond in the center.

"Will you marry me?" I asked, my heart pounding hard in my chest. Elsie's tears began to fall and she fell to her knees in front of me while nodding her head.

"Yes. A million times yes."

I started to cry too as I pulled the ring out of the box and slipped it onto her finger. I dropped the box and I pulled her close to me as I kissed her. Our kiss deepened as she wrapped her arms around me. We were about to start pulling each other's clothes off again when my stomach growled this time. We stopped our kissing and rested our foreheads against each other, panting at the slight loss of breath we were both feeling. We looked at each other and laughed.

"Food," I declared, and Elsie grinned at me and stood up, grabbing my hand in hers as she pulled me up.

She looked down at her hand and stared at the ring for a moment.

"It's beautiful," she whispered, looking back at me.

I kissed her gently on the cheek. "Just like my soon-to-be-wife," I declared and Elsie's cheeks flushed.

"Wife…I like the sound of that," she told me and I grinned.

We walked hand in hand to the kitchen where I had set up a small cooker. I let go of Elsie's hand and walked to the bench where I had stashed some cans of spaghetti. I pulled the tab, taking off the lid.

"Do you mind finding a pot?" I asked, looking back at Elsie who was admiring her ring. I grinned as I looked back at the can of food. It didn't take long for Elsie to find a pot, which she put down next to the can and then wrapped her arms around my waist.

"Have you ever cooked like this before?" She asked, distracting me as she started kissing the side of my neck.

"I've never left my home before now, so no, not exactly," I replied, trying to ignore the sensations brewing between my legs as Elsie's tongue trailed along my throat.

"You have to be careful with the gas," Elsie noted, her breath soft against my skin. I couldn't help but shudder as Elsie pressed her body against my back.

"Noted," I replied, tipping the contents into the pot. I then opened the side compartment of the cooker to connect the gas cannister, but I paused as Elsie's hands made their way under my shirt, along my belly and finally rested on my breasts. I could feel the cold metal of her ring against my nipple as she groped them, causing me to let out a moan.

"Elsie, I'm trying to cook us food to eat. You're not helping the situation," I whispered, as I leaned over to grab one of the gas cans. Elsie's right hand moved back down my belly, sliding down my pants where she didn't stop until her fingers were on my clit.

"Elsie," I moaned, but she just gripped my breast tighter and rocked her fingers back and forth against my core. I gripped the counter for support.

"I can think of something better for you to eat," she whispered in my ear and I moaned as she picked up her pace. I let out little whimpers as she continued to work me up to breaking point.

"Come for me, wifey," she whispered and I broke as my orgasm ran through me, taking over my senses. I fell back against Elsie, but she held me up by bringing her leg between mine.

She moved her hand from my pants and put it back on my breast, massaging my slickness onto my skin. I thought she was finished with me, but she started to move her leg back and forth, and she had put it in such a perfect position that I felt it rubbing against my already tender core.

"Elsie…" I pleaded, moving my neck back, which gave her the perfect opportunity to move her mouth onto my throat again. She started sucking my skin, while continuing to massage my breasts and move her leg against me. Soon another orgasm washed over me again, only this time I screamed in pleasure.

I felt Elsie's smile against my skin. She removed her hands from under my shirt and put her leg back down.

"Now you can cook us some food," she announced.

This made me look at her with my eyebrow slightly raised.

"Where did that come from?" I asked her, feeling slightly weak from her antics. I didn't know if I could even lift the gas can and put it in the compartment now.

Elsie smirked as she shrugged her shoulders.

"Just doing my wifely duties," she replied and I chuckled.

"We're not even married yet," I pointed out, but she shrugged her shoulders again.

"Not legally, but we are in heart and soul," she replied and I gave her a grin as I turned back to start the cooker.

Once I got the pot of spaghetti heating, I turned back around and walked over to Elsie, putting my arms around her waist and bringing her close.

"We have to travel to a place called Auckland to get married. We found a dodgy judge who was easy enough to blackmail. He'll marry us without informing the police," I explained to her.

"So you had this planned out, huh?" She asked, a smirk appearing on her face. I grinned as I nodded.

"The only thing that isn't going according to plan, is the fact that our parents aren't with us," I replied, thinking of Dad and Olivia and of course Techy, who was probably sitting in a cold jail cell as we spoke.

"Did Olivia know?" Elsie asked.

I nodded again. "I asked her for permission actually..."

Elsie's face reddened slightly.

"It's weird. I know I've only known her for like six months and only known she is my mother for two, but I feel like she's been more of a parent to me than he was," Elsie said quietly.

I gave her a small knowing smile.

"I know. That's why I asked her. She told me she didn't have any say in the matter, but she was honored that I asked. She said that she couldn't be more happier for the two of us," I told her and Elsie smiled.

"I had been thinking of legally changing my name to Elizabeth Swanson," Elsie said quietly.

"But now, I get to be Elizabeth Torres Alveraz and I couldn't think of anything better," she explained, which made my heartbeat quicken.

"I like the sound of that," I whispered as I kissed her. I could smell the food heating up, so before the kiss got any more heated, I pulled away from her and walked over to the pot.

It was bubbling away so I opened the drawers and searched for a wooden spoon. Once I found it, I stirred the spaghetti around. Luckily it just needed to be heated through, because my stomach rumbled again and it was beginning to hurt.

"Can you find some bowls please?" I asked, as I stirred. Elsie was at my side again, putting the bowls down on the bench top, only this time she walked away and went to another drawer and pulled out silverware for us to use.

She set the table, while I checked the temperature of the food. It was warmed through enough. I dished the spaghetti into the bowls while Elsie got us two glasses of water.

We ate in silence, but our hands were joined together with our fingers linked. Her ring was resting against my finger and I couldn't help but think how perfectly it seemed to fit. I grinned at her as I ate, glad to get some food inside me.

Once we were finished we cleaned up our dishes, putting everything back where we found it. I put the garbage in an empty plastic bag I found in the cupboard.

When we had finished cleaning the kitchen, we made our way back to the bedroom, only because it was getting rather cold. We cuddled up against each other, using our body heat as well as the blankets to warm us up. Elsie had her head on my chest and I had my arm around her, holding her close to me.

"We're going to have to go on the ferry to get to Auckland, aren't we?" Elsie asked. She started to draw circles on my belly, which made me want to tear her clothes off again. But it was cold, so I chose to ignore it and focus on her question.

"Or we can steal a boat," I suggested, remembering all the boats we had gone past on the way here.

"Do you know how to drive a boat?" Elsie asked.

I chuckled a little. "Do you mean do I know how to

pilot a boat?" I moved my hand to Elsie's wandering fingers and linked them in mine. "Dad owns one. He took me out sometimes and let me navigate the wheel."

"You always seem to be able to surprise me, L," Elsie stated, looking up at me. I grinned as I leaned down to kiss her.

"I think if we steal a boat, they will know by the time we reach the other island. They will be waiting for us," Elsie pointed out.

I let out a slight sigh, because she was right.

"I suppose. I guess we have to wear our best disguises and then hide out for about four hours, because that's roughly how long the ferry will take to get across the strait," I concluded with a small pout. I was secretly hoping Elsie agreed to the boat stealing idea, but the more I thought about it, the more Elsie made more sense.

"Do they have cabins?" Elsie asked and I leaned over to the bedside table to grab the phone off of it. We really needed to get a new one. Chances were that the police had our number now. It would only be a matter of time before they came for us. We should really leave in the morning. I opened the phone and waited for the data to load and looked up the ferry. There was a cabin.

"We should go tomorrow," I said, closing the phone and putting it back.

"You don't want to stay here a little longer and break in the other rooms?" Elsie asked, looking at me with a hopeful look on her face. I laughed.

"You've exhausted me, E," I pointed out, tightening my arm around her to hug her.

Elsie pouted and I leaned down to kiss her.

We didn't end up going to sleep until about two hours later. She managed to get numerous orgasms out of me and I got a few from her.

We knew each other's bodies so well we just seemed to know how to pleasure each other in ways that still brought me so much joy I was afraid she was going to stop wanting to do it again. I guess that's why I took it all while I could. In case she changed her mind and decided it was too much to bear.

Chapter Twenty

Elsie

I woke up the next morning after the best night's sleep I have had since *that* night. It was a way better sleep than the nights where I drank myself practically into a coma. Apparently having lots of sex had been the answer all along! This felt odd to me, considering the nightmares that kept me awake every night were from a sexual assault.

I woke up with Lu's legs tangled between mine, her head against my chest as she cuddled into me. My arms were around her, holding her close with my hands resting on her ass. We were still naked from the night before, with only the sheet and blankets covering us.

I moved myself to look down at her and could see that she was still asleep. I smiled at her as I shifted my hand from her backside and glided up her body, which made her let out a soft moan as her eyes flickered open. My hand grazed her breast, and in return she moved her leg, causing my breath to hitch as it moved against my core.

"Morning, *mi amor*," I whispered. She grinned back at me, as she moved her head to look at me.

"Morning," she replied, puckering her lips. I leaned in to meet her with a kiss. I ran my hand back down her body as I continued to kiss her. I was just about to reach between her legs, but she intercepted my fingers by linking hers with mine.

"Not right now, babe," she whispered, pulling her head back from kissing me.

She brought my hand up to her mouth and she kissed it. I frowned and began untangling my legs from hers.

"We have to leave to get to the ferry," Lu reminded me, as she lifted my hand back up to show me the shining ring that was on my finger. "If we start anything now, we won't make it and it will take longer for you to be my wife."

I grinned as I lowered myself back down and kissed her anyway. I wanted to kiss her more, but I knew she was right.

I unlinked my fingers from hers and I moved myself so I was at the edge of the bed and stood up. Lu got out of bed too and moved to the bag of clothes, grabbing out what we needed to get dressed.

We had decided that since the ferry had a cabin with a shower in it, we would wait to shower there. We thought it was better than having a cold shower here, considering there was no power for hot water.

We got changed and it took everything in me to keep my hands off of her. I wanted to think that feeling hot and horny for my fiancée was completely normal, but right now it reminded me of how I felt when I had to have a drink. I wanted her and I wanted her *now*.

So I left the room once we were dressed, walking to the kitchen to start cleaning it up. We may have broken into the house and probably had sex on every surface of the place, but we weren't going to leave it messy. Once the kitchen was clean and the rest of the house was in a respectable condition, Lu and I hopped back in the car to make our way to the ferry terminal.

We had decided that we were going to ditch the car before boarding the ferry. We would travel the rest of the way to Auckland by bus once we got into Wellington. We had done research the night before and booked all the tickets we needed. It was going to take us fifteen and a half hours to get to Auckland.

We stopped at a public toilet just before the terminal, where we put on our wigs and I put on my scarf. I put on a short brown wig that made me look like I was going to ask to speak to someone's manager and Lu wore a flaming red wig which made me want to rip off all her clothes and fuck her right there in the cubicle. I resisted the urge by balling my hands into fists and walking away from her, causing Lu to hurry after me with the bags I had left behind.

We walked the rest of the way to the terminal, only to find three police cars parked in the parking lot.

"Fuck," I gasped, grabbing onto Lu's arm as I spotted a police officer sitting in the driver's seat of one of the vehicles.

"Don't act suspicious!" Lu exclaimed, pulling my hand away from her arm and linking her fingers with mine. I could feel her bracelet vibrating, in warning. I was glad it was silent, or otherwise it would give us away.

"We're just two travelers about to board a ferry," Lu pointed out, but my heart quickened as the police officer opened the door and got out. He looked over to us, gave us a small smile and then headed into the building. I let out a sigh of relief and I felt Lu squeeze my hand.

"The only thing that is going to make them look at us, is you doing something to give us away. Just breathe, E," Lu continued. I nodded as I squeezed her hand back and we continued to walk into the building.

As we checked ourselves in, paying for our tickets with the cash that Lu had carefully removed from the bag, I tried my hardest to ignore the officers walking around the building. I knew that they were here for us and I swear my nerves were taking over my actions.

I needed a drink. I needed something to take the edge off. My heart was pounding and my hands were sweating. I could feel the sweat pouring off my forehead. I was hot, even though the weather was freezing. If it wasn't for the fact that I had my hands shoved into my pockets, they would be shaking with fear.

I hadn't even noticed that we had moved to the other side of the building, and sat down in the waiting area, ready for the boarding announcement. I really couldn't sit still.

My leg was jiggling up and down, which made Lu put her hand on my knee to stop me. I looked at her and she gave me a look of concern, but I shoved her hand away because all I wanted her to do was to take that edge away.

"Calm down, E. You're making it obvious," Lu whispered harshly, then gave an overly fake smile to an officer who walked past and looked at us. I stilled my leg jiggling and avoided the officer's gaze by reaching into the bag of clothes and pulling out a water bottle.

"She's never been on a ship before, she's just nervous," Lu said in her fake Australian accent, which I must admit now sounded legit. The officer laughed as she carried on walking and I took a gulp of the water, wishing it was something stronger.

"I'm sorry," I whispered, moving my hand up to my forehead to wipe away the sweat.

"This is more than nervousness, isn't it?" Lu asked me, just as the speaker above us started to announce that it was time to board. I put the water bottle back in the bag and noticed how badly my hand was shaking.

"I need a drink," I admitted and Lu let out a sigh of realization as she stood up and held her hand out for me to take to help me up. When I stood she wrapped her arm around my waist as we started walking behind the crowd going to board the ferry.

"You're having withdrawal," Lu whispered and I nodded, feeling ashamed. By now I had usually snuck in two of those small bottles of vodka. By now I was usually pouring more into a different bottle to try to pass it off as water. It had been two days since I had my last drink and I guess I hadn't realized how much my body had come to rely on it. I also assumed it was because the last two days had been filled with sex and sleep that I hadn't had the time to realize it.

"It'll be ok. I think I just need to sleep it off," I informed her, after handing over our boarding tickets to the employee.

An officer stood next to him, looking down at two photographs which I could only assume were pictures of us, but he didn't even look at us twice as we walked past him. Obviously our disguises were working. Lu squeezed my side as we continued down the walkway, and soon we were on the ferry.

We handed in our cabin ticket to the receptionist at the desk and in return we were given a room number and key. As soon as we were in the cabin, we took our showers and then snuggled up together on the single bed.

We were both on our sides, with Lu's body pressing against mine. I was the little spoon this time and having her arms around me helped ease the shaking.

I grabbed her hand and moved it between my legs and she didn't ask me what I was doing, as she knew what I needed.

When my orgasm hit, the relief I felt was instantaneous. The endorphins eased my pain and I felt relaxed as Lu removed her hand from me. Lu kissed my head and I closed my eyes.

"Thank you," I whispered, grabbing onto her hand to bring it close to my chest as I cuddled it.

"Anytime," Lu replied, with a soft chuckle.

I grinned as she linked our fingers together. Soon, thanks to my fiancée, the silence, the gentle rocking of the ocean and my newly at-ease mind, I drifted off into a dreamless sleep.

~.~

Three hours later we arrived in a city called Wellington. There were police surrounding the terminal again, but Lu and I managed to leave the terminal without anyone noticing us. We boarded a bus that was to take us to a station, where we could catch a bus that would take us to Auckland.

"Tell me again why we have to go all the way to Auckland to get married again?" I whispered as we sat down at the back of the bus, holding our bags close to us.

"We could only find one dodgy judge. He's from there," Lu whispered back, watching as a cop entered the bus and looked around.

I felt Lu tense as she hugged the bag she was carrying closer to her body. She had agreed to only carry her knife on her person, so both guns were in the bag. It was also still filled up with cash which would look suspicious in itself if anyone were to search it.

The officer nodded his head towards us with acknowledgement before walking off the bus again. Both Lu and I let out sighs of relief.

"Either New Zealand cops are useless at their jobs, or our disguises are flawless," I pointed out, as I moved myself so I could put my head down on Lu's shoulder.

"I'm going to go with our disguises are flawless," Lu

responded, putting her head on top of mine.

The bus started moving out of the parking lot. Lu and I sat in silence as the bus made its way to the station. It didn't take long for us to arrive, and once we got some snacks from the grocery shop, we were sitting on the new bus waiting to start traveling again.

Lu had brought four seats for our trip, so when we got on the bus, we went straight to the back of the bus and she suggested that I sleep on her, using her legs as a pillow.

I swear to god, at that moment, I wasn't against public sex. It didn't help that I had bought a blanket from the grocery shop, so really no one would see what I was doing. Right? I refused to give into the temptation, though, and lay down on her legs, facing towards the front of the bus.

Even though I was scared the nightmares would come, knowing Lu was right there gave me enough comfort to fall asleep about half an hour after the bus started its journey. She was running her fingers through my wig, which was both comforting and relaxing.

I slept for a good hour before waking up. Lu and I spent most of the rest of the bus trip eating, sleeping and talking about what our future would have been like if we weren't in this predicament.

"I would love to draw for a living," I stated quietly, sitting between Lu's legs and leaning against her, while she leaned up against the side of the bus. We both had our feet lying across the seats with the blanket covering us for warmth. It really was quite cold.

"What would you want to draw?" Lu asked. She lifted my left hand and started playing with my fingers.

"Portraits of families," I replied, smiling as I watched her twirl the ring on my finger.

"You can always tell how happy a family is by how long they can sit still together. Also you can see it in their eyes. If they were unhappy, I would be able to help them," I mused, looking at Lu. She looked back down at me, pausing the ring twirling.

"What about you?" I asked, wondering if she would want to work with her father or something.

 Lu looked away, resuming her twirling of the ring. She didn't answer me. I frowned slightly and pushed myself up so I could look back at her. Lu dropped my hand so I could use it to hold myself up.

"L?" I urged and her face turned red. It occurred to me that, outside of stealing, motorbikes and sex, I didn't know what Lu actually enjoyed. I didn't even know what she was good at.

"I always wanted to be a singer," Lu mumbled so low

under her breath, I didn't think I heard her right. I tilted my head slightly.

"I didn't quite hear you," I replied, a small smile creeping on my face because I had heard her, but I wanted her to repeat her dream.

"I want to be a singer," Lu replied, her face so red, I could almost feel the heat coming from it.

"I didn't know you could sing," I pointed out and Lu awkwardly nodded her head.

"I'm alright at it," she responded, looking away from me. I twisted myself fully, so I was facing her, sitting on my knees between her legs. I gently reached up and cupped her face, making her look at me.

"Why didn't you tell me?" I asked her, my heart bursting with pride. Apparently, taking music class wasn't because it was the least objectionable elective at all, but something she had chosen because she enjoyed it. Lu looked at me with her face full of embarrassment.

"Because I haven't sung in front of anyone since my mom died," Lu replied, her tone soft. I dropped my hands from her face and took her hands in mine instead.

"Not even in class?" I asked, giving her hands a small squeeze. Lu shook her head.

"Luckily I'm pretty good with a guitar, so I just used that in music," Lu responded, with a small shrug of her shoulders.

"But you must still sing, if you think you're good at it," I teased, trying to get her to smile, or at least be less embarrassed about it. Lu tilted her head and smirked as she looked back at me.

"You've been quite out of it when you've had a few drinks," Lu commented, making me turn red as well. "When you were dead to the world, I would use the time to sing. It beats sitting on the bed all night letting my mind wander."

"What do you sing about?" I asked her, turning myself back around so I could spread my legs back out and lean against her.

"You," she replied, matter-of-factly. I could tell my face grew redder, considering the heat that it caused.

"Will you sing something for me?" I whispered, looking around the bus. It wasn't too full. Most of the passengers had decided that the front of the bus was better to occupy, so we were pretty much alone in the back. Lu sighed a little as she moved her arms around my middle and hugged me from behind.

"Please remember I don't do this often," Lu said quietly.

"I'm sure however you sound, it will be perfect," I responded, looking up at her. She kissed me gently before taking a breath and began singing "How Can I Resist Her," by Split Endz, but the Robinson version. By the time she had finished singing, I was in tears. She was perfect. Her voice was like angels singing. I moved myself to face her again.

"That was amazing! Perfect," I declared and Lu let out a soft chuckle and kissed my forehead.

"You stole Techy's laptop didn't you?" I asked, with a grin as I looked back up at her.

"What makes you say that?" Lu asked with a laugh.

"You wouldn't know the way Robinson sang it, otherwise," I pointed out and Lu just grinned at me.

"Guilty," she said, reaching up to wipe my tears away.

"So do you think I could have become a singer?" She asked quietly. I leaned forward and kissed her.

"Absolutely. Promise me you won't stop singing, even if we get caught and have to go to prison," I whispered, aware that people were probably still in ear shot of us, even if they weren't sitting by us.

"As long as you promise not to stop drawing," Lu replied and I nodded in agreement.

"I promise," I added, as I leaned forward and kissed her again. Once we stopped kissing, Lu looked at her phone.

"We should arrive in Auckland in about an hour," Lu

commented, which made me turn and lean back into her. She lifted the blanket that had fallen down over us again.

"Let's sleep for the rest of the way, then when we get to Auckland, we will go shopping for wedding clothes. I reckon we could even dye our hair back to normal, now that everyone knows what we look like. We'll be in wigs most of the time anyway," Lu pointed out. She grabbed the bag of clothes off the floor and put it behind her head, using it as a makeshift pillow.

"I like the sound of that. I miss your pink hair," I said quietly, as I closed my eyes.

"And I miss your beautiful blond hair," Lu responded and I let out a soft laugh. It didn't take us long before we both fell asleep and soon we arrived in the heart of Auckland.

Chapter Twenty-One

Olivia

"They're in Auckland!"

The shout was surprisingly near. I got up from the bench I was lying on and looked towards the front of the cell. I heard Jorge swear behind me, which suggested he had heard the shout as well. I looked back at him, slight fear likely showing in my eyes, considering that the plan *was* for Lu and Elsie to be in Auckland right now.

A few seconds later, Special Agent Dick - sorry, Special Agent Lewis - was at the door and he was grinning through the window like he had just won something.

"Did you hear that?" He asked, his voice smug as he opened the slot in the door.

I stood up and walked towards him. "No, sorry, I didn't hear you above all the silence in this jail cell," I replied, rolling my eyes.

"They're in Auckland. You forgot to clear the redial and we finally tracked them down," Special Agent Lewis explained.

My heart stopped.

"What did you say?" I asked, wondering if I heard him right. Surely I wasn't the reason they were found, was I?

"The girls. They're in Auckland. Thank you for helping us track them," Special Agent Lewis repeated, loudly and slowly so there was no way I would miss his words.

I felt the back of my shirt being pulled roughly and then suddenly my back was slammed against the wall and Jorge was in my face, his teeth bared.

"I knew you would fuck this up for them!" He snarled as his forearm crashed against my throat, cutting off my air supply. My eyes went wide as I struggled to push him off. Techy had rushed from his seat and was trying to get Jorge off me too, but Jorge stood his ground, pushing his arm harder.

"Please," I choked, my hands gripping onto his arm. I heard screaming, clunking of keys, and opening of doors, but spots were forming in my vision so I couldn't see where they were coming from.

"Once a fucking pig, always a fucking pig. *Te voy a matar*," Jorge growled. I had no doubt in my mind that he wasn't joking about killing me. More spots grew and I thought that I was going to die knowing I was the reason Elsie was caught.

Just when I thought I was going to lose consciousness, Jorge was pulled from me. I fell down the wall on the ground and clutched my throat as I looked up. Jorge was struggling to get away from three police officers that were holding him back. His face showed how much he wanted to kill me and for the first time I had been with him, I was truly scared of him.

"I'm sorry," I whispered, my voice coarse. I looked at Techy who was being held back by another officer, but of course he wasn't struggling.

Agent Lewis stepped forward and grabbed my arm, pulling me up from the ground. He escorted me out of the cell, leaving the other officers, Jorge, and Techy alone. He walked me back into the room where I had made the phone call and he sat me down on the chair. He grabbed a chair that was on the other side of the table and brought it round to sit in front of me, his face full of concern.

"Are you alright?" He asked.

I looked at him with a slight glare as I rubbed my bruised throat.

"Peachy," I croaked.

The agent winced and left the room. He didn't lock the door; in fact, he left it wide open.

I could try to run, but what was the point? If the girls had been found, it was only a matter of time until we would be reunited. I leaned back in the chair, wondering where he had gone.

A second later, he walked back into the room with a glass of water and an ice pack. He carefully handed them over to me. I took them, taking a small sip of water before putting the ice pack against my throat.

"That wasn't my intention," he started.

I tilted my head slightly with my eyebrow raised. "You didn't think he would react to you announcing that it was my fault his daughter was found?" I questioned, my voice still clearly showing that my vocal cord had been crushed.

Special Agent Lewis grimaced.

"Not like that, anyway…I thought if I put the idea in his head, he would show me his true intentions towards you," he said quietly.

I raised my eyebrow further.

"I thought he was protecting you, saying he had kidnapped you because he loved you," he continued.

I laughed and instantly regretted it.

"Ouch! Don't make me laugh," I whispered. I took another drink of water, then put the glass back down on the table.

"First of all, gross. Secondly, like I've been saying since the beginning; I *was* kidnapped. I had no choice to come here," I lied. I was glad that my voice was quiet at this point. I was never good at poker. "Was it really from my phone call that you found them?" My heart was beating hard.

The agent gave me a look of shame as he shook his head.

"No…it was all to see your reactions to it. Two things were cleared up for me," Special Agent Lewis admitted.

I tilted my head slightly as I pressed the ice pack tighter to my throat to get it closer to my skin.

"Oh? And what were those two things?" I asked. I felt my blood pressure rising in anger.

"One, I think you're telling the truth and two, the girls really *are* in Auckland – it was purely a guess before that," he replied. I screamed internally. Of course, he was playing us.

"You really didn't know?" I asked. I was furious with myself. He shook his head.

"What makes you think I'm telling the truth now?" I asked, wincing from the raw pain in my throat. My voice was becoming even more coarse.

"Well, firstly, if you were in a relationship with Jorge Torres, I don't imagine he would have believed for a second that you made it possible for us to trace the girls," Special Agent Lewis started, getting out his phone and looking at it.

"Secondly, we've been given evidence that proves that you were telling the truth about being abducted," he finished, holding the phone out for me to see.

It was a picture of me being forcibly taken from my apartment with Jorge putting a gun to my head. Since this didn't happen at all, I could only assume this photo was photoshopped. Whoever did it was beyond a professional. Even I thought it was real.

I gulped a little as I looked at it, then back at the agent. He moved his thumb across his phone and there was another picture of me photoshopped to look like I was passed out on the back seat with my hands and feet tied up with rope.

"That must have been when they chloroformed me. I don't remember that at all," I muttered, feeling my heart quicken as I blatantly lied.

Special Agent Lewis pocketed his phone in response and nodded his head.

"I believe you were abducted and brought here against your will. But I also believe that you are putting your daughter's safety first, above the law," he stated.

I gulped again and looked away from him. This one I couldn't lie about and get away with it, because there wasn't anything I wouldn't do for Elsie.

"I believe you know where Elizabeth and Lucita are

and I know how hard it must be for you to push aside all your training and oaths," he continued in a soft tone, which was a contrast to the way he had been acting towards me for the last two plus days.

"I know, because there isn't anything in this world that I wouldn't do for my daughter, April. She's ten. I would slay the whole world for her if I had to and not give it a second thought. So I get it, I do. But the longer they are on the run, the more chances that this isn't going to end well for them. And I think you know this," Special Agent Lewis finished, which made me look back at him. He was getting right to the point, sympathizing with me to make me feel guilty. It was working.

"I know," I whispered, my eyes tearing up at the thought of Elsie being gunned down because she refused to let herself be caught.

"Tell me where they are heading. Tell me where they are and I will make sure you don't get prosecuted for your role in their escape. Tell me where they are and I promise to bring them in safely."

Tears started falling down my cheek.

Jorge already thought I betrayed him. Maybe telling the agent where they were wasn't such a bad idea. Maybe the time to end this was now.

It was only a matter of time before they got caught

being out there on their own anyway – what did two eighteen-year-old girls, who had never been in this country before, know about not being caught by the police? Sure, they had their disguises. Sure, they had money. But that was going to run out soon and certainly they could only use a wig so many times before people started to recognize them.

I closed my eyes tightly, taking the ice pack away from my throat and dropping it down next to the glass. "Take me with you when you go to arrest them." I kept my eyes closed so I didn't see his face. "Promise me that I can be there to make them come to you without any trouble and I will tell you where they are headed." My voice shock from worry and a bruised windpipe. I opened my eyes to look at the agent pleadingly. He nodded his head.

"I promise," he stated.

I looked in his eyes for a moment and could tell that he was telling the truth as a fellow officer of the law and wasn't just saying it to make me open up.

"They are going to the district court in Auckland. They're getting married," I stated.

Special Agent Lewis's eyes widened.

"Was that your idea? Since you know that spouses cannot testify against each other?" He asked, his tone more like it had been for the last few days.

I shook my head.

"Lu thought of it herself. I only said yes as Elsie's mother. Not that I have any say in the matter," I commented, looking away from him. "I don't know what you know about them, Special Agent Lewis, but those girls are in love. Marriage was just the next logical step for them. I guess being on the run made them do it a lot quicker, but I had nothing to do with it." I moved my hand up to my throat to rub it.

Special Agent Lewis looked at me for a moment before sighing and standing up.

"We're taking you to the hospital. Then we will get a flight to Auckland once you've been checked over," he told me, moving towards the door.

I got up to follow him. It felt nice not to have to wear cuffs as he escorted me through the station and out of the building. We got into his borrowed vehicle and he took me straight to the hospital.

Chapter Twenty-Two

Lu

By the time we got to the courthouse, Elsie and I were looking like our old selves. Even though my hair was a lot shorter now, having pink in it made me feel like I could be myself. Elsie's hair had been bleached and dyed back to her natural color and I couldn't help but feel grateful seeing my old Elsie back.

We had been shopping for more appropriate wedding clothes. Elsie had bought a beautiful white cocktail dress, gorgeous white heels with gold sequins on the top. I had bought a black suit and white shirt with boring black boots. Elsie insisted that I looked breathtaking but compared to her I felt a little underdressed.

We had also bought our wedding rings, a matching set of gold bands with a simple diamond in the middle of each. We didn't want to go too extravagant, in case we lost them.

I left my hair down, to show off the pink, but Elsie did hers up in a bun so she could show off her earrings and tattoo. Elsie would keep her tattoo covered with her scarf until we were in front of the judge.

I swear it took all my will power not to rip off that dress and have some fun, but we were under a time constraint.

We had to leave Auckland by nightfall, so we could find somewhere to stay for the night that wasn't busy with cops.

We walked into the courthouse, hand in hand, and straight towards a reception desk. A woman sitting behind it looked at us with her eyes slightly narrowed. "What can I do for you two today?" She asked, her eyes searching us. My heart squeezed as I thought about what could happen if she recognized us. I kicked myself internally for not thinking of wearing our disguises until we were safely in the confines of the judge's office.

"We are here to see Judge Matthew Wilson," I stated, my voice strong, despite my internal worries.

"Names?" She asked, looking at her computer.

"Claudia García Lopez and Veronica Marie Black," I answered. It wasn't until we were with the Judge that we were going to use our real names. Elsie squeezed my hand. I looked at her to find she was grinning at me. I could tell that she was excited. I grinned back at her and then back at the lady, who scrolled through her computer for a moment before looking back at us.

"He's been expecting you," she stated and then nodded behind us.

I turned to see a little waiting area.

"Sit there until he comes out," she explained. We

grinned at her, but our grins weren't returned and we hurried over to the seats.

We didn't have to wait long. About two minutes later, a short, bald-headed man in black robes hurried over to us. He looked nervous.

"Come with me, ladies," the man told us as he gestured us to hurry. We followed him back into a room that was behind the reception desk. Elsie was practically bouncing up and down with excitement. I couldn't help but grin at how she was acting. It reminded me of what she was like at the jewelry store.

I quickened my pace as Elsie pulled me along, trying hard not to let my thoughts turn dark, considering where we were and what we were about to do. The man shut the door behind us and walked to the front of the room.

"I'm Judge Wilson, but you probably already know that," he told us with a nervous laugh. He pointed to a spot in front of him.

"If you could please stand here and face each other," he instructed. We followed his instructions and Elsie and I stood face to face. Elsie took off her scarf and dropped it on the floor before she took hold of my hands.

"This is going to be short and sweet, ladies. I have done all the required paperwork and it's ready to be registered as soon as we finish up the formalities," Judge

Wilson explained.

I grinned at him before looking back at Elsie's excited face.

"Lucita, please repeat after me," the Judge stated and my heartbeat picked up in pace.

"I, Lucita Torres Alvarez, declare that I am freely entering into this marriage between myself and Elizabeth Rose Neilson," he started. I repeated the words, a grin on my face with every syllable.

"I invite everyone to witness that I, Lucita Torres Alvarez, take you, Elizabeth Rose Neilson, to be my legal wife." Again I repeated the words, my eyes actually beginning to tear up as I saw Elsie starting to cry.

The judge turned to Elsie who repeated everything I just said, switching our names as needed. I zoned out a little as the judge started to talk about the importance of the rings. I was too focused on the love of my life. It wasn't until Elsie squeezed my hand that I snapped out of it.

"Sorry?" I asked. The judge was looking at me expectantly.

"I now invite you to exchange rings," the judge repeated, his voice a little impatient.

I ignored it and grinned instead as I pulled my hand from Elsie's to take out the rings. I handed Elsie the one she was going to put on my finger.

"Lucita, please place the ring for Elizabeth on her finger," the judge instructed.

Smiling so widely that my cheeks hurt, I grabbed hold of Elsie's hand. Her hand was shaking, so I gave it a small reassuring squeeze, before I gently lifted her ring finger and slipped the wedding band on, nestling it against her engagement ring. They looked beautiful together. Elsie let out a small sniffle as she tried to hold back her tears.

"Elizabeth, please place the ring for Lucita on her finger," the judge directed Elsie, who lifted my hand in return and sobbed as she slid the ring into place. I wanted to wrap her up in a tight hug and kiss her senseless, but I had to wait.

"Lucita and Elizabeth, I now pronounce you to be legally married as wife and wife. You may now kiss the bride," he stated, finally. And thank God, because I didn't know how much longer I could wait.

I stepped forward, grabbed my wife, and kissed her roughly on the mouth. Elsie wrapped her arms around me, pulling me close to her body. One of her hands ran down my back and found its way to my ass, where she cupped it as she pulled me closer. My legs parted and her leg slipped between them, heat rushing to my core.

I was about to rub against her when the judge cleared his throat loudly, reminding us that we weren't the only ones in the room. Elsie and I pulled apart and I smirked as I wiped my mouth. Elsie's face reddened as she looked at the judge.

"Right, well, if I could just get you to sign these papers, you can be on your way," the judge stated, his face just as red as Elsie's.

He moved to his desk and moved several papers across it. One was our marriage certificate and something called Particulars of Marriage. I could see that it was already signed by someone as a witness, which I supposed had something to do with the money we were giving the judge to do this for us. Elsie and I signed the papers and so did the judge. He took a copy of the certificate, then handed us the original one.

"That's it, ladies. Congratulations, you're married. Now please leave," the Judge stated, nodding his head to the door. He looked worried and I couldn't help but frown.

Elsie picked up her scarf from the floor and wrapped it around her neck to cover up her tattoo again. When she was done, she grabbed my hand and we headed towards the door. It really was short and sweet – it had only taken a few minutes - I guess the judge was scared he was going to get caught with us.

I reached the door and I opened it, letting Elsie walk out first. She froze and I walked straight into her, causing me to let out a muffled *hmph.*

"Why did you stop?" I asked, looking at her. She had a panicked look on her face and seemed to be staring at something. I followed her gaze and my heart stopped when I saw about twenty police officers pointing their guns at us. My eyes went wide and I glanced down at the bracelet that was not vibrating.

"That got turned off the moment we had your exact location," a male voice said through the crowd. It didn't take long for the owner of the voice to step forward. My eyes narrowed as I saw the figure beside him.

Elsie let out a small squeak, which dripped in disappointment. My hand automatically went to my side, where I had placed a gun, but Elsie grabbed my hand to stop me and held it tightly in her grasp instead.

"Well, congratulations, you have us cornered. I suppose we have you to thank for that, do we?" I asked, my question directed at Olivia. Olivia looked at us with a look of both guilt and relief. Guilt for turning us in? Good. I ignored her relief.

"Enough is enough, Lu," Olivia said quietly.

Elsie's grip tightened even further. I had been in this

situation before. There wasn't any use trying to free my hand at this point.

"You betrayed us," Elsie whispered, barely loud enough to hear, but I could tell that Olivia had read her lips, because her guilt-ridden face deepened. She tilted her head to the side and I couldn't help but notice a long bruise along the front of her throat. I felt another noise come from Elsie, which only confirmed that she had seen it too.

Considering she had been arrested with my dad and was now here, I couldn't help but think he had something to do with the bruise. I hoped not, considering his views on violence against women, but I knew how angry he got, especially towards cops and those who threatened his family. I gulped as I looked away from her throat and narrowed my eyes further when I looked at her face.

"This has gone on long enough. It's time to come in quietly," Olivia started.
I rolled my eyes and pulled Elsie back into the room and shut the door. I locked it and I turned to find the judge had left the room, through a door at the back. I hurried over to it and locked that door too. I ran back over to Elsie and wrapped my arms around her. She was shivering.

I had hoped that by now we would be back in the

alley where we had stashed our stuff behind a dumpster, so she could at least have a jacket on to keep her warm. But now it looked like we wouldn't get a chance.

"What do you want to do?" I asked her, pulling away from her so I could take off my black jacket. I wrapped it around her shoulders before pulling her back into a tight hug. I hoped that, together with my body heat, would warm her up and kept her comforted from shock.

"We're surrounded, L. What are the chances there aren't cops on the other side of that door, too?" Elsie whispered, referring to the door I had just locked. I bit my lip, knowing exactly how likely it was. There was a bang at the door.

"Girls! Please. The guns are away. Please come out and we can go back home. Please come out and this won't get any worse," Olivia pleaded. Her voice was muffled, but I could hear the desperation in it.

"Your mother is a rat," I stated, looking over Elsie's shoulder towards the door, imagining Olivia's face. I wanted to punch the shit out of it.

"I can't believe she turned us in," Elsie cried and I hugged her tighter.

"I thought we were making progress. I thought she wanted us to be free. I never thought she would be the reason we were caught," she continued. I rubbed her back in support.

"We have to turn ourselves in, L. There is no other option. We're at a dead end," she continued. She pulled back from me, so I did the same and we looked at each other for a moment, before we both nodded in agreement.

"I won't let them separate us," I promised and Elsie nodded again. I grabbed her hand, walked back over to the door, and unlocked it.

"We're coming out!" I shouted, then opened the door slowly.

The door was violently shoved the rest of the way, whacking into my hand because I didn't get it out of the way fast enough. I cursed as large hands wrapped around my wrist, causing me to drop our marriage certificate.

"Be careful, asshole," I snapped as the hands grabbed my other wrist and harshly brought it behind my back beside my other one. The person cuffed me and I turned my head to see the male who had told me why my bracelet wasn't working.

"Lucita Torres Alvarez, you are under arrest for multiple counts of murder, larceny, criminal impersonation and evading arrest," he stated in a strong American accent. I noticed his jacket had 'FBI' written on it in big yellow letters.

"Awesome," I muttered, as he continued to read me my rights. I noticed Olivia had started crying as another officer hand cuffed Elsie and he read her rights to her.

"I have a gun under my shirt on the right," I declared. The agent ripped up my shirt, revealing both the gun and my stomach.

"No need to undress me," I snapped, moving my hip away from him. I could see in the corner of my eye that Elsie was struggling against the officer who was holding her. I looked up at her and she gave me a pleading look, which made me want to be by her side.

"It's alright," I mouthed, knowing she was just as good as me at reading lips.

The agent grabbed the gun, took the bullets out, and then handed it to another officer who put it in an evidence bag.

"Any other weapons?" The agent asked.

I shook my head, but at the same time Olivia pointed down at my boots.

"Check for a knife," she instructed. Elsie let out another noise at yet another betrayal by her mother.

"Bitch!" I snapped, trying to get out of the agent's grasp to get at her, but he gripped me tighter then shoved me down to the ground instead.

"Stop fighting, Ms. Torres, or this is going to get

worse for you," he told me as he put his knee on my back. I screamed as I felt the pressure of his body on top of me, but it didn't last long because I could hardly breathe. He removed both of my boots and I heard the clink of my switchblade falling to the ground.

"I can't breathe," I stated, my voice struggling to come out.

"Special Agent Lewis!" Olivia pled, rushing from her spot by the wall to come closer to where we were. A moment later the pressure was released from my back and I could breathe again.

My boots were roughly put back on my feet and I noted that there was no sound of the zippers being closed. I was awkwardly pulled to my feet by my cuffed wrists, which caused a sharp pain in my shoulders.

"You don't have to be so rough! I'm not resisting," I pointed out. Elsie had stopped struggling against her officer, but she was full-on crying now.

"Please, let me go to my wife," I begged, looking at Olivia, then down at the certificate that was down on the floor. No one had noticed it yet and I was hoping that if there was any chance that Olivia was still on our side, she would do what needed to be done to make sure our marriage was recognized in America.

Olivia nodded at me and picked the certificate up off

the ground. She carefully rolled it up and put it in her shirt pocket.

"Congratulations on the nuptials," the agent sneered, as he pulled me even further away from Elsie. I tried to turn back but he pushed me forward, forcing me to walk away from her.

"You'll be lucky if you're even in the same prison, if I have anything to do with it," the agent hissed, just loud enough for me to hear.

I stopped walking, my unpredictable rage boiling over as I felt the agent walk into my back. I lifted my loose-fitting boot and slammed it down on his foot, causing him to howl in pain. His hands let go of me to tend to his injury. Elsie screamed behind me as I turned my body around and brought my knee up to hit him in the groin.

I barely touched him when a fierce shock started at the base of my back and ran through my body. I fell to the ground, my body convulsing as 50,000 volts went through my body, causing the most excruciating pain I had ever felt. Everything around me went black.

Chapter Twenty-Three
Elsie

I screamed as Lu's body spasmed on the floor. The officer who had tasered her looked like he was going to be sick, but I couldn't care less. With all the strength that I could muster, I pulled away from the officer who held me and surprisingly it was enough for him to let go.

I hurried over to Lu, not caring in the slightest that more officers were now pointing their tasers at me. I was just glad that no one had decided guns were an option, now that we had turned ourselves in.

I fell to the ground next to Lu, ignoring the pain in my knees and throwing my body over hers protectively. Olivia ran to my side, shouting at the officers who were still pointing their tasers at me. The agent who had been holding Lu finally put his foot down, swearing at the situation in front of him. Olivia tried to lift me up from Lu, but I screamed and pulled my shoulders out of her grip.

"No! Get off me! No! Leave me alone!" I shouted, as I buried my head into Lu's neck. My tears wet her skin and I was sure that if she was awake, this would make her cringe, but I didn't care.

"Elsie, please, stop it. She's just knocked out. She will

be fine. She will just have sore muscles for a while. She'll wake up soon, her body is just recovering," Olivia pleaded with me as she tried to get me to sit up again.

"Get off me, you traitorous bitch," I snarled after she managed to pull me up enough that my face was no longer buried in Lu's neck.

Olivia let out a noise that suggested I hurt her feelings. I wanted to lash out at her, but I wanted to comfort and protect Lu more, so when she let go of me, I buried myself back into Lu, trying to hug her as much as I could with my hands cuffed behind my back.

It wasn't long before someone tried to move me again, but this time, I felt two hands on either side of my arms and they had no trouble lifting me up. I kicked and screamed, trying to get away.

"ENOUGH!" The agent bellowed, causing me to stop at the shock of his sudden temper. It reminded me of *him*. I looked towards the ground, away from the agent, because at the moment, I felt like *he* was in front of me.

"You are going to be escorted to a police car and you're going to do it without resisting," the agent declared.

I hung my head and nodded.

"Yes, sir," I whispered, my heart pounding in my chest.

"Good," the agent retorted. Soon I was led out of the courthouse. I looked back at Lu, who was being lifted up by one of the other officers. I was tugged forward, forcing me to look back to the front and we walked through the doors where paparazzi were waiting with their cameras.

Flash after flash went off, capturing one of the most horrible moments of my life. All I wanted was Lu by my side for all of this but instead she was unconscious, and it was being recorded for the whole world to see.

I kept my head down as I was escorted to the car, put in the back seat, and buckled in. The officer on my right sat in the back next to me. The other officer went to the driver's side and got in, starting the car. We waited for a moment and then Olivia opened the front passenger side door and got in too.

"Does she have to come with us?" I asked.

My question was ignored.

Once they were all set, the officer who was behind the wheel put the car into drive and we made our way out of the maze of media. I leaned back against the seat, with my arms sitting awkwardly behind me.

I stared out of the window, wondering how long it would be until I was locked up and I wouldn't be able to see buildings, people and possibly even the sky again. I know it sounds silly, but surely that sky right then was different than the sky I would see behind locked fences and security gates, right?

The ride was so silent that you could hear a pin drop. The only sound was from Olivia, who was letting out little sniffs, which I could only guess meant she was crying. I had to roll my eyes at that. She didn't get to cry. It looked like she was now a free woman. She wouldn't have to be locked up like Lu and me.

"Would you stop feeling sorry for yourself!?" I snapped after her fiftieth sniff.

I raised the leg that wasn't connected to my bad hip and kicked at the back of her seat, though I only kicked once since the officer beside me put his hand on his taser. I knew it was an idle threat, that he wouldn't shoot me with something that had high voltage in such close proximity, but still, I got his message. At least the sniffing had stopped.

"You don't get to be sad. You're not the one going to prison," I pointed out, angrily. "Let me guess - telling them where we were got you a get out of jail free card."

Sniff.

"I thought I meant something to you, *detective.* I thought you would do anything to keep me safe," I finished, leaning back into the seat again. The handcuffs were chaffing my wrist. Damn it.

Sniff, sniff.

"You mean everything to me, Elizabeth," Olivia began.

I raised my eyebrow slightly as she looked at me through the rearview mirror.

"And by doing this, I *am* keeping you safe," she insisted.

I snorted, then rolled my eyes.

"Please, you have to understand." She turned around in her seat to look at me. "If this went on any longer, if you and Lu continued to evade the law, as fugitives, anything could have happened. There would be rewards for your capture, bounty hunters. Most of the time the rewards state dead or alive."

I could see the pain in her eyes.

"I had to turn you in. You've been portrayed by the media as a danger to society. At least this way, it won't get any worse. At least you won't be killed," she pointed out.

I relaxed my shoulders slightly as I looked at her. Her eyes were all red and swollen from her crying. She had blotchy cheeks, like this wasn't the first time she had cried today.

"I love you, Elsie. I know we've only known each

other as mother and daughter for two months, but I've loved you since the day you were born. This was the best thing for you," she stated with finality.

I narrowed my eyes and watched her carefully. She didn't look away. I sighed and looked out the window, slumping against the seat as my own tears started to well up again.

"Lu is hurt," I pointed out, watching as we drove past some children playing in a field.

I'll never get to do that again, I thought.

"She'll be sore for a while, but she'll be ok," Olivia noted quietly.

"She could have been shot," I added, my heart squeezing tight at the thought.

"But she wasn't," Olivia stated.

The officer beside me moved uncomfortably in his seat. Clearly, he wasn't liking this conversation.

"Have you got something to say, officer?" I asked, turning to look at him.

"She's lucky Constable Henderson didn't use his gun. He had every right to do so – she assaulted an FBI agent," he commented.

I narrowed my eyes at him.

"That FBI agent said something to her. He provoked her," I retorted, feeling annoyed.

Olivia cleared her throat and I looked at her as she shook her head, pleading with me not to argue.

"There better not be any lasting effects," I commented, turning back to look outside.

We had come to a stop at a traffic light. Olivia turned back to the front and my heart started to pound as I saw the signs for the police station just up the road from us.

"What's going to happen now?" I asked, my voice quiet.

"You will be detained until a flight to America is available," the officer who was driving stated.

"How long will that be?" I questioned, looking at the back of his head.

"Could be a couple of hours, could be a week. You'll get used to the waiting – you've got nothing else to do."

I narrowed my eyes.

"Great," I said sarcastically.

When the lights turned green, we drove on and soon pulled into a driveway that led to the back of the building. The officer pulled into a basement garage, parked the car and turned off the ignition.

Olivia hopped out of the car first, followed by the officer sitting beside me, then finally the driver. The officer who had been sitting next to me walked around the car, opened my door, leaned over to unbuckle my seat belt and then grabbed my shoulder to start pulling me out of the car.

Once I was out, he lowered his hand to my forearm and started to lead me towards a door. Olivia walked beside me, often glancing at me to see how I was doing.

I felt like I was about to burst out crying, but I had to be strong, because really, I had no one else to blame. This wasn't Olivia's fault at all and I was being unfair by being angry at her. This was my fault. Mine and Lu's. We had gotten ourselves into this mess.

"Do I get a lawyer or something?" I asked as we walked through the station.

"Once you're back in Sutton," Olivia promised.

I gave her a small nod. I hoped whoever Mr. Torres got to represent Lu would represent me too, otherwise I was fucked. And not in the enjoyable way, which I craved so much right then. That, or a strong drink.

We walked through a room that was surrounded by uniformed officers. When they turned to look at me, some actually clapped. My heart stopped, realizing that they were congratulating the officers for capturing me. I lowered my head to avoid looking at anybody as we continued our way through the room. I was taken to a room where they took my photograph and fingerprints, entering them into their system.

I was then led down a corridor, into another room, where the officer took my handcuffs off me. He took a step back and nodded to Olivia, who walked up in front of me and gently began to take my scarf off. I grabbed onto her hand to try and stop her, but she shook her head.

"I have to take it," she explained.

I frowned.

"So I don't kill myself?" I asked.

Olivia looked at me with her teary, sad eyes as she nodded her head. I wasn't going to, but I would be a liar if I said it hadn't crossed my mind.

Another officer walked through the door, a female, holding folded clothes, including a white bra and tank top, socks, underwear and a pair of white sneakers.

"I'll be on my way then," the male officer stated, leaving the three of us alone.

"I have to get changed here?" I asked, looking down at the gray sweatpants and matching sweatshirt. The female officer nodded as she passed the clothing to Olivia and pulled out a clear plastic bag.

I sighed as I took off the jacket that Lu had wrapped around me and handed it to the officer. I slipped my heels off then turned, so the officer could unzip my dress and I awkwardly got out of it. I was freezing already but taking off both those layers made it even worse.

I shivered as I reached behind myself to pull off my bra.

I hadn't been naked in front of anyone other than Lu, so when my face started to warm up, I wasn't surprised. I grabbed the bra on top of the pile and turned myself around, so I wasn't facing them. I handed my bra back to the officer and put on the new one, which I noticed was wire-free. Wow. They had pulled out all the stops.

I grabbed the underwear, noting the lack of elastic and quickly got out of mine and slipped them on. My face was hot as I turned to hand my underwear to the officer, who put them in the bag. Olivia handed me the sweatpants first and I hurriedly put them on.

"Your navel piercing," the officer said, holding out her hand. I groaned as I unscrewed the little ball and pulled out the stud. I closed it back up and put it gently in the officer's hand.

I then put on the tank top followed by the sweatshirt and then the socks. Finally, I slipped on the sneakers and grimaced as I looked down at myself. I was a prisoner and this outfit just confirmed it.

"Your earrings," the officer stated, pointing to the side that had the most. I glared at her before starting to remove them one by one. Once they were all off and in the bag with clothes, she looked down at my hand with the rings on it. I immediately used my other hand to cover them and shook my head.

"No, not the rings please. Surely there isn't a way I could kill myself with these," I begged, putting my hands behind my back. The earrings I kind of understood. I mean they had stabby bits and if Lu had taught me anything, it was that getting stabbed in the right, or in this case, wrong, place, could possibly get you killed.

Olivia gave me a pained look as she stepped forward and held out her hand.

"I'm sorry, Elsie, but everything personal needs to be put away in the lockup. That includes your rings," she noted, sadly.

I watched her carefully for a moment, before letting out a disheartened sigh and bringing my hands back to the front. I began to take off my wedding ring, then my engagement ring, my hand shaking. I put them in Olivia's hand, tears forming in my eyes. I watched with horror as Olivia passed them to the officer, who just chucked them casually into the bag with my dirtied clothes, like they meant nothing.

Once the officer zipped up the bag, she knocked three times on the door and soon the male officer opened the door and the female left. He handcuffed me again and then led me further down the corridor to where the cells were located.

He walked me to a solid door that had a small viewing window and a slot, which I guessed was for sending food in. He unlocked the door and opened it.

Inside the cell was a cot with a single mattress and one blanket. On the other side of the cell was a toilet and a small basin. There was also a small window with bars across it, letting the light from the sun stream into the room.

"Get used to your new accommodations," he chuckled as he pushed the door open fully. "You're probably going to be in a room like this for the rest of your life."

He unlocked my handcuffs which gave me instant relief from the chaffing of the bracelets. I heard Olivia sniff and I turned to see that she was crying again. The officer pushed me gently into the room and shut the door, locking me in. He opened the small slot in the door and then left, leaving Olivia and I alone.

It was weird that I could only see her through a clear windowpane. I put my hands through the slot and Olivia took them in hers.

"Will I really be in prison for the rest of my life?" I asked, my voice strong with fear as I thought of the first officer's comment.

Olivia finally broke down and her tears came out in full.

"If you get a good lawyer, they could try to lessen it to twenty-five years," she noted through her crying.

My legs felt weak.

"Twenty-five years?" I repeated with a cry.

"Twenty-five to life," Olivia whispered.

I felt like I was going to be sick. I tugged my hands away from Olivia and slowly made my way over to the small cot and sat down.

I needed Lu. I needed her hold. Her touch. I needed my wife. I brought my hand up to eye level and looked at the place my rings were meant to be and breathed in and out slowly like she had taught me. I pictured kissing her in my mind, touching her, loving her.

My heart slowly came back to a normal rhythm and I lowered my hand as I looked back at Olivia, who had lowered herself slightly so she was looking at me through the slot.

"What's happening with Mr. Torres and Techy?" I asked, biting my lip.

"And what happened to your throat?" I added, remembering the bruises I had seen earlier.
Olivia put her hand on her throat and cringed slightly.

"Jorge reacted to my supposed betrayal," Olivia said, her face reddening even more. I raised my eyebrow. So much for being against violence towards women.

"But you *did* betray us," I pointed out and Olivia shook her head slightly, before sighing.

"Not at that time. The FBI agent, Special Agent Lewis, played us. He guessed your location, making it sound like I had told him, and Jorge confirmed it. If it wasn't for Jorge's reaction, they wouldn't have known anything," Olivia explained. "It wasn't until afterwards, that I decided that the best way to help you was to let them catch you."

Silence.

"Jorge and Techy are already on their way to America," Olivia added. There was a noise to the right of us and another officer appeared with a chair for Olivia. She took it and sat down. The officer left immediately, leaving us alone again.

"Do you know what is happening with Lu?" I asked, wondering if she was alright. She would be sad to learn that she was now in a different country than her dad.

"She's been taken to the hospital," Olivia explained.

I bit my lip as I looked back at her.

"Just to get checked over. She had 50,000 volts go through her body. I'm sure it's just a precaution," she informed me.

I sighed and lay down on the cot, groaning slightly at the hardness of it. I hoped the prison beds were more comfortable.

"Are they going to keep us separated?" I questioned, noting the fact that there was only one cot in this cell.

"For the time being," Olivia replied quietly.

"They won't put us in separate prisons, will they?" My heart pounding at the thought.

"It's up to the judge and prison wardens."

I breathed in and out slowly, trying to return my heart to a normal rhythm again, but it was no use when I was thinking of being apart from Lu.

I closed my eyes tight and tried to imagine us being put in the same cell in prison. That we weren't separated. That we would be together. Because I could handle twenty-five to life if I was with her. I wouldn't last a week if I wasn't.

~.~

I must have fallen asleep, because when I opened my eyes again the light that had been coming through the window had been replaced by a fluorescent light in the ceiling that hadn't been on earlier. I sat up and looked out the front of the cell to see an empty chair. Olivia had left.

"Lu?" I shouted, wondering if she was in the cell next to mine. The walls were solid cinderblock, so I had no idea who could be in the other cells, or even if there was anyone else.

No one replied. I was alone.

I shivered as I grabbed the blanket from the foot of the bed and wrapped it around myself. Where was she? Did the taser actually do more damage to her than anybody had thought? Her body was so slim it could have felt twice as bad for her. Where had Olivia gone?

I stood up and walked to the front of the cell, trying to see anything. There were tiny lights on the wall, but other than that it was eerily quiet. I looked up in the corner of the room where there was a camera pointing down at me and I gave it a little wave. I felt stupid, but if anyone was watching, maybe they would send someone in to come and talk to me.

My stomach grumbled, another clear indication that I had been sleeping at least for a couple of hours. I heard a door open and soon Olivia walked into view, carrying a tray of food.

I gave her a small smile when she reached the cell.

"I asked them to let me talk to you. I have some news and you're not going to be happy about it," Olivia stated, her face not showing any indications of being happy to see me again.

I frowned as she passed the tray through the slot. It was a sandwich and a bottle of water. I grabbed the tray,

walked over to my bed and placed it down. The food
could wait. I walked back over to her and put my hands
through the slot. Olivia grabbed hold of them.

"Is it about Lu?" I asked, my stomach dropping at the
thought. If I had been asleep for hours and she still
wasn't back then something must have happened to her.
The look on Olivia's face told me it was very bad. When
she nodded, I let out a small gasp of fear and she
squeezed my hands.

"She went into cardiac arrest shortly after arriving at
the hospital," Olivia told me quietly.

I blinked as I looked at her, processing the words in
my mind.

"Is she…?" I started, but I couldn't bring myself to
finish the sentence. My mind went to worst case scenario
and I pictured my wife dead on a hospital bed,
surrounded by doctors, nurses, and cops.

"She's alive, but they're keeping her in the hospital
for a few nights for observation," Olivia stated.

I let out a relieved sigh before bursting into tears. I
took my hands out of Olivia's and sunk down to the
ground, resting my head on the cold door as I sobbed.

"I thought you were going to tell me she was dead.
Olivia, she must be so scared," I sobbed.

I couldn't see her anymore, but I could tell she had

lowered herself, because the shadow through the crack of the door had moved.

"She's all alone after that ordeal. You have to go to her, please. I'll be fine here," I exclaimed as I lifted my head from the bar and looked at her through the slot in the door.

"You said she would be fine," I whispered.

Olivia let out a groan.

"Cardiac arrest is a side effect of being tasered, but it usually only happens to people who take drugs or have heart defects. I didn't think…" she started, but I sobbed loudly so she stopped talking.

"We haven't smoked a joint since we left the cannabis in the plane," I told her, then my eyes went wide with realization.

"She overdosed on cocaine when she was younger…would that have weakened her heart?" I asked, my own heart squeezing tight at the thought.

"Maybe…or maybe she had an underlying heart condition that nobody knew about. It could have been anything, Elsie, but she's fine now and with excellent medical people to keep her safe," Olivia reassured me, as much as she could without seeing me.

"Would you go to her, please? I want her to know she's not alone," I whispered, loud enough so she could hear me.

Olivia didn't respond at first.

"Alright," I heard her agree.

"She probably won't be happy to see you but tell her it's for me. Tell her that I love her," I whispered.

Olivia cleared her throat.

"Alright. I'll go, but please, Elsie, eat. Eat what they give you, drink all the water you can. Please don't do anything that will comprise your health."

I lifted my hand to my eyes and wiped away the tears.

"I'm not going to starve myself," I told her, frowning at the thought. Why was she acting like I was suicidal all of a sudden?

"Els, you drank yourself to the point where you would black out, you didn't eat for days at a time and drank instead, you sometimes refused to get out of bed and now you're in a situation that you can't get out of. You have gone through multiple traumas, *survived* those traumas, but you had those coping mechanisms to stop the reminders, but now you don't have access to those," Olivia started, and I gulped as she pointed everything out.

"I know you don't want to hear this, but you are depressed. All of that, plus the fact that now you're going to be worried about Lu, makes me worried. I will go to her, but you need to promise me," she finished.

"I promise. I promise I won't starve myself. I promise I won't do anything to hurt myself and I promise I love you and Lu too much to ever think about doing anything like that," I whispered. Olivia let out a little choked noise at my last promise and I let out a little laugh.

"Yes, *mom*. I love you. Even though I'm probably going to spend the rest of my life in prison, I know you're going to come and see me every visitor's day. We're going to talk on the phone every time I'm allowed to use one. I'm not going to do anything to sabotage the time we will get to spend together," I commented, tilting my head slightly.

"Mom…" Olivia started and I laughed again. "You are my mom. It's about time I acknowledged you properly," I stated.

I watched as fingertips came through the bottom of the door. I smiled as I put my own against them.

"You are brave, my daughter," she told me and I couldn't help but roll my eyes. I was nowhere near as brave as I should be.

"I will be braver when I know that Lu isn't alone," I noted.

Olivia sighed and then removed her fingers from under the door. She must have stood up because the shadow moved again. I stood up too, so I could see her again through the windowpane. She nodded her head towards my tray of food.

"Eat," she demanded, then gave me a small smile.

I stood up, walked over to the bed and sat down. I picked up one half of the sandwich and took a bite.

"Happy?" I asked, my mouth full.

Olivia chuckled as she shook her head.

"Ecstatic," she responded.

"I'll call the station with an update on Lu. They are keeping an eye on you, so if you need anything, just wave at the camera again," she said with a wink.

I nodded as I continued eating.

Olivia walked away and I put the rest of my sandwich down, carefully putting the tray on the ground. I was going to eat, but I couldn't just yet. I felt sick. I needed to know that Lu was alright. I would wait until I heard from Olivia first. Once I knew that my wife was okay, I would eat.

So instead, I lay down on the bed, bringing the blanket over me and closing my eyes. I pictured myself in the hospital bed next to Lu, taking care of her. Holding her as she slept soundly against me, her heart monitor beeping steadily, telling me that she was going to be alright.

Chapter Twenty-Four

Olivia

"What the fuck are you doing here, *soplona*?" Lu spat as a form of greeting as I walked into her hospital room.

She tried to sit up, but she was connected to a heart monitor and her left hand was handcuffed to the bed. She swore as she tugged at the handcuff, but it only made her heart monitor start to beep out of rhythm and a nurse hurried in to try to get her to lie back down.

"You need to relax, Ms. Torres. Any stress on your heart could put you back in cardiac arrest. You don't want that do you?" The nurse questioned her as I stood in the doorway, with my shoulder leaning on the door frame. Lu leaned back on her pillows and glared at me as she took in deep breaths and let them out again, trying to calm her heart rate.

"Of course I don't. That is an experience I never wish to go through again. But this *soplona* is messing up my zen," Lu complained, as she tried killing me with her eyes.

She kept calling me a snitch. I couldn't exactly tell her to stop calling me that, considering that was exactly what I was. I let out a sigh and walked further into the room, only stopping because the nurse looked from Lu's heart monitor to me and gave me the same 'if looks could kill' glare. I threw my hands up in front of me and took a small step back.

"Look, I know I'm the last person you want to see right now, Lu, but you almost died. I'm not about to leave you alone," I stated.

She folded her arms across her chest, well, as best as she could, considering there was a handcuff stopping her.

Her heartbeat was settling back into a normal rhythm, so at least that was something. She looked at the nurse and nodded her head, like they were having an internal conversation. The nurse patted Lu on the shoulder, then turned to walk past me. When she got to my side, she leaned in slightly.

"If you make her heartbeat rise even just a little bit, I will have security kick you out. I'm not about to have an eighteen-year-old girl die because of something you've said or done," she said to me.

I just nodded my head in agreement. I didn't want that either – especially because that eighteen-year-old girl was now technically my daughter-in-law.

"Roger that," I replied and the nurse narrowed her eyes at me slightly before continuing out the door. Clearly, she only thought of me as a police officer, because no one else was allowed in Lu's room besides her doctor, the charge nurse, and police officers. I would have been wary of me, too.

I continued to walk closer to Lu's bedside, where there was a chair next to her bed. I sat down and she looked away from me, staring at her monitor. After a moment of silence, Lu finally looked at me.

"Why did you turn us in?" Lu asked.

"I did what I did, because, believe it or not, prison is probably the safest place for you right now," I started, stopping because Lu opened her mouth to contradict me, but I shook my head and continued.

"If they had found you two without me being there, that taser could have been a gun. If they had found you, without my help, egotistical males would have taken it personally that it took so long to find you and gotten trigger happy. At the time I thought being hated by the two of you would be easier than you both being dead." Lu just looked at me, her tears threatening to take over. "I did hate you," Lu whispered, and I nodded in understanding.

"I know. I'm a *soplona*," I commented, with a small smile. Lu smiled back and my heart pounded at the fact that I was getting through to her.

"I wanted to shoot you," Lu admitted.
I grimaced. I thought I had seen her hand move to her

hip. If it hadn't been for Elsie stopping her, who knows what would have happened?

"Well, I'm glad you didn't," I stated, my eyes flicking over to her heart monitor and watching the lines go up and down in a steady rhythm.

"If you did, I obviously wouldn't be sitting here talking to you, but you wouldn't be here either. It was a good thing Elsie stopped you."

"Where is Elsie?"

I leaned back in the chair.

"She is at the police station," I answered.

Lu's eyes finally filled with tears. This was the first time I had seen Lu visibly upset since we all went on the run. Sometimes I wondered if she'd ever let her emotions show through her rock-hard veneer. I frowned as the tears fell down her cheeks.

"I always felt like I couldn't be upset when I was around Elsie," Lu started.

I reached up to grab her handcuffed hand, which was still awkwardly folded against her chest. I expected her to pull away, but I was pleasantly surprised when she let me hold it.

"I wasn't the one who was assaulted. I wasn't the one who got stabbed with a knife..." Lu continued in a whisper. "But I killed people, Olivia. I killed a man who was defending his shop. I killed a man who did unspeakable things to the woman I love. I am a murderer and I had to keep it all in because Elsie was breaking apart at the seams. I had to be strong for her, because if she saw me break she would have fallen completely apart."

My heart broke for her. I gave her hand a squeeze and nodded with understanding.

"What you both went through was very traumatic. People handle things in different ways. Elsie was handling it on the outside, while you internalized things," I noted .

Lu let out a half-hearted laugh. "I internalized it so much that I broke my heart," she joked, looking down at the leads that were connected to her chest.

I followed her gaze and grimaced slightly as I saw part of the red mark left behind by the paddles that restarted her heart.

"And you would never have known you had something wrong with your heart if you hadn't had 50,000 volts go through your body," I pointed out, biting my lip slightly, remembering the way her body seized when the electrodes connected with her skin.

"What made you attack Special Agent Lewis like that, anyway? What did he say to you?" I asked.

Lu looked down at our hands and let out a small sigh.

"It seems stupid now, with everything that happened afterwards…but he said he was going to try and keep Elsie and I separated and I kind of, well…lost it," Lu told me.

I raised my eyebrow.

"Don't worry, he said plenty of things to me and I wanted to punch his face too. He likes to provoke people," I pointed out. I squeezed her hand to make her look at me again.

"You're going to get a lot of people trying to provoke you from now on, Lu. You need to keep your temper in check, even more so now that your life literally depends on it," I commented.

She winced slightly.

"Have they told you what's going to happen to me now? How long do I have to be here? What happens once I'm in prison?" Lu asked.

I shook my head.

"I'm not your next of kin; I'm not privy to that information," I told her.

Lu pulled her hand out of mine and looked down at the ring on her finger. I was surprised they hadn't taken that off her by now. Perhaps they were waiting for her to get out of the hospital.

"You're basically as close as I'm going to get, with my dad in jail," she said. "I will make sure to tell them that they can tell you everything."

"Alright. But you should know – your father is probably halfway to America by now, along with Techy," I said quietly.

Lu put her hand back down and her tears filled up in her eyes again.

"I've really fucked everything up, haven't I? I'm sorry I got Elsie in trouble. I'm sorry I killed that man and I'm really sorry that I put Elsie's life in danger twice," she apologized, then burst into tears.

I stood up and wrapped my arms around her, pulling her close to me. Her heart monitor started beeping, but there was nothing I could do to calm her down. She cried and cried and I could feel her pulse quickening.

"Shh, it's okay, Lu. I know you're sorry," I said, trying to calm her down.

"It's all my fault. Elsie, Dad, Techy, you," she sobbed, her head on my shoulder.

I shook my head.

"No, no…you didn't put a gun to their head to force them. To force us. We all chose what we did with our own free will. Elsie chose to do everything she did. It's not your fault," I whispered.

She shuddered against me.

"It's my fault she got assaulted. It's my fault she got stabbed. If it wasn't for the fact she was with me, then she wouldn't have been targeted," Lu countered.

I had to bite my lip.

"If it wasn't for me, she wouldn't have gotten suspended. She wouldn't have come with me to town that day, so she wouldn't have gotten arrested. If she hadn't gotten arrested, her father wouldn't have beat her up. If it wasn't for me getting my father to blow up Mr. Neilson's car, she wouldn't have remembered stuff from her past. I made her remember. I made her get to the point that made her shoot him. Everything is my fault, Olivia, and you can't tell me otherwise."

I leaned back to look at her. She looked up at me, her eyes red and her face puffy.

"So you *did* have something to do with that car bombing," I said with a slight smirk.

Lu let out a small laugh and hit me gently on the shoulder.

"It's not funny, Olivia. I'm being serious," she stated, the hint of a smile quickly fading from her face.

I sighed, I lifted my hand up to her cheek and started to gently wipe away her tears.

"I know you are, honey, but like I was trying to say,

you didn't make all those things happen. Richard Neilson was a terrible man who did horrible things to Elsie behind closed doors. No one knew what he did to her – he was abusive, manipulative and cunning," I began, noting that because Lu was now listening to me, her breathing had started to even out.

Her pulse was starting to steady and the beeping was starting to die down. Hopefully this meant I wouldn't get a visit from the charge nurse and get kicked out.

"Now as for the other events, yes, maybe those things wouldn't have happened if she wasn't your girlfriend, but you didn't force any of those people to do what they did. You didn't make Dante assault her," I continued, pausing for a moment as Lu grimaced.

"You also didn't put the knife in the man's hand that stabbed her," I finished.

I took her hands in mine again. Her heart was beating at a normal rhythm now and she had stopped crying. I felt like she needed to hear this from me. The last time we spoke about any of this was when we were still on the plane.

"I'm sorry if I ever implied that I blamed you," I said quietly and Lu bit her lip as I looked at her.

"I don't blame you and you shouldn't blame yourself either. This is not your fault. It was just a series of events that started off as a small snowball, which rolled down a hill and became so big that it blocked the road ahead of it," I stated.

"The road being our future," Lu retorted in a whisper.

I gave her a sad smile and nodded my head. "Unfortunately.

Lu leaned back on her bed and let out a yawn. It was like the nurse was waiting for that cue, because as soon as Lu finished yawning, she came into the room.

"Right, it's time for Ms. Torres to rest. Detective, I need you to leave now," the nurse ordered, so I let go of Lu's hands and stood up. I didn't want her to get security.

"Actually, Irene, this is my mother in-law. Can you please let her stay with me for a while? And can you tell her everything about my heart please?" Lu asked, looking between me and the nurse.

Irene gave me a look of scrutiny as she examined me. Since I was only thirty-four and I still looked as if I was somewhere in my twenties, I'm sure she was wondering how I could be an eighteen-year-old's mother in-law. Irene was an older woman, who I was sure would think it would be a scandal that I had a child so young.

"I had my daughter when I was sixteen," I commented, watching as her judging eyes narrowed. I was surprised that this woman was so kind to Lu, considering she had a police guard outside her door and was handcuffed to her bed.

"Right, well, if you would like to come with me, so Lu can get some sleep, I will update you on her situation," she instructed.

I looked down at Lu before nodding.

I followed the nurse out into the hallway and she closed the door behind me. The police officer who was standing in front of her door gave me a nod in greeting and I nodded back with a small smile. Irene took me into a room just a few doors down from Lu's and shut the door behind me as I walked in.

"The taser caused Lu to go into cardiac arrest shortly after getting into the ambulance. We obviously managed to get her heart started again, but further tests have concluded that she now has ventricular arrhythmia," Irene explained.

I nodded my head, trying to take in the news.

"Irregular heartbeats," she added, like I didn't know what that meant.

"I know what it is," I said quietly. I folded my arms across my chest and rubbed my arms up and down, in a way to comfort myself. This was some serious news.

"Does she know this?" I asked.

Irene nodded her head.

"I don't think she quite realizes what it all means. She shrugged it off when I explained it to her," Irene admitted.

I couldn't help but let out a grim laugh. That was so Lu.

"Is it something that will go away with time?" I asked.

"It might be something that will get better with medication and a heart-healthy lifestyle, but it could also get worse before it gets better, due to stress she's about to endure. Not to mention her temper," Irene started, shuddering slightly.

"Oh, you've seen that already?" I asked raising my eyebrow.

"When she realized that her wife, your daughter, wasn't with her," she said. "When she leaves here, she's going to have to wear a bracelet that monitors her pulse. If it goes too fast, or too slow, it will beep at her. If it beeps, she needs to stop what she is doing and get her heart rate back to normal. If she doesn't, she could go back into cardiac arrest." Irene continued.

I grimaced. What were the chances that if she did go into cardiac arrest, someone would be there to start her heart again?

"She'll need to stay here for a week or two. I have already cleared it with Special Agent Lewis," Irene carried on.

I had to raise my eyebrow at that.

"It's amazing what seeing a young girl have a heart attack can do for changing someone's mind about something," she commented.

I grimaced again as I nodded. If I had to be honest, I was glad I hadn't been there to see Lu in that state.

"She will need to be on medical watch through processing and wherever she is held. She will need a checkup once a week," she told me.

I couldn't help but let out another small laugh. "Lu really isn't going to like that."

Irene smiled for the first time since I've met her.

"No, from what I've seen from her already, I don't doubt that she will hate it," Irene finished. She looked at her fob watch then cleared her throat.

"I must get going. Please let Lu sleep for at least an hour. She hasn't rested since she got here," Irene stated before turning to leave out the door.

I followed her, deciding that I needed to find a phone so I could get in touch with the station to check on Elsie. I thought it would kill some time if I used a public phone, rather than the cellphone I was given and which was sitting in my pocket. I couldn't shake the feeling that she didn't keep her promise about eating her food. When I got to the phone, I rang the station and it was answered after a couple of rings.

"Constable Rosh, it's Olivia Swanson. How's Elsie doing?" I asked. Rosh was the officer who helped Elsie with her change of clothes.

"I'm pretty sure she's gone back to sleep," she replied.

I leaned my head against the phone case.

"Did she eat?" I asked, closing my eyes as I prayed that the answer was yes.

"Doesn't look like it, I'm afraid," she replied.

I groaned internally.

"Maybe she's waiting on news about Lu. Are you able to tell her that she's up, alert and she greeted me by calling me a *soplona*?" I asked, opening my eyes. I'm sure Elsie would know Lu was perfectly fine if she could still insult me.

"What's a *soplona*?" Constable Rosh asked, and I let out an awkward laugh.

"A snitch," I responded.

She let out a noise of understanding.

"I'll be back," she stated.

I heard the phone get put down on the bench. I moved

myself so I was leaning against the wall as I waited.

About five minutes later, I heard rustling and some clear their throat.

"Are you there, Olivia?" Constable Rosh asked, waiting for me to reply.

"Yes, I'm here," I answered.

"I think you're right about waiting for the news. As soon as I told her about the *soplona* comment, she laughed and picked up her food straight away. She even asked for more," she told me.

I sighed with relief.

"I know it's your job to keep an eye on her but can you do me a favor and you know, *keep* an eye on her?" I asked, hoping she knew what I meant.

"Of course. I will ring the hospital if I think there is anything of concern, but I really just think she's worried about her wife. I'm sure she'll be fine," she stated.

"I know, but like I told you earlier – she got herself addicted to alcohol. I'm not sure what happened in those few days we were apart, but she's likely to have withdrawal symptoms, so just make sure she doesn't like, you know, choke on her own vomit or something," I commented, grimacing slightly at the thought.

"Gotcha. Look, Olivia, I have to go. Don't worry about her, we have eyes on her," Constable Rosh stated.

I was about to thank her, but I could hear the dial tone already.

I sighed as I hung the phone back up again. It had only been twenty minutes since I left Lu's room, so I pulled out my cellphone and decided to bite the bullet and do something I hadn't done in over two months. Call my parents.

Chapter Twenty-Five

Lu

I spent two weeks in the hospital after I almost died. During those two weeks, I was not allowed to leave the hospital room. I was either handcuffed to a bed or had a police officer standing outside the door while I went to the bathroom or took a shower. I was only allowed to walk up and down the corridor directly off my room, to demonstrate that I was able to tolerate mild levels of activity without my heartrate spiking before they could release me.

It was hard enough to walk for the first few days of being tasered since my muscles were so sore after they had all spasmed.

I had been released with a bunch of medical pamphlets about my new condition to go over. It was something called ventricular arrhythmia, which basically meant I now had an irregular heart rate and it could easily put me into cardiac arrest if I either got too excited or upset.

The only thing I could keep thinking about was what if I died during an orgasm? I was too scared to give myself one, in case the nurse asked me what I was doing to get my heart rate up. I had to admit that even to me, she was quite intimidating.

In those two weeks, I had not seen or spoken to Elsie, not even once. So, to say I was excited to be released to go to jail was an understatement. Which was why I was sitting in the back of the police car, smiling like a maniac as we left the hospital parking lot, even though I had my hands cuffed together and was about to lose my freedom.

"You might want to wipe the smile of your face, Lu. They might mistake you for being jubilant," Olivia suggested as she leaned over and put a hand softly on my lap. My smiled faltered only slightly.

"I'm only excited to see Elsie, that's all," I pointed out, loud enough so Special Agent Lewis, who was driving could hear. He had been nice to me since the taser incident. He had apologized for provoking me and told me he wasn't going to press charges for assault against a law officer, which I was grateful for, but in the scheme of things, that charge was at the bottom of the pile. It made me wonder if he felt bad about me almost dying.

Olivia frowned ever so slightly and squeezed my knee, just as Special Agent Lewis cleared his throat awkwardly. My smile vanished.

"What?" I asked, feeling like I was about to be told bad news.

"We have to keep the two of you separated," Special Agent Lewis explained through the rear-view mirror. I felt my heart stop. Literally. It hurt. I gasped and at the same time my new bracelet started beeping in warning. It was like the police bracelet, but much noisier.

"Lu," Olivia said, in a hurried voice. She grabbed my hand and I looked at her.

"Breathe. In and out slowly," she said to me and I nodded as I followed her instructions. My heartbeat started to calm, but the beeping continued. I focused on Olivia who helped me by breathing with me. After a moment, everything went back to normal, but I was still shaking.

"Please don't keep us separated," I whispered, but Olivia gently shook her head.

"It's not our country, Lu. We have to go by their rules and they keep criminals who do crimes together separate," she explained.

I frowned slightly.

"But you were with Dad and Techy," I pointed out.

"We were in a different city. At the time, they had the other cells full. They had no choice. This precinct is a lot bigger and can accommodate a larger amount of people," she explained.

I lowered my head, so I wasn't looking at her.

"It's been two weeks…I haven't gone this long without seeing her since we first started dating," I told Olivia and from the corner of my eye, I could see that she was giving me a small half-hearted smile.

"Does she know that I'm coming in today?" I asked. Olivia nodded.

"Do you think I will be able to see her even briefly?" I asked, looking back at her. I looked up at the rear-view mirror to see that Special Agent Lewis was looking at us closely.

"She'll have to stay in her cell and it can only be for a short time. You won't be able to touch," Special Agent Lewis stated, watching me carefully.

I continued to breathe in and out slowly, not wanting my heart to react to the news, in case it set off my bracelet.

"Okay," I whispered, even though it was far from okay. I had no choice about it though, and I knew I only had myself to blame.

I leaned back in the seat and took Olivia's hand in mine as I looked out the window, watching everything as we went past it, possibly seeing the outside for the last time.

It wasn't long until we reached the precinct and parked in lot right next to the building. A female officer opened my door when the car was turned off. Olivia unbuckled my seatbelt and leaned slightly against me, to see who was at my door. Special Agent Lewis had already gotten out and left us to go into the precinct.

"Morning, Constable Rosh. How's Elsie doing this morning?" Olivia asked, as the officer gently grabbed my upper arm, gesturing for me to move. I got out of the car and then Olivia followed on the other side, looking expectantly at the officer for an answer. I looked at the officer too, waiting.

"She's the same as yesterday," Constable Rosh replied, her face frowning slightly.

I looked between her and Olivia. Olivia's face told me something wasn't right.

"What's wrong?" I asked as Constable Rosh unlocked one wrist from the handcuffs, gently moved my hands to my back and then re-cuffed me.

"Elsie hasn't been sleeping very well," Olivia admitted, her voice sounding concerned.

"She's been waking up with night terrors," Constable Rosh elaborated.

I groaned slightly. Of course she was. She had nothing to help her overcome them and I wasn't there to help soothe her.

"We've been getting her to see a therapist twice a

week, but I don't think it's helping much," Olivia said quietly.

"You have to let me see her properly, please?" I asked, looking from her to the constable again.

"You can talk to her, but I'm afraid, that is all we can allow," Constable Rosh said quietly.

I gritted my teeth as she started walking us into the building. I wanted to argue, but I was in enough trouble as it was. I had to hold my tongue and breathe so I didn't get upset.

The constable took me into a room, where she took my photograph and then my fingerprints. I supposed it was in case we ever tried to get into their country again.

After that, they took me into another room where I had to get changed. Everything was taken from me, except for my medical bracelet. I watched with bitterness as my wedding ring disappeared inside the bag with my clothes.

Once I was changed into clothes that I couldn't possibly end my life with, unless I was really creative, I was escorted to the cell area.

They had handcuffed me again, but this time it was at the front. I had a feeling that even though they had said I couldn't touch Elsie, they made it so it might be possible.

I knew straight away which one was Elsie's because

as soon as I walked passed a cell with the slot open, I heard a scream and the palest hands appeared through the hole in the door.

"LU!" came Elsie's voice. When I saw her hands poke out of the hole, I managed to slip the grip of the constable and run to the cell door. I grabbed onto Elsie's hands, cursing the damn door for being in my way.

"Elsie, baby," I cried, as I gripped onto her hands like my life depended on it. Elsie started crying too and as I watched her through the windowpane, I could see dark circles under her eyes and how pale her skin was. She was not all right.

"I missed you so much," Elsie cried and she squeezed my hands. She moved one of her hands up my arm as much as she could, I suppose to try and hug me, but she only reached my elbow.

"Please," I begged, as I looked back at the constable and Olivia, who was trying to hold back her tears.

"Please let me hug her," I pleaded, squeezing Elsie's hand tightly.

"Please. Even if it's just for a couple of seconds. We promise not to do anything stupid," I bargained, looking at them with hopeful eyes.

"Yes! Promise!" Elsie squeaked from the other side of the door. The constable looked at Olivia carefully, each having their own internal conversation. Constable Rosh sighed and took a step forward, pulling out the keys from her pocket.

"All right, stand back. You have two minutes and that is *all*. As soon as I say it's time, you won't argue, or I will put you in the cell furthest away, instead of the one next door. Got it?" She asked.

I nodded my head quickly.

"Got it!" I responded and Elsie agreed. I took a step back and stood next to Olivia, who took my upper arm.

The constable opened Elsie's door and as soon as it was open, I got out of Olivia's grip again and ran forward, putting my cuffed hands around Elsie's shoulders. She immediately put her arms around my waist.

"Elsie," I whispered before pulling her as close to my body as humanly possible and kissing her hard. Elsie kissed me back, but I felt a hand on my shoulder, pulling me back.

"I said yes to hugging, not kissing," the constable demanded.

I didn't want her to separate us before our two minutes were up, so I moved my lips away from Elsie's and put my forehead on hers instead.

"I've missed you," I said quietly, pointing out the obvious.

"I've missed you too," Elsie whispered back.

"You really scared me, Lu. I thought you were going to die," she told me and my heart skipped a beat.

"I know. I'm sorry. I will try not to do it again," I replied, breathing in and out slowly to try and settle my heart.

"We are a pair, aren't we? Damaged lung, damaged heart," she stated.

I laughed slightly. "We need to keep the taking of each other's breath away to the bare minimum," I pointed out and she chuckled. I missed that sound.

"You haven't been sleeping?" I questioned, quietly.

"I keep having nightmares. The latest one has been of Dante Moretti shooting you right in your heart, then passes the gun to Richard who aims the gun at my head and pulls the trigger. I always wake up before the bullet gets to me though," Elsie explained, shuddering against me.

I tried to pull her closer, but the constable cleared her throat again.

"Time's up," she declared and because I didn't want to be in a cell that was far away from Elsie, I lifted my arms back from her shoulders and Elsie let me go.

Olivia took a step forward and took my arm again, pulling me back as Elsie walked backwards into her cell. The door was shut and relocked and I took another step towards the door, allowing Olivia to keep hold of me.

"They are both dead, Elsie. There is no way they can hurt us now. You have to remember that," I said quietly.

Elsie sniffed as she held back her tears.

"I know. I just can't seem to stop them," Elsie explained in a whisper.

"You have to go into your cell now," Constable Rosh said quietly, grabbing my arm so Olivia let go.

"Will we be able to talk to each other through the walls?" I asked, turning away from Elsie.

"If you talk loud enough, you'll be able to hear each other," Constable Rosh replied with a nod of her head.

I breathed out with relief. At least there was that. I turned back to look at Elsie through the windowpane.

"I love you, my beautiful wife," I said to her, with a small smile. She smiled back.

"*Te amo, mi bella esposa*," she replied, putting her hand on the windowpane as I was escorted towards the cell next door. She had echoed everything I had just said to her in Spanish. She was a quick learner.

Constable Rosh unlocked and opened the door, then turned to uncuff me.

"We'll be back in a few hours with lunch. Special Agent Lewis is finalizing the details with the airline to get the three of you back to America. I suspect you won't be here for more than a couple of days," she explained as she took the cuffs off my wrist. I stepped into the cell and she shut the door.

"Thanks, I guess," I called back, just before the door shut. She gave me a small smile and then left. Olivia waved at me through the windowpane and I heard something shut, which I assumed was Elsie's door slot.

I walked over to the wall that was next to Elsie's and I sat down, leaning my ear against it. I winced at the coldness of it, but I just had a feeling Elsie was doing the exact same on the other side.

"Everything will be ok, E. We're together now," I called out, hoping I was loud enough for her to hear.

~.~

I was in the cell for a total of six hours. I was given lunch, then suddenly I was given jeans, a top and a sweater, thanks to Olivia buying us some travel clothes and then we were hurried off to the Auckland Airport.

Unfortunately, they drove the two of us in different cars, so I didn't even get to spend the drive with Elsie.

When we got to the airport, they still kept us

separated as we were quickly moved through the security procedures and then ushered aboard the plane.

Olivia was allowed to stay with Elsie which I was grateful for, because I knew that traveling meant that Elsie was more than likely going to fall asleep and if she had a nightmare in the middle of the flight, at least someone would be there to calm her down.

They had put Elsie and Olivia at the front of the cabin and I was sitting beside Special Agent Lewis at the back. Since we were the first to board, we had to wait awhile for all the passengers to arrive and be seated.

Because we had to be hand cuffed the whole duration of the flight for 'the safety of ourselves and others.' Special Agent Lewis had agreed that we could both have a blanket. This meant that we could cover ourselves, so no one knew what we were hiding.

This was a relief, because as soon as people starting boarding, those closest to where we were sitting started whispering. They could tell who we were, considering our faces had been plastered all over the TV and newspapers. I was just glad that they couldn't see our handcuffs. One less thing for them to talk about.

I looked over the tops of the seats to where Elsie was sitting. She was looking back at me, as if she had turned and knelt on her seat. I could see that Olivia was trying to tug at her arm, probably trying to get her to turn around. I smiled at her as I went to stand up, but Special Agent Lewis tugged me down fast. I turned to scowl at him and by the time I had looked back up, Elsie was already back in her seat.

It wasn't long until everyone had boarded the plane. The flight attendants gave us the safety briefing, playing a video and showing us the emergency exit aisles and life vests. I gulped at the thought of us having to use one but decided that where I was going was probably much scarier.

Not long after that, the flight attendants did a once over down the aisles, checking that everyone was buckled in, tray tables stowed away, window shades and seat backs, up and aisles clear. When a female flight attendant made her way past me and Special Agent Lewis, she gave him a brief smile and looked at me like I was a killer. Well, I guess she wasn't wrong.

She hurried back up the aisle and I watched as she left, chuckling slightly about the fact that people thought I was dangerous. I was only dangerous to those who hurt Elsie. Surely that was obvious? I wasn't a serial killer.

"What are you laughing at?" Special Agent Lewis asked, leaning back in his seat and looking at me, with a slightly raised eyebrow.

"It's just funny that people think I'm dangerous," I admitted, shrugging my shoulders.

"Well, you have killed a lot of people, Lucita. People will be a bit wary of you," he pointed out.

I rolled my eyes and looked out the window as the plane started moving onto the runway.

"Whatever," I replied, not wanting to talk about my crimes - or lack thereof - without my lawyer. I guess they were still trying to pin the Moretti gang deaths on us.

I couldn't help but think of my dad in that moment. I wondered where he was and how he was doing. Had he already been sentenced? Was he in prison and calling all the shots already, or was he keeping his head down? Had he gotten off of his charges because of his lawyer? I hadn't asked much about him, especially around Olivia. I felt bad that he had choked her. I didn't think he was capable of doing something like that to a woman. Considering she was pretty much a part of the family, it actually devastated me.

I refused to ask Special Agent Lewis, even though he had been acting very friendly since my heart episode.

I watched as we rolled down the runway, clenching my hands as the plane moved to the beginning of the runway. When the plane started to lurch forward, picking up speed as it went, I held in my breath. We shot down the runway and then up into the air. I let my breath out as my bracelet started beeping under my blanket.

Special Agent Lewis bumped me gently on the shoulder.

"There's nothing to be afraid of. Flying is the safest way to travel," he stated.

I tried to laugh off my nervousness, breathing in and out slowly to try and settle the bracelet down. When it stopped making noise, I gave him a fake grin.

"I know. It's just the funny feeling of my stomach dropping that gives me the *escalofríos*," I explained. I had to laugh again when Special Agent Lewis looked at me in confusion.

"What you would call 'the heebie-jeebies,'" I offered.

He nodded his head in understanding. I shook my head, amused then looked out the window again, watching as we started climbing higher than the clouds.

"Well, I'm going to see if I can sleep straight through. Wake me up if anything interesting happens," I said with a sigh. I turned my body around slightly, so I was leaning against the side of the plane. I pulled my legs up, so they were against my chest and my feet were tucked just beside Special Agent Lewis's leg.

I heard him scoff, but I pulled my blanket up and over me and rested my head against the seat, closing my eyes.

I was pretty exhausted. I seemed to get tired more easily since my heart had stopped and had been shocked into restarting. Now I knew how Elsie felt. It didn't take long for the noises around me to fade away and I was soon in a deep sleep.

Chapter Twenty-Six
Elsie

Richard was hovering above me, holding the gun he had snatched from me, pointed directly at my face. He charged at me so fast that I hadn't had time to react, so when he pushed me to the ground, I fell in a heap. Everyone around me laughed, including Lu, who had come to stand next to my so-called father and Mrs. Taylor was on his other side.

"You really are pathetic, Elizabeth. You can't even get shooting me right," he taunted, while Mrs. Taylor held her belly as she sneered at me. Lucita took a step forward with the most hateful look on her face.

"You're so pathetic that it was easy for me to get what I wanted. You were so desperate for love and acceptance that you would have chosen anybody. You were just convenient because you were so easy," Lucita told me, as she pulled someone from behind her. My eyes widened as Olivia stood next to her.

"You're so pathetic that when you were born, I just had to get rid of you. Elias wanted to die just so he didn't have to know you," Olivia jeered.

I bit my lip as I tried to stop myself from crying, but as I looked to Olivia's left, I couldn't help myself. Dante stood next to her.

"You're so pathetic that I couldn't even bring myself to enter you. I would rather fuck a dog than you," he sneered and I tried to move away from him, covering up my legs with my torn dress as I did so. I stopped as I felt myself bump against someone. I turned my head and saw Ryleigh staring down at me with a nasty look on her face.

"You're so pathetic even your adoptive mother wanted to die to get away from you. You ruin everything you touch. You're a waste of space. You're stupid. No one loves you. No one will EVER love you," Ryleigh goaded, picking me up roughly from under my arms and lifting me up so I stood in front of everyone.

She pushed me towards the row of people, the rest of the school bunching up behind them. Giovanni stood next to his nephew, holding his knife threateningly in his hand.

"You should be dead. No one wants you here," he told me as Ryleigh pushed me closer to them again.

Richard stepped forward and put the gun against my head. Grabbing my hand, he forced the gun into it, making it so I was holding the gun and my finger was on the trigger.

"Do us all a favor," he goaded, making my finger tighten.

"Do it," he sneered and I let out a cry as I pulled the trigger.

"ELSIE!" came the sound of Olivia screaming in my ear. I woke up with a start, panting and breathless. I blinked a few times, looked at Olivia and then burst into tears. The people around us looked at me and began talking amongst themselves. I threw my hands over my face, trying to hide from everyone, forgetting that I had handcuffs on.

I heard gasps now from the people around me and I cried even more. Olivia wrapped her arms around my shoulder and pulled me close to her. I buried my head into her and cried.

"It was just a dream, Elsie. None of it was real," Olivia said to me, rubbing my back. I sobbed, moving my hands away from my face. I felt the blanket go back over my hands, shielding them from wandering eyes.

"I was back at the school. Everyone was telling me how pathetic I was. Why everyone hated me," I whispered as Olivia continued to rub my back and make shushing noises.

"You're not pathetic, Elsie. And nobody hates you. We love you," Olivia pointed out and I couldn't help but pull back and look at her.

"But you got rid of me," I whispered. Olivia was

about to respond to me, but she was interrupted by a loud shout.

"Let me go to her, you fucking *puerco*!" Lucita shouted, so loud I could hear her from the back of the plane. My heart pounded as I sat up and turned around in my seat to look back at Lucita, who was being held back by Special Agent Lewis, halfway out of her seat and into the aisle.

Clearly, I had made enough noise that she could hear me from where she was. Every single person on the plane was now looking at Lu, who was screaming and hitting the agent and her bracelet was beeping in warning that her heart was getting out of rhythm. If she didn't calm down, chances were that her heart would stop all together.

I unbuckled my seat belt and stood up, the blanket falling to the ground. People looked between the two of us, wondering what I was going to do.

"Lu!" I yelled, loud enough that she could hear me over what she was doing. She stopped and turned her head to look at me. I could see her eyes widening and that she was panting. I brought my hands up to my heart, then gestured to her to calm down by moving my hands in a downwards motion. I then pointed my finger to my eye, then my heart and then pointed to her. I hoped that would acknowledge to her that I was all right. She smiled at me and nodded her head and I smiled back, noting how she was now breathing slower and the beeping had started to lessen.

Special Agent Lewis was still holding her. I guess he was aware that she could easily try to get out of his grasp and run down the aisle to get to me. I watched as he pulled another set of cuffs out from his pocket and while she was distracted, he slapped one side on her right wrist just above the other and then tugged her back down, so she was sitting again. I heard a noise of the other cuffs being secured to something solid, which I could only assume was the arm barrier between the seats or something.

The passengers went back to what they were doing before, clearly satisfied that there wasn't going to be anything dramatic to watch. I turned and sat back down, letting out a big sigh.

Olivia bent down and grabbed the blanket that had fallen and put it over me again.

"First of all, that girl has a set of *cojones* on her," Olivia chuckled and I gave her a pointed look as I turned my head to look at her.

"Secondly, I didn't get *rid* of you. I had no choice, I've told you this," Olivia stated with a frown.

"You could have fought for me," I pointed out.

"You don't think I tried? Elsie, I loved you the moment I found out I was carrying you. I fought tooth and nail to keep you, but I was only sixteen. My parents, your grandparents, wouldn't listen. Not once did I ever not want you," she told me, pulling me into another hug.

"And despite what your nightmares tell you, I would never, ever, make you feel unloved or unwanted," she added.

I buried my head back into her chest, wishing I could hug her back.

"I know, Mom, I'm sorry," I whispered, feeling like I was going to start crying again.

But I wasn't going to. No, I was stronger than that, despite my mind telling me I wasn't. I pushed myself away from Olivia and she looked at me carefully.

"I need to go to the bathroom," I announced and I stood, the blanket falling to the ground again. I turned to look towards the back of the plane, hoping that Lu was looking in my direction. She was.

She was awkwardly craning her neck so she could see over the head of the people in front of her. I could see that Special Agent Lewis wasn't looking; he was too engrossed in a book. I lifted my hands up and put them in a T position to indicate to Lu that I was going to the bathroom. I hoped she got why I was telling her this. She raised her eyebrow slightly, but then it was like a lightbulb turned on as she widened both of her eyes and gave me a smirk. She nodded her head and I turned to look at Olivia, who was watching me, shaking her head, as she knew exactly what I was trying to do. I gave her a pleading look, as she stood and moved out of her seat and gestured for me to follow.

"The less I know, the better," she informed me. She grabbed my upper arm and walked me towards the toilets. There was three of them at the front and two were at the back of the plane, but luckily the two at the back were already in use. I had no doubt that Lu could con her way to the front of the plane.

Once we were in front of the bathrooms, Olivia got a key from her pocket and unlocked the cuffs around my wrists. I opened the middle door and stepped in. When I shut the door, I didn't bother to lock it. I quickly went, as I really did need to pee. Once I was done and I was washing my hands, the door opened and I turned to see Lu stepping in. She kept her head poked around the corner.

"I'm going number two, so don't bother waiting. It might take a while. That jail food hasn't agreed with me," she announced and I had to put my hand over my mouth to dampen the noise of my laugh. Lu shut the door, then locked it before turning to me, grinning. I grinned back as we began wrapping our arms around each other.

The stall was tiny – it barely fit the two of us in it. The toilet was digging at the back of my legs and the sink was close to our sides. It was really uncomfortable, but at the same time, I didn't want to be anywhere else.

"I've missed you," I whispered against Lu's ear and she shuddered slightly as my breath hit her skin. She moved her head, so she was looking at me and leaned forward to kiss me. When our lips met, it felt like the hole in my heart had been fixed. I parted my mouth and her tongue slipped in and I pulled her body closer to mine. I could feel her heart pounding and it made me reluctantly pull away from her.

"Is what I want to do with you right now going to kill you?" I asked, moving my hands from her waist to settle them on her ass. I gave her cheeks a gentle squeeze and she let out a moan.

"Probably," she answered, then lowered her mouth to my neck and gently started sucking me there. I closed my eyes and let out a moan of my own as her hands wandered from my back and moved around to my front.

"But what a way to go out," she added, forcing me to

turn so I had my back against the stall's wall.

I had no doubt that this was the most unhygienic place we could possibly do this, but there was literally a club that people belonged to, so I knew we weren't the only ones to do it in here.

"It's not funny, Lu," I gasped as she kissed down my neck and moved her hands up my top to squeeze my breasts. I pulled at her ass to bring her front closer to mine and she retaliated by moving my bra to the side and pinching my rock-hard nipples.

"In all honesty, I don't know what will happen," Lu commented as she lifted her lips from my throat and looked at me.

"So let me taste you again and that will satisfy me enough," she announced, making my heart flutter and my cheeks warm.

"All right," I agreed, not that I was going to say no.

Lu grinned and moved her hands from my breasts to the front of my jeans. She unbuttoned them, then pulled them down, along with my underwear. She closed the lid to the toilet and grabbed my hips, turning me and forcing me to sit down.

She lowered herself to the ground and pulled my clothes fully from my legs, freeing her to spread my legs apart. I moaned as she grabbed my right leg and put it over her shoulder, immediately starting to trail kisses down my inner thigh until she reached my already aroused pussy.

When her tongue pressed on my clit, I let out a small whimper and moved my butt slightly forward on the seat so she had better access. She gripped my thigh and I moved my hand to her hair and tangled my fingers through it, pulling it tightly, knowing how much she loved it. She let out a groan against me and I shuddered at the feeling.

"Naughty," she mumbled and she started to eat me like she had been starving for weeks.

"Fuck," I moaned, dragging the word out as her tongue moved like magic. She licked my clit up and down, moved her tongue in circles, devouring me into a puddle.

The noises I was making were getting loud, so it didn't surprise me when the hand that wasn't gripping onto my thigh to hold me down came up and covered my mouth. I moaned into her hand as she continuing making magic. Her hand on my thigh moved and I let out a little scream against her hand as she pushed her fingers inside me.

She started pumping them in and out of me as she continued to move her tongue. I tugged at her hair again, pushing her head closer to my core and I put my other hand on the wall to hold myself up.

I felt my orgasm begin and I guess Lu did too, because as I started to tighten around her fingers that were exceptionally pounding in and out of me, I felt her teeth bite me. Her hand tightened over my mouth as I let out a pleasurable scream.

"Lu!" I dragged her name as I came undone. I felt the orgasm rip through my whole body, the euphoria hitting me everywhere. My legs were shuddering against Lu as she continued to lick me through the orgasm, only stopping when I slumped forward, panting like I had run a marathon.

Surely, if I had done this to Lu, her bracelet would have told everyone what we were up to, not to mention I probably would have killed her. My heart was going bonkers.

Lu licked the length of my pussy down to her fingers, which she removed them, only to replace them with the tip of her tongue. I moaned, as she licked up my juices, then she removed her mouth from me, grinning as she made her way back up to my mouth, moving her hand from my lips and putting her fingers in there instead. I looked at her as I sucked on her fingers, tasting myself.

There was a knock on the door and Lu removed her

fingers, moving back slightly so I had enough room to stand up.

"Hurry up!" called the voice of Special Agent Lewis. I giggled quietly as I grabbed some toilet paper to wipe myself up before lifting the lid to flush it down the toilet.

"You're the one who fed me the awful food!" Lu shouted back, a grin on her face as she moved to turn the tap on. She washed her hands and I grabbed my jeans and underwear from the floor. I awkwardly put them back on and then buttoned my jeans back up before I pulled Lu into a tight embrace. We kissed for a moment, before there was another rattle at the door and we both froze when it began to open.

Three people stood on the other side: Special Agent Lewis, who had his arms folded against his chest, with a look of pure anger on his face; a female flight attendant who looked very highly amused - this was not her first rodeo - and Olivia, who looked like she wanted to die from embarrassment.

"What gave us away?" Lu asked, as she brought her hand up to her mouth and licked it. If it wasn't for the fact that I had just had an amazing orgasm, I probably would have been embarrassed by that gesture, but instead it oddly turned me on even more.

Special Agent Lewis stepped forward and grabbed

both of Lu's hands, roughly pulling her out of the cubicle. He handcuffed her behind her back this time, then shoved her into the arms of Olivia before turning his attention to me.

"It was kind of obvious when two other people came out of the other bathrooms," Special Agent Lewis stated as he grabbed my upper arm and yanked me out.

He proceeded to handcuff me too, roughly forcing my hands behind my back. I couldn't help but think he was more pissed off at the fact that we outsmarted him than he was about anything else. I grinned at Lu, who was grinning back.

"Clearly, I can't rely on Olivia here to be impartial," he continued, turning his gaze to Olivia, who looked down at the floor, her face red. She had done me a favor by pretending she didn't know what I was up to. Now she was in trouble. I stopped grinning, feeling slightly ashamed. I was glad the flight attendant had gone off into the cabin to help a passenger who had pressed the call button, so she didn't have to hear Olivia getting in trouble.

"I thought by giving you professional courtesy you would take this seriously, Olivia. Clearly, you can't put aside the need to make your daughter love you, even if it means going against the rules," the agent continued.

I couldn't help but start to feel angry.

"Hey, she doesn't need to *make* me love her. I already do. And if you're going to blame anyone, blame me. She didn't see which stall I went into," I pointed out, not exactly lying, considering I'm pretty sure she was watching the agent and Lu come up the aisle when I got into it.

"Be that as it may, it's no longer appropriate for Olivia to be minding you," Special Agent Lewis declared and then turned his attention from me back to Olivia.

"Take Lu back to her seat and take mine instead. We will talk about this when we're back on solid ground," he told Olivia, who looked at him, still red, and nodded.

When she turned to look at me, I mouthed 'sorry,' and she shrugged her shoulders slightly, before pushing Lu gently to start her walking.

"Have a good sleep, babe," Lu announced, looking over her shoulder at me, with a smirk before turning and walked down the aisle, ignoring all the passengers who watched her. I looked at the agent, who was turning slightly red from her comment. He wouldn't know it of course, but Lu knew that because she had just given me an earth-shattering orgasm, I could now sleep without the nightmares. It worked every time and I had no doubt it would work again.

Special Agent Lewis huffed as he gripped my upper arm and pulled me to my seat. He sat me down, not bothering to rearrange my handcuffs, which made it very uncomfortable to sit.

"Are you going to make me sit like this for the rest of the trip?" I asked, moving my head back to look behind me. The agent buckled his seat belt up, then reached over me to buckle mine also.

"Maybe you should have thought about the consequences before doing everything you could to join the Mile High Club," Special Agent Lewis retorted.

My face warmed.

"Maybe you shouldn't have kept us separated for so long," I pointed out, turning away from him to look out the window. It was getting dark.

"How much longer until we get to New York?" I asked, changing the subject.

"We have about ten hours left," the agent answered.

I knew we had to eat at some point in our flight but considering I had gone days before I took a bite of food, refusing to eat until I heard about Lu, I knew I could wait another ten hours until we got to JFK.

So that's what I did. I put my head against the wall of the plane, closed my eyes and soon drifted off into a nightmare-free sleep, thanks to Lu working her magic tongue and fingers.

Chapter Twenty-Seven
Olivia

The rest of the flight was uneventful. I had rearranged Lu's hands so she could have them in front of her, so we spent a few hours playing cards and then the rest of the time we spent sleeping. I unfortunately had to handcuff her to the seat again when I felt myself drifting off to sleep. She didn't seem to mind though.

When we got to JFK we had to wait until the plane had been emptied before we could take the girls off the plane. We went through special security and customs clearance to get us back into the United States, which took about an hour.

During that time, Elsie and Lu were allowed to be near each other, but Special Agent Lewis said they couldn't speak. They held hands the whole time. I couldn't help but feel grateful to the agent, considering what had happened on the plane. He could have easily punished them more by keeping them separated.

Once we cleared customs we went to retrieve our bags. We had sent most of our possessions through air freight, along with Elsie and Lu's personal items, including their rings.

After leaving the airport, we soon found ourselves in

the back of two vehicles; Lu and I in one and Elsie and Special Agent Lewis in the other as we traveled back to Sutton.

The drive took about an hour and a half and soon we pulled into the parking lot of the police station. I got out of the car, my heart pounding at the anticipation of seeing my father. The last time we spoke, he had told me he remembered our last conversation and he wasn't convinced that the photos he had been shown of me being kidnapped were real.

He had told me I had put him in a difficult position because he knew what I had done. He had said that my fate would be decided when I returned home. Then he had gone to find my mother so I could talk to her. She was over the moon about hearing from me and clearly didn't share the same opinion as her husband.

When I closed the car door, I looked up to find that several officers had come to take over custody of Elsie and Lu. I went to say goodbye to Elsie, but a firm shake of the head and a grim look from Special Agent Lewis made me stop in my tracks.

"It'll be all right," I called out as the girls were led into the station. Elsie looked over her shoulder at me and gave me a weak smile. I awkwardly gave her a little wave.

When she turned back around and disappeared through the doors, Special Agent Lewis cleared his throat, making me drop my hand and turn around to look at him.

"Your actions keep contradicting the purported fact that you didn't break the law to be with them, you know," he commented, looking from the girls to me, giving me a knowing look. I gulped slightly.

"Despite everything that happened to me, I still want what's best for my daughter," I pointed out. "And my daughter in-law."

Thanks to the fact the marriage certificate was legit and processed before the girls were arrested, the marriage had been accepted by the American government before we left New Zealand.

Elsie and Lu were officially wife and wife and I couldn't be happier for the two of them. And it had little to do with the fact that they couldn't testify against each other, if they pled not guilty to the charges and went to trial.

Special Agent Lewis looked at me for a few moments longer before shaking his head and heading off in the direction the girls were just taken.

"Come on, your father is waiting for you," he announced and I gulped again, wondering what was about to happen. I forced myself to follow the agent and soon we were inside my old workplace.

Some of my colleagues came up to me, shaking my hand, welcoming me back. I returned their polite gestures with a forced smile, because I couldn't help but wonder how many of them believed I had chosen my daughter over the law. I'm sure most of them thought I had broken the law before the photos were found and I knew a lot of them would doubt that they were real.

However, no one said anything and unless my father spoke up about what I had said to him the first time I called him, I didn't think anyone would.

Special Agent Lewis waited for me to get through the crowd, before knocking on my father's office door.

"Come in," came his voice, and the sound of my heart beating drowned out all other sounds. Special Agent Lewis opened the door and gestured for me to walk in first. I forced my leaden legs to move one step at a time and was surprised to see my dad start smiling when he saw me.

"Olivia!" He exclaimed, his arms open wide, the biggest smile on his face, as he stepped around his desk and practically ran to wrap his arms around me.

"Dad," I breathed in relief. I hugged him back and put my head against his chest. He was taller than me, so his chest was the perfect height for me to sink into him.

"I would like to talk to my daughter alone for a few minutes, if you don't mind, Special Agent Lewis. Why don't you go and make sure Torres and Neilson get processed correctly," Dad stated.

"Yes, of course, Captain Swanson," Special Agent Lewis replied. I lifted my head and watched as he exited the room, shutting the door behind him. I looked back up at my dad, wondering if this was just a show he put on in front of the agent.

"I've missed you," Dad commented and I gulped, leaning back from him slightly. He moved his hands from behind me, put them on my arms and rubbed gently.

"I meant what I said about you putting me in a difficult position, squirt," he told me, calling me by the nickname he had given to me as a child. I was always the shortest in my classes at school and even now in the police force I was shorter than most. He liked to remind me sometimes. My cheeks started to warm at his comment.

"I know," I whispered, feeling ashamed. He knew that those photos were a lie, he knew that I had intentionally broken the law, and he knew that I was now lying about it. I'm sure he knew I would continue to lie, even if that meant committing perjury on the stand. He rubbed my arms a bit more before letting out a sigh.

"As far as anyone is aware, the last time I spoke to you was when I took your badge and gun," he stated, letting go of my arms then moving back around to his desk. He lifted up a couple of photos, showing me the pictures of my fake abduction.

"As far as anyone is aware, I believe these to be real and I feared for your life, until I got a phone call from Special Agent Lewis stating that he had found you," he continued.

I bit my lip as he put them down and looked at me with his stern, parent face that had a mix of captain in it.

"As long as you stick to the story and tell everyone exactly what they need to know, no one will be any the wiser," he declared.

"Right," I said quietly.

"That being said, I am glad you came to your senses and told the agent everything you knew. That will help get your gun and badge back quicker," he commented and I bit my lip again.

"About that …" I started and my dad lifted his head from where he had been looking down at his desk.

"I don't know if I want to come back, just yet …I mean, after I'm cleared and go through everything I need to go through, I think I want to take some time off, to focus on helping Elsie," I explained, moving to the chair and sitting down.

Dad just frowned, but he followed suit and sat down at his chair too, putting his elbows on his desk and linking his fingers together so he could rest his chin in his hands.

"I don't think there is much you can do to help her, at this stage, squirt. She's committed several felonies and fled the country. She would have to have a damn good lawyer to get her off those charges," he pointed out.

I lowered my gaze and nodded my head.

"I wasn't talking about legal help," I said quietly. I wasn't sure how much he wanted to hear, but when I saw him move his hand and hold it out for me to take, I looked up at him and put my hand in his. Tears started filling my eyes.

"Tell me," he said quietly, giving my hand a squeeze. "She's been through so much in her eighteen years of life. I think prison is going to be the final straw for her," I whispered.

"I want to be able to see her whenever there are visitors' hours. I want to be able to take her phone call as soon as she calls. I want her to know that I am there whenever she needs me. If I'm on the job, I won't be able to stop what I'm doing to take that call. I have enough vacation days, right?" I asked, and Dad looked down at his desk at a file I assumed was mine and he nodded.

"You haven't taken a day off until this whole ordeal. Not that you could call it a day off," he stated.

I cringed.

"All right, I will sign off for your sabbatical," he said after a moment.

"How bad is her mental health?" He questioned, his captain voice completely switching off, as all I could hear in his voice was concern. Concern for his granddaughter, perhaps? Or maybe just concern at how upset I was about it.

"She keeps having nightmares. She hasn't slept properly in weeks, was a borderline alcoholic, from which she had to go through withdrawal, cold turkey. She doesn't eat every meal, sometimes skipping a day or even two," I started.

His frown deepened.

"If she's separated from Lu in prison, I really think she'll do something to get herself to get out of the hell she is living with inside her head. Lu seems to be the only person who can bring her back to reality," I said quietly, feeling my heart break just at the thought of it.

"We can send our recommendations, but it's up to the warden," Dad pointed out.

I knew that – once they were in the care of the prison, we had no say what would happen.

"Can I say something that you might not like to hear as a cop, but might understand as my dad, as her granddad?" I asked, giving his hand a squeeze as I looked at him. He shifted uncomfortably for a moment, before nodding his head.

"I hope the La Dragones loves their leader's daughter enough to pay the warden to do what they say. I hope Jorge Torres Rodriquez has told them to pay whatever they need to pay to make sure they are safe and happy," I stated, biting my lip as I waited for his response. And to my surprise, he nodded his head.

"Jorge is in the country, being held at New Haven Correctional Facility on remand until his sentencing. He pled guilty to all charges including abducting you and the warehouse murders. His only request is to talk to you," Dad exclaimed.

He pled guilty? He must have had a tactical reason to do that. I was about to reply when Dad nodded his head towards the door. I turned and saw a shadow behind it, which meant that Special Agent Lewis was waiting for us.

"You know what to do," he added, gesturing for me to leave.

I nodded my head, as my mind replayed the conversation we had just had, around in my head. Did he just tell me to go talk to Jorge in prison to make sure this happened? Yes. Yes, he did.

~.~

The prison was cold. I walked into the facility wearing a long-sleeved shirt, a sweater, long woolen pants and a scarf, but I was still shivering.

I was escorted by a corrections officer into a room that immediately made me feel uncomfortable, as it was bare except the seats, the bench top and the glass partitions that separated me from the inmates' side.

I sat down on one of the seats, jiggling my knee up and down, with my hands clasped together between my legs to keep them warm as I waited for Jorge to be brought in.

Surprisingly, it hadn't taken long for me to get permission to visit him. He had apparently made arrangements to allow me to visit him, which I couldn't help but find a bit shocking.

I had received a letter in my mailbox when I finally got back to my apartment. I had filled out the requested form and it was only two days later when I received a phone call saying that I had been granted permission to visit him.

Because I was a detective, the warden had granted me special permission to visit him outside of visitors' hours, which I was grateful for, because I had helped put away most of the inmates in this prison and I wouldn't want anyone to recognize me. Even with the glass partition separating me from them, I still felt nervous.

The officer who had escorted me to the visitation area stood on the other side of the open door frame, allowing me a bit of privacy, but I knew he would still be within ear shot. I hoped I could get out what I wanted to say to Jorge, without getting into any trouble. I didn't want that for him, or for me.

I gulped nervously as the door on the other side of the partition opened and Jorge was escorted through. He was wearing a two-piece khaki uniform, with his wrists and feet handcuffed together and connected by a chain. It looked very awkward to walk in. He was followed by another officer, who stood by a wall, lazily resting his hand on the side of his belt. I wondered briefly what weapon he might be concealing.

I stood up as Jorge approached his side of the partition, only sitting down again after he sat down. He was looking at me with a smirk on his face, which made my heart pound with anticipation.

It wasn't, an 'I'm going to kill you' kind of smirk; it was more of a 'I know something you don't know' one. I gulped once again as I shakily reached up to the phone on the side of the booth and waited until Jorge grabbed his one.

"Hello, *wife*," he stated.

I narrowed my eyes.

"I am not your wife," I responded with a hiss, and he smirked even more.

"Oh, but for all intents and purposes, you are," he countered, leaning forward slightly, giving me a look that made my heart pound. I narrowed my eyes more, scowling at him.

"Is that how I got access so fast?" I asked, feeling anger build up in my chest, rather than the nervousness I was feeling earlier. He gave a slight nod of his head.

"I knew you would come and see me after betraying us. I had to make it work for me," he stated.

I let out an annoyed sigh.

"I didn't betray you. It was a rouse of Special Agent Lewis. If anyone gave away the girls' location, it was *you*," I retorted. I didn't come here to have this argument, but if it got me on the good side of a gang leader again, then perhaps it wasn't a bad idea to set the record straight.

"Oh, he explained everything," Jorge replied with a dismissive tone, leaning back in his seat,.

"Though, I've been kept up to date with everything since we parted. You took them straight to the girls. You put my daughter at death's door, because you had a guilty conscience," he exclaimed.

I bit my lip slightly as I watched him.

"Lu didn't have to react the way she did," I said quietly, but he ignored my comment.

"You've been in the back pocket of that FBI agent ever since, now that you think you can get away with helping them escape the country with those fake photos," he continued and my eyes widened. He let out a laugh.

"Yes, I know about the photos. Who do you think had them made? Techy doesn't do anything unless I tell him to," he stated.

My eyes flicked to the officer who was standing behind Jorge, pretending not to listen.

"Don't worry about him. Or the other officer. They're paid to not pay attention to anything I say or do," he commented and I gulped. He already had the correctional staff on his payroll.

"Anyway, let me guess what you came in for. You want me to make sure Elsie is protected in prison, am I correct?" he asked, shifting in his seat.

"As well as making sure the girls are kept together," I added with a nod.

Jorge's smirk grew.

"I've heard that the State wants to keep them apart, they fear the girls will cause trouble," he stated.

I bit my lip more. I was also scared of that.

"It would cost a fair bit to get the warden on our side," he continued.

I watched him as he pondered.

"What will you do for it?" He asked, shifting again and leaning forward.

I frowned.

"Well, I was hoping, you would, well, just do it because it's what's best for Lu," I answered quietly.

"Lu can take care of herself. If she's separated from Elsie, she will hurt for a little while, but she will get over it. Sure, she might think Elsie is the love of her life, but with plenty of woman to choose from, she'll move on quickly enough," he commented with a shrug of his shoulders.

I gaped at him. How could he say that?

"No, I will be doing *you* a favor. A huge one, one that you couldn't possibly pay back," he continued and his smirk grew to the point that I dreaded what he was going to say next.

"If you want me to do this - if you want me to make Elsie's prison sentence seem as if she's at a summer bootcamp, rather than paying for her crimes - then you have to do something for me," he continued.

I groaned inwardly.

"What?" I said quietly, wondering why I was even asking. I'm sure what he wanted me to do wasn't legal.

"I want you to bring merchandise into the prison," Jorge said matter-of-factly, leaning back in his chair.

My heart stopped and my mouth went dry. I dropped the phone and looked around the room, noticing that the officer behind Jorge had not even batted an eye and the officer at the door was standing calmly as if we talked about the weather. I picked the phone up with trembling hands.

"I can't do that … I won't do that," I stated, to which Jorge responded with a shrug.

"Elsie will just have to get over her separation anxiety then, because she's going to have to get used to being alone in another state," Jorge retorted. "Not to mention, how you will have to get used to being in prison yourself. I'm not sure if you've heard, but inmates don't play nicely with *la poli*." He raised his eyebrow knowingly.

"Especially woman," he added.

I gulped. I knew exactly what they did to police in prison. I wouldn't last a day if the female inmates found out I was a cop.

"Are you blackmailing me?" I asked, gripping the phone. That was a rhetorical question, obviously.

"Do you not think I have evidence that would put you away for a long time? Well, if you don't get shanked the moment you enter your cell, that is," Jorge said with a slight sneer in his tone. He was getting angry now.

"Do you not know that I have video camera footage of you entering my car without my knowledge? Video footage of you in my car waiting while I saved your daughter from being stabbed to death, with you doing nothing to stop it? That I have video footage of you running and climbing into my car, voluntarily, when the police were moments away from Maria Sanchez's clinic?" He listed.

"I even have the recording of your conversation with your dear old parents. You know, the one where you told your father that you won't tell him where the girls were and that you, and I quote, 'have a duty to protect my daughter'?" He added.

This led to my eyes filling up with tears.

"That's right, Olivia, I have everything in my power

to fuck up the lives of you and your daughter," he declared.

I tried to hold back the tears, but I couldn't as they had already started slipping down my cheek.

I felt completely useless. Dumbstruck. Afraid. He was right. He could let the state place Elsie in whichever prison they saw fit and if he was right about the rumors, then she could end up on the far side of the state, where she would be left to fight her demons on her own. Without Lu. Without me.

He could put me away for a very long time with that evidence. The chances were I wouldn't even live long enough to get out. I was a cop. I was screwed. I bit the inside of my lip again, trying hard to focus on that, rather than my thoughts. Soon I could feel a metallic tang of blood throughout my mouth. I swallowed it, trying not to get sick.

"How?" I whispered.

"Well, you see, as my wife, we have certain perks that other visitors do not," he started, and I let out a groan.

"I'm not having sex with you," I stated, quickly.

Jorge merely rolled his eyes.

"*Como si quisiera follar con un cerdo,*" he replied and my face burned. Like he would want to fuck a pig. That really did wonders for my ego.

"Please stop calling me that," I pleaded.

He ignored me.

"With conjugal visits, we will be left alone in a room. All you have to do is pass your search and give it to me. There will be no cameras running properly during our visit. I have the officer in charge of security footage, as well as the officer who is always the guard outside the room, on payroll. There will be no official record of our conjugal visit, as it will only state you are visiting during normal hours," Jorge continued, as if I hadn't said anything.

"As long as you can get it through the doors and to me without getting caught, you will be in no danger. How you do that is up to your imagination," Jorge told me with a smirk.

My cheeks reddened. I knew what he was implying. I was not going to be putting drugs up my vagina.

"How will I get the drugs?" I asked, shifting uncomfortably in my seat.

"You will visit Fingers at my home on the morning of our scheduled visits," Jorge told me.

I had met Fingers at the abandoned warehouse. I grimaced at the thought of missing an appointment with him. I had heard about how he had gotten that name.

I shuddered slightly and gripped the phone even

tighter. Jorge noticed my movement, as his eyes flickered over my fingers.

"I wouldn't advise missing those meetings. He has told me how he has thought about breaking your bones before snipping them off one by one. He doesn't take kindly to traitors, cops, or snitches, and you happen to be all three," Jorge commented. I'm sure my face was now white instead of red.

"If I agree to do it, you'll make sure the girls are together, right? That Elsie will be protected? That you won't release the footage?" I asked, definitely feeling more nauseous than before.
Jorge nodded.

"That is correct," he responded.

"All right," I gulped, feeling like I was making the worst mistake in my life. But the thought of Elsie being alone and unprotected in prison, overrode any logical thinking.

"I agree."

Chapter Twenty-Eight

Lu

Three days had passed since we'd been back in Sutton. The first thing they did when we arrived at the police precinct was to make us put on hideous orange jumpsuits that did nothing whatsoever to help my complexion. I got a glimpse of Elsie wearing hers and couldn't help but think how stunning she looked in orange, before they whisked her away to a separate cell.

I wasn't sure why they had separated us, considering the cell units they had were set up with several bunk beds, so they could each hold several offenders who were waiting for their day in court. I tried asking, but no one would talk to me when they came to give us our food. I was also ignored when we got twenty minutes of time outside to get in our daily vitamin D, where it was very obvious within the first five minutes of our first outing that Elsie was not in my group.

I hadn't seen Special Agent Lewis since he helped process us and I still hadn't seen a lawyer. I was sitting on my assigned bed, which was on the bottom of a bunk bed, staring angrily at the opposite wall. The woman who was assigned to the bunk above me smelled like she wasn't using our assigned shower times to actually shower, which made my eyes hurt and my mood sour. Add this to the fact that sleeping with several other women who pretty much snored, farted, or tossed and turned all night made it impossible to sleep properly, and it was hardly a surprise that I was grumpy.

The women were sitting at a table, playing cards, which they had invited me to play. I told them I wasn't interested and chose to stare at the wall instead. I was thinking about Elsie, trying to brighten my mood, but I was finding it harder and harder as each hour went by, not knowing where she was or how she was doing. It made me feel even angrier.

My heart started pounding as I thought about her and before I knew it, a loud beep started coming from my bracelet. One of the women swore, one toppled out of her seat and the others started looking around for the source.

"What the fuck is that?" shrieked one of the women, who called herself Shorty, apparently due to her height. She seemed to be the one who had been here the longest, as she kind of acted like she was leader of the women here. Rolling my eyes, I stood up from my bed and held up my wrist.

"It's just my heart monitor bracelet," I explained, breathing in and out slowly to try and smooth out the pounding in my chest. The woman who fell off her chair, Emmy, nicknamed that because of her emerald-green hair, glared at me like I had physically pushed her off it as she got herself off the ground. The one who swore, named Legs, because of how long her legs were in comparison to her body, seemed to find it amusing that I had startled her.

"You got a broken heart or something, Pinky?" She asked and I lowered my arm again with a slight frown.

"Depends if you mean literally or metaphorically," I commented, feeling slightly more relaxed at the use of my new name. I had learned pretty fast that no body used their real names around here.

"Because it would be a yes to both, I guess," I answered before she could respond. I breathed in and out a bit more, until finally the beeping stopped. I sighed and went to sit on the seat next to Shorty and the woman I had named Smelly, as I actually didn't know her name. She either didn't want to talk or she was mute, because I hadn't heard her speak since I got here.

"Something to do with that Elsie chick you keep asking the pigs about?" Shorty asked, and I nodded my head.

"She's my wife," I answered, my stomach lurching as I said it out loud. It wasn't because I was ashamed or anything; I was pretty certain that Shorty would understand, as she was the most butch looking woman I had seen. I think it was because I was actually becoming more anxious by the second, not knowing where she was. Shorty's eyes lit up, confirming my suspicions.

"Settling down before you're even old enough to tie your shoes by yourself," Shorty chuckled and I narrowed my eyes.

"I'm not that young," I snapped, feeling the sudden need to defend myself. "I turned 18 last month," I added and she laughed more.

"You two must have done something really bad if you're stuck in here with us oldies and not down the road at the juvie center," she retorted.

I bit my lip slightly as I nodded my head again. I didn't want to talk about it. If they hadn't heard about what we'd done, then I didn't want to offer anything up that they could use against me. Besides, I had always thought there was an unwritten rule about not asking other inmates what they did to get put inside. I guess that didn't really matter if you were only at the pre-court stage.

"You don't have to tell me. This isn't my first rodeo, so I can pretty much narrow down what got you here. You've either stolen something that was worth something, had a fuck ton of illicit drugs in your possession, or you murdered someone," she stated matter-of-factly.

I avoided her gaze so she couldn't see which ones I reacted too.

"If I was a gambler, I would take a guess that it might be the drugs, because you don't look like someone who could kill someone," Shorty added.

I looked at her and she let out an awkward chuckle.

"Lucky I'm not a gambler then," she noted, just as Smelly leaned across me, giving me a whiff of her murderous armpits, to hit the pile of cards in front of Shorty to get her to pay attention to the game.

I groaned quietly as I tried to hold back the instant feeling of nausea and pushed my chair back from the table, walking to the front of the cell where the bars were. Shorty chuckled again before returning to the game. Emmy, Legs and Smelly all looked mighty pleased with themselves that they had the attention of their fourth player back.

I sighed and spotted a shadow coming around the corner. I stepped back just as one of the cops came into view. It was Officer Adams. I had managed to not see him over the last few days, but I guess I couldn't be lucky forever. When he saw me, a smirk appeared on his face.

"I always knew you would be in these cells one day, Torres," he stated as he stopped in front of me.

I glared at him.

"That jumpsuit was made just for you," he continued, to mock me.

"Ha. Ha," I responded, spacing my words. "Are you here for a reason, or just to jibe at me?" I questioned, starting to feel irritated again.

"Your lawyer is here to see you," he responded and gestured for me to move back with a flick of his wrist.

I took a step back as he reached for his keys on his side belt and unlocked my door. He grabbed his handcuffs before opening the door and looking at me expectantly.

I walked out of the cell and as per procedure, I turned and put my hands behind my back. He grabbed my wrists and cuffed them together, then put his hand on my upper arm, pulling me back in the direction that he had just come from.

"Where is Elsie?" I asked, wondering if he would actually tell me, considering he knew our history.

"She's been having a vacation in the loony bin," he responded with amusement in his tone.

I stopped in my tracks and looked at him, causing

him to swear and force me to start walking again.

"What do you mean she's been in the loony bin?" I asked.

"She's in the medical unit, being monitored," he clarified, as he pushed open a door with the hand that wasn't holding onto me.

"Monitored for what? She's not crazy!" I retorted, feeling desperate. I had to see her and had to see her *now*!

Officer Adams smirked and shrugged his shoulders slightly, as he pushed me to walk through the door.

"It was ordered by Captain Swanson. Who are we to question his reasons?" He answered, my heart skipping at the name. A relation of Olivia's? Which meant he was related to Elsie, somehow. Officer Adams stopped outside a door and knocked on it before looking at me.

"Captain Swanson is Olivia's father. Their connection isn't exactly a secret around here. I would say he's just concerned about her mental health. From what I've heard, she can't seem to sleep more than an hour at a time or hold down food. But if she's married to you, I suspect she's a lot stronger than everyone is giving her credit for. I wouldn't worry too much," he stated, his tone growing softer as he tried to make me feel better, but at the same time, still make fun of me.

I gave him a weak smile. The man might get on my nerves, but at least he was trying to be nice. He didn't smile back – instead he motioned for me to turn around with a twirl of his finger, which I obeyed and he uncuffed me.

"You've been requested to be uncuffed when she sees you, but that doesn't mean you get to misbehave," he warned as I turned back around. I nodded my head, wondering why on earth he would think I would misbehave now, knowing cops in the States use both tasers *and* guns.

Officer Adams pushed the door open, revealing a woman I had only seen a few times with my father. She was the one who always got him off his drug charges when he was arrested. Considering the police always had enough evidence to put him away for life, I knew she was good.

She was wearing a black pencil skirt and a white blouse that even I had to admit did wonders for her figure. Her hair was done up in a sleek ponytail and she was wearing glasses. I think her name was Camilla. She gave me a small smile then nodded her head to the corner of the room and cleared her throat a little.

Elsie was sitting in a chair, staring at her hands in her lap. I let out a little squeal of excitement, which even surprised me a little, as Elsie lifted her head and her eyes caught mine. She leapt off her chair and ran towards me, just as I opened my arms. When we collided I grabbed her in a tight, you're-never-getting-away-from-me-again type hug. I heard a chuckle behind me just before the sound of the door shutting, indicating that Elsie and I were now alone with our lawyer. Obviously, she had been paid to represent both of us, for which I knew I had my father to thank.

"Elsie," I murmured against her hair, as I buried my face in it. Her hair smelt like vanilla. Whoever was in charge of looking after her was doing a good job, considering the shampoo and the conditioner that I had to use smelled like plain old soap.

"I've missed you so much," I told her, even though in reality it had only been three days since we had been separated this time. The last time had been at least two weeks. I guess I had felt this one a lot harder, because I had known she was in the same building as me, but no one would tell me anything about her.

Elsie put her hands on my hips and pushed off me slightly, making me move my head away from her so she could lean back and look at me. Her eyes had dark circles under them, meaning she hadn't been sleeping. Her face was pale and drawn, like she hadn't been eating. I let out a surprised noise and her cheeks flushed slightly pink, giving her color to her fearfully white face.

"What's going on Elsie?" I asked, looking from her to the lawyer, wondering if she could tell me exactly what was happening to my wife. Elsie looked down and I brought my hand to her cheek and lifted her face up to look at me again. She bit her lip, like she was ashamed.

"Elsie has been put on psych hold," the lawyer offered, in a tone that suggested she didn't agree with it.

I looked up at her with a frown.

"The precinct's captain has it in his head that Elsie is a danger to herself," she continued and I let out a scoff.

"That's absurd," I declared, looking back at Elsie, who looked like she wanted to avoid my gaze.

"That's not true, is it?" I asked, quietly, wondering if it had anything to do with the scream she let out when we were on the plane. I knew she had awakened from a nightmare, but surely that's all it was right? A nightmare?

"The captain is my biological grandfather," Elsie said quietly.

"Olivia mentioned to him that she was concerned for my wellbeing and he ordered for me to be put in a room that is monitored by a nurse at all times," she explained.

My bracelet beeped in warning that my heart rate was getting high, reminding me again that I literally wore my heart on my sleeve. I cursed under my breath.

"It's okay! I've been able to sleep longer than I ever have before," Elsie said quickly, moving her hands from my hips and grabbing my hands instead.

"I've been given sleeping pills which help immensely. Now they're just working on a way to help me keep my food down. For some reason I can't even take a bite of food without throwing it back up immediately," she explained.

I couldn't help but groan.

"You didn't tell me. When did that start?" I asked, thinking back, wondering if I had missed it.

"Not long after I was taken to the police station after being caught at the district court," Elsie admitted, looking ashamed again. "I didn't want to worry you," she added.

I squeezed her hand.

"I'm more worried with not knowing what is going on with you, E," I told her, running my thumb over the back of her hand.

"I'm sorry," Elsie whispered and I moved my hands out of hers and pulled her into another hug.

There was a sound of someone clearing their throat

and I suddenly remembered we weren't alone. I pulled away from Elsie, quickly giving her a kiss on the lips, before turning to look at the lawyer.

"Sorry to interrupt, but time is ticking," the lawyer stated, tapping her wristwatch lightly with the pen that she was holding.

I nodded and let go of Elsie, grabbing the second seat to sit down, while Elsie grabbed the other chair and brought it next to me before sitting down herself.

"I don't think I've ever formally introduced myself to you, Lu," she started, then looked at Elsie and gave her a small smile.

"I am Camilla Pérez Moreno and I have been hired by Jorge to be your lawyer," Camilla stated.

I reached over to Elsie and grabbed her hand. She responded by giving it a gentle squeeze.

"I would say it's nice to officially meet you, but under the circumstances ..." I started, but Camilla just waved her hand lightly and pulled out her seat to sit down herself.

"Now, your arraignment is tomorrow," Camilla started and I gulped.

"You will be read the charges against you by the judge and then asked if you understand those charges," she explained.

"You will then both be asked how you plead to the charges. You have three options. One, guilty; two, not guilty; or three, no contest, which basically means you don't agree that you've committed the crime, but you're willing to accept a conviction," she continued.

My heart started pounding a little quicker. *Breathe, Lucita, breathe.*

"I can only suggest that you plead not guilty, which gives me time to come up with your defense," Camilla stated.

I was guilty for some of the crimes, but there was no way I was going to go down for the murder of Dante – sure I had killed him, but it was to protect Elsie.

"What if I want to plead guilty to some of the charges against us?" I asked.

Elsie squeezed my hand again. I looked over to her and I could see that she was getting anxious, because her leg was jiggling up and down. I squeezed her hand back, trying to reassure her that I was asking this for the benefit of both of us. I looked back at Camilla and she looked at her notes for a second before looking back at me.

"Well, if you're referring to the theft charges and the felony murder of Keith Miller, evading arrest and fraud - " Camilla started, and I nodded my head.

"Then it's up to you. Considering you left a tidbit of information for the detective to find when she woke up after the crash," she paused.

I cringed. That seemed to be a good idea at the time.

"I admitted we were H.E.L.L, but I didn't admit to the murder," I retorted, my cheeks warming. "But yes, there's no point arguing against those charges, because it's clear that we are guilty." I absentmindedly tightened my hand around Elsie's. She let out a little noise and when I looked at her and she looked down at her hand. I immediately let go.

"Sorry," I murmured, only for her to grab my hand again, this time linking our fingers together.

"But I'm not pleading guilty to the murder of Dante Moretti. Or any other murders they're trying to pin on us. Dante was self-defense on behalf of Elsie. Also, Elsie shouldn't plead guilty to the murder of Richard Neilson, either. She suffered years of mental and physical abuse from the man; she just snapped," I finished, looking at Elsie, who was looking at her lap again.

I leaned over and kissed her gently on the cheek. She looked up at me and gave me a small smile. Camilla cleared her throat again and we both looked at her.

"Like I said, it's only my suggestion what you plead. But if you plead not guilty to any of those crimes, normally bail will be set," she continued, moving her notes to the side and putting her pen down. She linked her own fingers together and put her hands on the desk before leaning forward.

"Obviously, because of the fact that the two of you fled the country, you will both be remanded in custody," she stated.

Both Elsie and I nodded our heads in understanding.

"You both will be taken from the court and transferred immediately to New Haven Women's Correctional Facility, where I will meet you there and discuss more options," she explained.

I felt my stomach drop. I had gotten used to staying with the ladies in my cell for the last three days, but prison was going to be a lot harder. At least Elsie would be with me.

"So we're going to be in the same prison then?" Elsie questioned quietly. I looked over to her.

"It's just that I overheard the nurse talking to one of the officers and he was telling her I was going to be transferred to a prison in New York," Elsie whispered, the color and a hopeful look returning to her face.

This was obviously why she looked so depressed.

Camilla gave Elsie a reassuring smile.

"I got confirmation this morning that you are

definitely going to be in the same facility," Camilla announced and the odd feeling in the pit of my stomach finally let go. I hadn't realized how anxious I was about that. I leaned over to Elsie again, just as she turned her head to look at me, and we kissed.

"That's fantastic news!" I stated, once we pulled apart again. This was the happiest I had felt since we were arrested.

"Will they keep me separated?" Elsie asked, her smile fading. "I'm not a danger to myself, I promise. I don't want to die. I just want to be with Lu," she promised, her voice cracking slightly.

I frowned. They thought she was suicidal? I just thought they were worried about her sleeping. I squeezed my fingers against Elsie's and she looked at me. I gave her a look.

"I'm not. I promise. I haven't even thought about it," she added, but I had a feeling in the back of my mind that she was lying to me and to herself. I didn't blame her – I would be a liar too if I said it'd never crossed my mind.

When I almost died after using cocaine, I had told my father that I wished I hadn't awakened. When I killed Keith Miller, if Elsie hadn't taken away my knife, I had thought about using it on myself.

She was still having vivid nightmares after three months.

 She had told me herself that those nightmares felt like she was reliving that night. So much stuff had happened to her over her eighteen years of life that I didn't blame her at all.

"I love you, E and don't you ever think that you're going through this alone," I whispered to her and she nodded her head.

"I know. I don't," she told me. "I love you too," she added, with a smile.

I smiled back then looked at Camilla expectantly.

"I believe they have a psychiatrist lined up to make an assessment. They will confirm your sleeping arrangements after that," Camilla explained, and my heart squeezed slightly. We were still going to be separated after the court hearing. Hopefully it was only for a short while.

"I also have an independent psychiatrist lined up for your defense, Elsie," she continued, looking between the two of us.

"You both have to get used to telling your story over the next couple of weeks, because there will be many interviews, not to mention the actual trial. I suggest putting any feelings aside, get your stories straight and get ready to be in the limelight," Camilla warned.

I nodded my head.

I wasn't completely oblivious to the fact that this wasn't exactly going to be a secret. Sutton was small and our actions over the past several months would have been the highlight of everyone's year. We made Sutton the talk of the country. People, mainly that bitch Ryleigh, were suddenly on TV, giving them their five minutes of fame.

There was a knock on the door and Camilla gathered up her notes and put them in her briefcase just as the door opened, revealing Officer Adams and another officer, which I assumed was there to get Elsie.

Camilla stood. "It was nice to meet you girls, despite the circumstances. I will see you both tomorrow," she announced with a smile.

"Thank you," I said quietly. She nodded then left the room, making the officers step aside for her to pass.

Once she was gone, Officer Adams entered the room first, gesturing for me to stand. I did, but so did Elsie who unlinked our fingers, then took a step towards me and wrapped her arms around my middle.

"Please don't separate us again," Elsie begged, holding me tight like she couldn't let go. I rested my arms over her, trying to hug her back. Her chin went on my shoulder and I leaned my head into hers and closed my eyes. I didn't want to be away from her any longer either. I looked at Officer Adams with pleading eyes, who looked at the other officer. He stepped forward and walked behind us.

"Sorry, Neilson, but rules are rules. You only have one more night here, don't make this any harder," he warned, putting his hand on his side.

I gulped, thinking he was threatening to use his gun, but I noticed that his hand was on a yellow-colored syringe. I frowned. What the fuck? They were going to drug her?

"Surely, if it's only one night, it wouldn't hurt for us to be together?" I said quickly, looking away from the officer's belt back to Officer Adams.

"Take me to the room she needs to be in," I begged, but Officer Adams shook his head.

"It's against protocol, Torres. Let go of her," he instructed, but I shook my head and tightened my grip on her arms. She was squeezing me tightly now.

"Don't make me do this, Neilson," the other officer warned, taking a step closer and pulling out the syringe. He uncapped it, so the needle was sticking out.

"I've told you, it's *Torres Alveraz*," Elsie snapped, making my heart skip a couple of beats. My bracelet beeped in warning.

"Ok, girls, that's enough. Clearly, we don't want to have to drug you. It's just one more night and you can see each other at ten tomorrow morning when you get transferred to court. Don't make this any harder, please," the officer with the syringe pleaded.

I tapped lightly on Elsie's arm. She let out a sigh and loosened her hold around my stomach. It was enough for the officer to recap the needle, put it back in his belt and step forward to pull her away from me. Elsie was handcuffed and forced out the door. She looked back at me, tears rolling down her cheeks.

"I love you, babe!" I called out to her as Officer Adams stepped forward to handcuff me.

"I love you too, *mi amor*," Elsie called back, just before she was out of sight.

"This is totally unfair," I pointed out as Officer Adams secured the second cuff. "She's not suicidal. She's just having nightmares. She shouldn't be put in a psych hold because of that," I protested and he let out a grunt before pushing me slightly to get me to start walking. We headed out the door and towards the cells.

"Better to be safe, than sorry," he retorted.

I rolled my eyes. We walked the rest of the way in silence and soon I was back at my cell, where I was uncuffed again and pushed into the room.

The group of women were still playing cards, only this time they finished quickly to let me join. I accepted, only because I wanted to keep my mind off of Elsie, who was probably still very upset.

Chapter Twenty-Nine
Elsie

When I woke up the next morning, I had a pounding headache. I had not had any nightmares and slept right through the night for the first time since I had stopped drinking, or without having sex beforehand. The headache I had woken up with was worse than my hangovers and I had to put it down to the fact that I had cried for hours after leaving Lu. Everything was sore - my eyes, my head and even my chest. I felt stuffy and gross, which the crying also explained.

I had been awakened at 8:00 a.m. by the nurse who had been caring for me during the nights. She had given me some painkillers and a pill that helped me keep my food down. She stayed with me while I ate my breakfast, which, surprisingly, stayed in my stomach. Clearly the pills were working, because it was then 9:30 a.m. and I still hadn't vomited. Unfortunately, my headache hadn't been affected by the painkillers. The nurse had finished her shift and, since it was my last morning, there wasn't another nurse taking her place.

Instead, an officer was assigned to watch me like a hawk while I got changed into my court clothes. I wanted to hide myself away from him, but he wouldn't have it.

"Get used to it, blondie. Where you're going, you won't even get to shit without someone watching you," he declared, which made my heart drop and my gaze lower as I changed into the white blouse and black dress pants that Olivia had organized for me.

At least I didn't have to change my underwear in front of him. I took a shower the night before and changed them then. Apparently, they didn't have an endless supply of wire-free, lace-free and string-free under garments to distribute like candy so I had gotten used to only changing my underwear every two to three days. Gross.

Once I finished getting dressed, the officer took me to the bathroom so I could relieve myself, brush my teeth and make my hair look presentable. By the time I was done, it was 9:45 a.m. and I was handcuffed behind my back and escorted to a transfer van.

Several other people were being loaded into the back of the van, so it took me a moment to find Lu. She was already in it, looking rather annoyed at the fact that she had been one of the first people to be put in. She was closest to the security screen on the right side.

I was the last one to be loaded into the van, my arms still handcuffed awkwardly behind me and hooked onto an anchor point, keeping me from moving. I looked over at Lu, wishing that I had some kind of superpower that made me strong enough to break away from my chained position to be near her. Instead, I gave her a wide smile and mouthed 'I love you,' because there were two other woman and three other men inside the van and I didn't want to draw attention to us. She mouthed it back just as the van started moving.

The journey to the courthouse was silent. No one was looking at the others, though Lu and I stole glances at each other. Everyone had their heads facing down to their laps.

Someone was sobbing, but I couldn't tell who, as they were doing it so quietly that the only reason why I noticed was because I heard them sniff occasionally. To be fair, if I had any tears left after yesterday, I would be crying also. I was petrified. This was the start of the end of our future.

Lu wanted to plead guilty to most of the crimes we had committed. I knew why – there was no point trying to plead not guilty, when we pretty much had admitted it all anyway. But she wanted to plead not guilty to the murder of Dante and she wanted me to plead not guilty to the murder of the man who abused me.

I knew her reasons for me to plead not guilty made sense. I could probably use temporary insanity as a defense, but what was the point? We were going to go to prison regardless. I felt torn, because I did feel guilty. I had done it. I kept doing it in my dreams. Over and over again. Like I never really left the school hallway. Would pleading not guilty and having to go to court to defend myself cause more distress for me?

I looked up from my lap to see Lu staring at me. When our eyes caught, she gave me a small smile.

'Are you ok?' she mouthed to me and I returned her small smile with a nod. I would be even better if I could hold my wife in my arms.

We turned a corner and the van slowed down to a stop. We felt the van shut off and soon the officers in the front seats got out and opened the van's back doors. The van was inside a metal wire cage, which made escaping impossible. There was even a roof. One by one, we were unhooked from anchor points, uncuffed and re-cuffed in the front and then chained into a line. I was at the back of the line, while Lu was at the front. I'm not sure why they kept us separated, considering we were going to be together soon anyway.

We were taken into the courthouse, stopping periodically as a prisoner was unhooked from the line so they could be put in a room with their lawyer to await their arraignment.

Soon it was just Lu and me left. The officers took each of our arms to escort us to the last room. One of the officers knocked on the door and then waited for Camilla to answer before opening it. They uncuffed us and as soon as we were in the room with the door shut, Lu and I embraced. I had to feel sorry for Camilla, considering we hadn't even acknowledged that she was in the room with us.

"Are you alright?" Lu asked me, pulling back from the hug and kissing me hard on the mouth. I kissed her back, moving my hands to grab her blouse to pull her closer to me. When we parted, I put my forehead on hers and closed my eyes.

"I am now," I replied, softly.

Camilla cleared her throat and Lu and I reluctantly pulled apart and sat down on the two seats in front of the table.

"Your arraignment is at 10:30 a.m.," she announced and I glanced at the clock on the wall behind her and gulped. We had ten minutes.

"As I told you yesterday, be ready to hear the charges, agree that you understand the charges, then you will get to say your plea. Most of your charges are the same, so you will both say how you plead. When it comes to the separate charges, please don't speak until the judge looks at you and has finished talking," she continued and we both nodded in understanding.

"Lucita, I have been warned that you have a temper. Today is not the day to react. The judge on your case doesn't take kindly to unsolicited comments, gestures or noises. If you act out, you will find yourself in more trouble and it's just not worth it," Camilla stated.

Lu actually let out a huff.

"Like that – do that in there and you'll regret it," she said, raising her eyebrow warningly.

"Right, got it," Lu responded, her voice slightly higher than normal as she tried not to react to being told that she had a problem. I reached over and grabbed her hand.

"I won't be doing much talking in this hearing, as there is nothing I could say or do that will keep you from being remanded to jail until your trial," she continued, ignoring Lu's subtle glare.

"Ok," I said with another gulp.

"Any questions?" Camilla asked.

I looked at Lu who shook her head. I looked back at Camilla and bit my lip slightly, as I always did when I was nervous about something.

"Will Olivia be there?" I asked, wondering if I would get to see my mom before I was transferred to prison.

Camilla gave me a small smile and nodded her head.

"She's been here since the court opened. She's waiting in your designated court room. You are allowed to hug and talk to her before the judge enters the room, but you are not allowed to talk to her after he enters, understood?" She asked. I nodded. My heart was pounding, both in fear and in excitement to see Olivia.

I glanced at the clock again. Five minutes. There was another knock on the door and Camilla called out for the person to enter. It was a court officer and one of the officers who came with us in the van.

"It's time," the court officer announced and Camilla stood up and gestured for us to do the same.

We stood, clutching each other's hands. We walked behind Camilla, following her lead, out the door. We stopped, in front of them and the officers handcuffed our hands in front of us. Then they took us by the upper arm and made us continue walking.

We were led through a door and found ourselves in the front of the courtroom. There were several court officers and police officers around the room, standing guard. I cringed noting that all of them had tasers and guns.

I forced myself to look around the room. There was a raised wooden platform at the front of the room, which I assumed was where the judge sat, and what looked like a wooden box with seats in it at the side along the wall, which I could only assume was for the jury. There were two wooden tables in front of a barrier that separated us from the public. At the table closest to the jury box, there was a man sitting down, looking over his notes. He must be the prosecutor. I felt sweat break out on my brow.

My eyes flicked over to the public gallery, which was full of people who had come to see our fate. I swear the whole of Sutton was there. Olivia was sitting in the first row behind the empty table and looked anxious. When she saw me, she jumped to her feet and gave me a smile. I smiled back.

We were led further into the room and I looked around a bit more to see that there was another wooden box next to the judge's, which had to be the witness box. I swallowed nervously thinking of who might testify against me.

We were led to the empty table. Camilla had taken the seat at the end. Lu took the one in the middle and I took the one on the other end, which was directly in front of Olivia.

Once the officers left to stand at the side of the room, I turned around and Olivia threw her arms around me, hugging me tightly. It was impossible to hug her back with my hands behind me, so she was practically leaning over the rail as she tried to pull me closer, which led the court officer to move from his spot, to give us a warning. Olivia let out a small laugh as she let go of me and leaned back, so she was safely behind the barrier.

"How are you doing?" Olivia asked, her hand coming up to cup my cheek. I felt Lu's shoulder against mine as she stood close to me. It was the best we could do, considering I couldn't hold her hand.

"Crappy," I admitted.

Olivia's smile dropped.

"You're sleeping though right? Eating?" She questioned and I nodded. I knew she had something to do with me being put in the hospital wing and despite how upset I was to begin with, I was grateful that I wasn't feeling my stomach eat itself because it was so hungry. I couldn't help but love her more for it.

"Thanks to you," I said with a genuine smile. I felt Lu nudge me, so I looked at her.

"I slept right through the night, last night," I told them.

"And my breakfast stayed down."

Olivia smiled at that and was about to say something, but a man – the bailiff - walked through the door and stood near the judge's seat, followed by a lady that sat down behind another table that housed a computer and keypad.

I turned around to face the front, adjusting myself so I was again shoulder to shoulder with Lu. I started to shake.

"All rise," said the man. Since Lu and I were already standing, we only had to wait for the rest of the court to stand. The only person who wasn't standing was the lady who was at the keyboard, typing away. A man in a black robe walked through another door at the front of the room and walked up on the platform. The first man continued to talk while the judge walked.

"The court is now in session. Honorable Judge Edgar Rogers now presiding. Please be seated," the bailiff instructed, finishing just as the judge sat down. I sat down along with everyone else, my heart now beating so loudly it was the only thing I could hear. The judge looked over at the man at the other table. He stood up and leaned into a microphone in front of him.

"Cooper Wyatt for the prosecution, Your Honor," said the man.

"Thank you, Mr. Wyatt," the judge spoke, then looked at Camilla.

"Camilla Pérez Moreno for the defense, Your Honor," she announced, standing up as she spoke. The judge nodded. She sat back down.

"Thank you, Ms. Moreno," he replied and I couldn't

help but wonder why no one ever called Latinos by their full last names. The judge turned to the bailiff.

"Please continue," he instructed.

"Docket number 1725362 - State of Connecticut versus Elizabeth Rose Neilson."

I felt my stomach drop at the mention of *that* name. I had spent the last two and a half weeks trying to correct people, but clearly no one got the message. I was not Elizabeth Neilson anymore. I was Elizabeth Torres Alvarez. I must have been shaking hard, because Lu bumped her shoulder into me again, so I looked at her.

'It's ok,' she mouthed. I gulped and nodded my head, then turned my attention back to the Judge.

"Miss Neilson, since this is your initial appearance, I want to remind you that you have the right to remain silent; you don't have to say anything at all, at any time regarding these charges. Anything you do say can be used against you. Do you understand?" he asked me.

My mouth went dry. The judge looked at me and my knees started to shake. I stood up, hoping I wouldn't fall on my ass.

"I do, Your Honor," I replied.

He nodded. "Bailiff, please continue."

"The charges are robbery in the first degree, felony murder, larceny in the second degree, manslaughter in the first degree, criminal impersonation and escape from custody."

I noticed that there were only two murder charges. Obviously, they couldn't prove that I had anything to do with the murders of the Moretti family. That, or Jorge, my now father-in-law, had confessed to them.

I was shaking from head to toe. I was glad I didn't have a warning device like Lu, as it would have disrupted the court with a constant beeping.

"Do you understand these charges, Miss Neilson?" The judge asked.

I wanted to correct the name he was calling me, but I remembered Camilla's warning about talking out of turn.

"I do, Your Honor," I said, my voice shaking, as I leaned over to talk into the microphone that was in front of me.

"How do you plead?"

I glanced down at Lu, who was watching me intently with her beautiful eyes that I wish I could get lost in, rather than be there right then.

I flicked my eyes over to Camilla and she gave me a small nod of her head, urging me to hurry up and answer.

"I plead guilty to all except for manslaughter, Your Honor. For that, I plead not guilty," I told him.

I heard what sounded like a relieved cry come from the direction of the public gallery. It didn't take a genius to guess that it was one of Mr. Miller's family members, relieved that I had pled guilty to the crime of murdering their father or grandfather.

Camilla stood up.

"Not guilty, by reason of temporary insanity, Your Honor," she clarified.

My heart was pounding so fast I thought I would pass out, but instead I focused on the judge as he nodded. He looked over at Mr. Wyatt, who looked confused and stood up.

"No objections, Your Honor," he stated and then sat down again. The Judge looked back at me.

"Thank you, Miss Neilson, please sit down," he instructed and I did, thinking it was just in time, before I really did pass out. Lu leaned over and bumped my shoulder. I looked at her and she gave me a small reassuring smile, but I knew she was feeling just as anxious as I was.

The judge turned his attention to Mr. Wyatt, who was still looking slightly puzzled. I guessed he hadn't expected me to plead guilty to any of my crimes. Mr. Wyatt stood and leaned closer to the microphone.

"The prosecution requests remand, Your Honor," he

stated and the judge merely nodded.

"Granted," he replied, so Mr. Wyatt sat down. "Bailiff?" The bailiff went on to call out Lu's docket number. She was charged with the same crimes as me and she pled guilty to all but one. She was also remanded.

Camilla had said her reason for the not guilty plea was because she was claiming self-defense. I sure hope it worked when you were defending someone else. When Lu was sitting back down again, the judge looked at us.

"You will now be transferred to New Haven Women's Correctional Facility, where you will be remanded until your next court date," he told us.

I merely nodded that I understood and lowered my head to look at my lap.

"Court is now adjourned." The judge banged his gavel on his desk, causing me to jump. The bailiff took a step forward.

"All rise," he instructed.

We followed his orders and stood. The judge stood up and left the room.

When the door closed behind him, noise around the room started up. I saw the two officers who brought us move towards us. I didn't know how much time I had, so I turned to look at Olivia who had tears falling down her cheek.

"That was brave of you," Olivia noted, and she put her hand out, which I leaned my cheek into. She rubbed her thumb gently on my face.

"The prosecution might offer you a deal to change your plea," she said quietly and I just nodded, trying to fight back my own tears.

"What deal could they make that would make us change our mind about fighting that charge?" Lu piped up, resting her chin on my shoulder. The officers had come up next to us by this point, which meant that Lu didn't stay there very long. She let out a groan and moved her head before she was pulled off.

"Perhaps a lesser sentence?" Olivia suggested, giving Camilla a hopeful glance.

"Maybe," Camilla responded, but she didn't sound convincing.

I shuddered slightly as I felt a hand on my upper shoulder and Olivia let go of my cheek.

"I will come and see you as soon as I can," she promised and I nodded as I turned to face the officer.

"Murderers!" I heard someone call behind me. I turned to look at where the noise had come from and saw a group of kids from school. My heart stilled when I saw Briar Millar, red-faced and tear-streaked. She was the one who had called it out. An older woman was crying too, holding Briar so tightly I could only assume that it was Briar's mother. She must have been the daughter of Keith. The owner of the jewelry store that we had stolen from. On the other side of Briar, holding her hand and looking at me like she didn't know who I was, was Ryleigh. My heart started beating again, but with a sense of anger brewing.

"You killed my granddad for no reason other than the fact that you two had a hard on for stealing! You even killed your father, Elsie! We saw you! How could you plead not guilty to that?" Briar went on, Ryleigh nodding along in agreement.

I wanted to say something back to that comment, to explain, to tell them to ask Ryleigh how my father abused me, but there was a bump at my side. I turned to look at Lu, who was being forced back by the police officer.

"Just ignore them, Elsie," Lu pleaded, and I was tugged along by the court officer. I was escorted around the table and towards the side door we had come into the room through and soon Lu and I were in the back of the van, getting transferred to the women's prison.

Chapter Thirty

Olivia

It was two days after the arraignment trial that I was finally allowed to visit Elsie. I had received a personal phone call from the warden, Robyn Kennedy, as she happened to be an old friend from high school. Even though we lost touch after I left school to give birth to Elsie, I had run into her a few times over the years because of my job as a police officer.

When she had heard that my daughter was coming to her prison, she had called personally to tell me that she was aware that Elsie was my daughter and all I had to do was text her if I wanted to see her. I had told her I didn't want special treatment, just because she knew me, but something in her voice suggested that wasn't the only reason she called.

I thought back to how Jorge had told me he would sort everything out and I couldn't help but wonder if he had threatened her. It made me feel anxious, because I didn't know what she had been threatened with, but also because I didn't know what Jorge had told her about our situation.

When I arrived at the prison that morning, I was personally welcomed by Robyn. She was waiting on the other side of the reception counter, which was surrounded by a clear screen separating the staff from the public.

Robyn had her hair tied up in a tight bun; not even one loose strand of hair could be seen. She was wearing a navy-blue pencil skirt and white blouse and a matching dress jacket with the logo of the facility on the front. I smiled as I walked up to her, but my smile quickly faded when I noticed that she didn't look at all happy to see me.

"Good morning, Robyn," I said tentatively as I approached her. I held out my hand for her to shake, as I hadn't seen her in a while and I thought trying to hug her would be a bit inappropriate, considering the situation. Robyn nodded her head and shook my hand, before grabbing a clipboard that had been put through a hole in the clear screen by the receptionist. There was a pen attached to the clipboard, which was soon thrust into my hand.

"Fill this out, then we can talk in my office," Robyn announced.

I gulped, suddenly feeling like I was about to be taken to the principal's office, which in all honesty probably wasn't too far from the truth. I filled out the paperwork, signed it and was soon following Robyn through the facility. She had a card attached to her skirt that she used to open every door.

Soon we were walking down a hallway that seemed brighter than the rest of the building, which could only mean that it held the administration offices. Robyn led me into a room at the end of the hallway, unlocking the door with a key this time, and letting me walk through before she shut the door.

"What the fuck, Olivia? You married the head of a Spanish mafia?" Robyn breathed out, clearly having enough of holding it in.

My heart pounded. Of course he had told her we were married.

"Not by choice," I mumbled, looking away from her judging eyes.

She didn't say anything for a moment before letting out a heavy sigh. She walked behind her desk and sat down. I looked up to find her gesturing me to sit in the chair in front of it. I did, awkwardly putting my hands between my knees to stop them from shaking.

"I have agreed to house Elsie and Lu in the same block. At the moment, they are separated, because Elsie is still being seen by a psychiatric doctor. But as soon as she has finished all her evaluations, she will be with Lu. Unfortunately, without causing a full-on riot, they can't be put in the same cell," Robyn started.

I bit the inside of my lip to stop myself from interrupting her, as she didn't sound like she was finished.

"Elsie is in prison for murder. One that, unfortunately, has been talked about throughout the prison, which was beyond our control. Other inmates will try provoking her, so there is only so much I can do to help protect her, if she wants to be kept in the general population.

"Unless I keep her in isolation, she won't have eyes on her 24/7. She'll have to learn to stick up for herself, in ways that doesn't end up getting her put in solitary confinement," she continued.

"Despite what your *husband* wants from me, I won't allow any bad behavior in my prison. Rules are rules for a reason and if I am shown to be giving special treatment to certain inmates, not only will it cause a riot, but it will put a target on your girls' heads. If they break one of my rules, they will be punished accordingly," Robyn stated, looking at me with her stern eyes.

I think our friendship might have ended the moment she was threatened.

"I wouldn't want it any different," I replied with a hard swallow.

"If Elsie misbehaves, by all means, punish her. She

needs to learn that there are consequences for her actions," I stated.

I winced as Robyn raised her eyebrow.

"Not that I'm saying she hasn't learned that already… I want to believe that being in here right now has given her a wakeup call," I added quietly.

Robyn let out a 'hmph' and leaned back on her seat, pulling out a file.

"The only reason I accepted his money, is because the government won't fund the facility to get new library books. It's the only reason I said yes. Do not think that I took his money for personal gain," Robyn told me.

Why was she telling me this? Did she think I was judging her?

"You don't have to explain anything to me. I'm just grateful that you are willing to let Elsie and Lu stay together," I said quietly, moving my hands from between my knees now that I was shaking a bit less.

"To help keep her safe," I added.

Robyn's eyes flicked over my hands and she frowned, eyebrows furrowed.

"Where is your ring? You don't want to announce to the world that you're married to a criminal?" She guessed, venom in her voice.

I turned red.

"Like I said. It's not by choice," I replied, crossing my arms to hide my hands again.

"If anything, I was put in the same position as you," I stated, lowering my gaze.

The room was silent for a moment, until Robyn cleared her throat.

"I guess I should take you to your daughter then," she remarked, as she stood and walked towards her door again.

I stood and followed her. She led me back through the hallways, scanning her card at every door, until we walked into a hospital ward. There were several beds, each separated by a blue curtain.

There were a few inmates occupying the beds, some with injuries that looked like they had been in a fight and others that looked like there was nothing wrong with them at all. I avoided their gaze as I was led past them and was soon brought to the last bed in the room.

All the curtains that surrounded it were shut, so Robyn opened one, revealing Elsie. She was wearing an orange jumpsuit. She was lying on her side, staring at the curtain opposite her, her arms folded and tucked closely to her chest.

"Elsie," I breathed and she rolled over, unfolded her arms and grinned when she saw me.

"Mom!" She exclaimed and I ran over to her and wrapped my arms around her.

"The blond bitch gets a personal visit?" I heard one of the inmates shout, which prompted Robyn to move from outside the curtain to address whoever had spoken. There were no more outbursts after that.

"How are you?" I asked, pulling out of the hug and putting my hand gently on Elsie's cheek. Her eyes widened as she looked at me. At least they weren't dark like they were a couple of days ago when I saw her in court.

"The pills they have given me to help me sleep without nightmares, are really working," she announced with a smile.

"That's good, honey," I smiled and I sat down on the edge of the bed. "How are you feeling though?" I asked, moving my hand to grab hers.

Elsie looked away from me for a moment.

"Depressed," she admitted. "I've been diagnosed with post-traumatic-stress-disorder, severe depression and anxiety. They've given me pills for that too, but I've only started them this morning, so they haven't kicked in yet," Elsie explained in a whisper.

My heart pounded, as I squeezed Elsie's hand. This news didn't surprise me at all.

"Once I'm moved into the general population, I have to come here in the mornings to get my medication," she continued, looking a bit pale. "I don't think I've ever taken so many drugs in my life and that was even with all the pain killers."

"Yeah, we can call her Skittles, cause she's pretty much got every color pill and she has a skittish brain," called out the same voice that, moments ago, had complained about my visit.

"That's enough, Floyd! Don't make me send you to the SHU," I heard Robyn bark out.

I couldn't help but laugh silently when I heard the inmate curse under her breath. She must have been in the next bed over if I could still hear her.

"She's been calling me names since I've been here," Elsie whispered, though by her smile I don't think she minded.

"Skittles is her best one yet," she added with a grin. "I don't mind being called something that has the colors of the rainbow in them."

Her face changed slightly and I couldn't help but wonder where her mind went. I didn't have to wait very long.

"I miss Lu," she sighed and I gave her hand a squeeze.

"You shouldn't have to wait much longer. Have you

had your assessment with the psychiatrist Camilla has hired for your defense yet?" I asked.

Elsie turned red and nodded.

"I would think you should be put near Lu soon then," I concluded. I gave her a small smile.

I heard someone clear their throat and, turning towards it, I saw Robyn standing at the edge of the bed.

"I'm sorry to have to cut this short, but I really can't have you here much longer. The inmates will start wondering what is going on; we don't want them to think she's getting special treatment," Robyn explained, quietly, just so Elsie and I could hear her.

I squeezed Elsie's hand again, nodding.

"I won't get to see you again until your court date. It sounds like Camilla has persuaded the court to start your trial quickly, so your sentencing can happen faster," I said quietly.

"Great. Can't wait," Elsie said sarcastically. I bit my lip, but she just let out a low chuckle and shook her head.

"It's fine, Mom. It is what it is. I did the crime, so I have to do the time," she stated and my heartbeat quickened. At least she was admitting it.

I nodded then leaned forward to give her a hug.

"I love you and I'm on your call list, so call me when you're allowed. I will answer no matter what I'm doing,"

I reminded her as I pulled back and gently moved my hand to tuck a strand of her hair behind her ear.

"I love you too," Elsie whispered and I gave her a weak smile. I stood and turned to follow Robyn, giving Elsie one last wave before leaving the room. I didn't want to say anything else, because I didn't know if I could get myself to leave if I did. Once we were out of the hospital wing, Robyn escorted me out towards the entrance of the facility.

"I've heard a rumor that the trial is set for next Monday," Robyn commented and I nodded.

"I guess because it's such a high-profile case, they want to get it out of the media as soon as possible," I said quietly. "I think if the girls had pled guilty to all charges, they would have been sentenced right then and there at the arraignment." I didn't want to think how long Elsie could be sentenced for.

"Let's hope that their defense lawyer will do what they can to help lower the sentencing," Robyn spoke so quietly, that I knew she was now talking as my friend again rather than the warden. If she wasn't, I'm sure she wouldn't care what they got sentenced. I gave her a small smile as we stopped at the entrance door that we just arrived at.

"Thank you, Robyn," I said quietly, then held out my

hand for her to shake. She just shook her head and pulled me into a tight hug.

"I should have known that you wouldn't marry a criminal on your own accord," she whispered in my ear. "Stay safe and stay out of trouble. I don't want to see you back here for the wrong reasons," she added, then let me go.

I leaned back from her, my face red, as I tried to shake off her words.

"I will," I choked out. I was about to smuggle drugs into the male prison. If I got caught, she would be *my* warden. Robyn waved goodbye and I left the facility, wondering if the next time I was there, I would be in an orange jumpsuit.

Chapter Thirty-One

Lu

It turns out that when you're still waiting for your sentencing to happen, you're put in a different block from the rest of the inmates. You're put in different colored jumpsuits and have different workstations. I was housed in F block, wearing orange, and was forced to do floor mopping duties.

I was mopping the bathroom floors, which, despite how much I put my body weight behind the motions of the mop going back and forth, it felt like I wasn't actually getting any of the muck off. It was disgusting, but at least I didn't have to clean the showers. That was being done by Shorty who happened to be transferred to the prison a day after me and Elsie.

I stared absentmindedly at the wall as I continued to move the mop, wondering if Elsie was okay. It had been three days since we got here and she was still being held in the hospital wing. At least this time I was given updates.

There was a correctional officer who seemed to work the night shift who had come to me every morning so far to tell me if Elsie had slept through the night or not. I had a feeling he was only telling me because he was made to, as he often mumbled something horrid under his breath as he left me. I swear this morning he had called her Skittles.

"Move it, Pinky," snapped the Correctional Officer or, C.O., who was currently watching me, Shorty and another inmate named Roo, because, yes, you guessed it, she was from Australia and still had the accent even though and had become a U.S. citizen over 20 years ago. She was cleaning the toilets. Gross!

I regripped the mop handle that had started slipping because I wasn't paying attention and put it in the bucket of disgustingly brown water. The C.O. was holding onto her two-way radio and had taken a step closer to me, making me realize that she had said something else before she told me to move it and I hadn't heard her.

"Are you deaf, girl?" the C.O. asked, as I dropped the handle, letting it fall against the side of the bucket. I glared at her and glanced at her name badge. B. Rizzo. I wondered if this was the C.O. everyone referred to as 'bitch.' Bitch Rizzo.

"No, I'm not deaf, I just wasn't listening to you," I stated.

C.O. Rizzo narrowed her eyes slightly.

"I said your lawyer is here to see you, so you need to take your mop and bucket back to the cleaning closet," she repeated.

I gulped slightly.

When I had last seen Camilla, after we had been officially processed into the facility, she had told me she wouldn't see us again until the start of the trial, unless the prosecution had a plea deal for us.

Shorty looked up from cleaning her second shower floor and gave me a thumbs up. Since I had been with her in the police precinct and I didn't have Elsie to talk to, we had become kind of close over the last week. She had this supportive 'older sister' vibe. I wouldn't go as far as saying a mother vibe because, while she was definitely old enough, she had made it clear that she wasn't a mothering type and snapped at someone who had called her mama bear only a day after arriving at the prison.

I had told her what Camilla had said about the plea deal and she had advised me to take it, because going through a trial could potentially fuck with my brain. She indicated that the prosecution would dig up every dirty secret about me and my family. Since my past was filled with secrets that I would rather stay buried and not come up in public, I had hoped that something like this would happen. I just hoped it was a good deal.

I picked up the heavy bucket of dirty water, leaned

the handle of the broom against my chest and started walking to the door. C.O. Rizzo opened the door for me and followed behind as I walked to the cupboard down the hall. I put down the bucket and opened the door.

The cupboard wasn't that big – it had a sink and several other mops hanging along the wall. There were a few more buckets stacked on top of each other that were pushed into the corner, allowing just enough room to stand in to empty the water into the sink.

I pushed the lever of the bucket with my foot and drained the water from the mop. I hung it up with the others, then picked up the bucket and emptied it into the sink. Putting the bucket near the others, I shut the cupboard door then turned to face C.O. Rizzo, who was impatiently waiting for me, hands on her hips.

"Hurry up, I have to get back to the others," she stated and I couldn't help but roll my eyes.

"I'm clearly done. Are you blind, Officer?" I asked, before I could stop myself. C.O. Rizzo's face turned red. She looked like a tomato. She stepped forward and grabbed onto my upper arm tightly.

"That's a shot, Alvarez," she declared.

My heart pounded at hearing my mother's name.

I didn't often get called that, because white people tend to forget that Hispanic people have two last names.

Usually I was just called Torres. It was only ever Torres Alvarez when it was something official.

"Just stick with Pinky, then you won't embarrass yourself by calling me by the wrong name," I pointed out, trying to loosen her grip as she started pushing me to walk in the direction of the lawyer rooms.

"And another," she noted and I had to bite my tongue to stop myself from saying something else. I didn't want to end up in the place they called the 'SHU.' Shorty had said that solitary confinement was another place that fucks with your brain. I stayed quiet for the remainder of the way.

The only sound was the beeping from the card that C.O. Rizzo used to unlock the doors. I noted that I would need to steal one of those if I wanted to escape.

No, Lucita. No.

When we got to the part of the prison that had several empty rooms big enough for a few people to meet at a time, C.O. Rizzo knocked on the door and opened it. She let go of my arm, but not before she dug her nails into my skin, causing me to yelp.

"Problem?" She asked, raising her eyebrow.

I put my hand on my arm and glared at her. Yep, she was definitely the bitch. She was looking at me like she was daring me to say something. I knew she could turn around, just like that, slot me or give me another shot which could affect any deal I got offered so I dropped my hand and shook my head. There was no point trying to say something against her.

"No, no problem," I mumbled, through my gritted teeth.

"Thought so," she replied and then grabbed the door and shut it in my face. I wanted to scream, but instead I took a deep breath and turned around to find Elsie and Camilla sitting, waiting for me. Elsie was looking at me with concern and Camilla looked uncomfortable, like she knew what just happened, but didn't want to say anything.

"I'm fine," I stated with a grin and hurried over to Elsie, who had stood up, and wrapped my arms around her. I buried my head into her neck and she squeezed me around my waist.

"I've missed you," I whispered and pulled back to look at her. Her face had brightened in color and she no longer had dark circles under her eyes.

"You look better," I stated.

She grinned at me. "I feel better too," she replied.

I beamed. We sat down on the chairs, grabbing onto each other's hands as we turned to face Camilla.

"Please say it's good news," I said, my heart beating

faster in anticipation. I hoped it wasn't too much of a change in my rhythm, because the last thing I needed was for my bracelet to start alerting me that I needed to calm down. It was bad enough that the noise was infuriating, but now it also sent an alert to the prison doctor who would tell someone to get me. At least I wasn't around other inmates right now. Camilla nodded her head with a small smile.

"Somewhat good news," Camilla stated. She leaned forward and grabbed something out of her opened briefcase. She pulled out two sheets of paper and put one in front of me and one in front of Elsie. They had our names on the top and lots of words underneath that I could not be bothered reading.

"Want to dumb it down for us?" I asked, with a slight laugh.

Camilla shook her head slightly in amusement.

"Basically, the prosecution has offered a lesser charge if you change your plea to guilty. For both charges, it would be manslaughter in the second degree. Elsie, yours is with a firearm, so instead of twenty years, you would be given the minimum sentence of one additional year for that one crime," Camilla explained, pushing Elsie's paper a bit closer.

I saw Elsie screw her nose up slightly and I wondered

what was going through her head. I gave her hand a squeeze and she looked at me, her eyes glistening with the tears that were threatening to escape.

"Lu, if you agree to the change of plea, you will also get an additional year for that crime," Camilla continued, turning her attention to me.

I took a deep breath. One additional year was better than another possible twenty years. I was sure with the felony murder, for that crime alone, I was going to get twenty-five years at least. I continued to look at Elsie, who was focusing on me as she tried not to let the tears fall.

"What do you think?" I asked quietly.

Elsie let out a sob.

"I don't want to change my plea. I've had a lot of time to think about it and I know I wouldn't have done it if he hadn't abused me for years. If he hadn't caused me so much pain and suffering. I shouldn't have to plead guilty, when I no longer feel guilty about doing it," Elsie whispered and I squeezed her hand again.

This was her choice. She had the right to fight against that charge. But I had made my mind up about mine. Even if I had to be in prison a year longer than Elsie, I was going to change my plea. If she was found guilty and had to serve more years because she got the maximum sentence for manslaughter in the first degree, then I would have to deal with that when it happened.

"I think you would have a good chance of being found not guilty due to temporary insanity," Camilla agreed.

I turned to look at her and I saw she was watching me closely.

"What about you, Lu?" she asked and I gulped looking back at Elsie for a moment. She watched me closely and then nodded her head, like she knew what I was going to do. I let go of her hand and held mine out towards Camilla, motioning for her pen.

"Alright. I'll agree to the deal," I stated, my heart fluttering. I started breathing in deeply as Camilla handed me her pen. I breathed out as I brought the pen to the paper and literally signed my life away. For a year anyway. Elsie's hand found its way to my thigh and she gave it a small squeeze. I put the pen down and let out a large sigh.

"What are we looking at in terms of sentencing for the other crimes?" I asked, wondering for the first time since I pled guilty, if we had made a mistake for not trying to fight it. If pleading not guilty was enough to lessen the charge and get a lower sentence, maybe we should have taken Camilla's advice and said not guilty for all.

Camilla linked her fingers together and let out a small

sigh. I think she was annoyed that we hadn't taken her advice too.

"For the felony murder alone, you could get anywhere from twenty-five to life," she told us and Elsie let out a gasp, like she had been holding in her breath. I put my hand on hers, moving it so I could link my fingers with hers. I held onto her hand tightly.

"Five years for the robbery charge, up to ten for the larceny charge, one year for the criminal impersonation and ten years for the escape," Camilla listed. I let out a groan.

"So, we're pretty much fucked for life then?" I responded, gripping Elsie's hand tighter. She was squeezing mine just as hard. I'm pretty sure the circulation in our hands was getting cut off. Camilla gave us a sad look, which confirmed it all.

"If the judge is considerate, you might have the chance to get parole after serving a number of years. However, that depends on your behavior while you're in here," Camilla offered, raising her eyebrow at me.

"I can behave," I replied, feeling slightly defensive.

"You've been here for three days and you're already in Rizzo's bad books," Camilla countered pointedly.

"Yeah, well. She's a bitch," I retorted, shrugging my shoulders.

"This isn't high school, Lucita. You are in prison. Your misbehavior can get you in serious trouble. I have had clients that have spent weeks, months even, in isolation due to their behavior and they do not come out the same," Camilla explained.

I shivered slightly. I had heard this before.

"Years could be added to your sentence, if it's bad enough. You could say something to the wrong person and get yourself killed. You have to watch your mouth," she pleaded.

I shifted uncomfortably in my seat.

As soon as I was moved to my permanent unit after sentencing, the first thing I was going to do was make myself a shiv. There was no way I was going to be walking around unprotected. I would have to make one for Elsie too.

"I will try," I stated.

"You have to do more than try, Lu. Your father has asked me to make you promise. Promise on your mother," she stated, giving me a look that made me realize she had more of a relationship with my dad than I had first suspected. He would have never brought my mother into the promise if it wasn't. He would do what he could to get that message to me himself.

I closed my eyes and took a deep breath again.

"Sometimes I can't control it, no matter how hard I try," I pointed out, after I breathed out again.

"Just think before you speak," Camilla suggested.

I let out an awkward laugh.

"Easier said than done," I countered. "But I will promise to try my best."

Elsie tugged her hand out of mine and put it on my cheek, making me look at her.

"I will distract her with my mouth, if she looks like she's about to speak out of turn," Elsie stated and my eyes went wide at the thought of her going down on me in front of C.Os and other inmates.

Camilla awkwardly cleared her throat.

"Kissing!" She clarified quickly, looking horrified. "I meant I would kiss her to stop her talking."

I laughed.

"But, that would definitely come later," she added.

"Are you trying to be helpful, or just make me want to speak my mind on purpose?" I asked, with a grin. "Because that would definitely make me want to bad mouth the bitch, if it means I will *come* later."

Elsie groaned and Camilla grabbed my signed piece of paper and then Elsie's, trying to ignore us.

"I'll just shut up now," Elsie declared, her face turning red as she let go of my cheek.

I grinned.

Camilla closed her briefcase and stood.

"Your trial starts on Monday. Lucita, you will state your change of plea, then it will be all about Elsie. It shouldn't take longer than a week, but it will get tiring. I suggest you both keep your heads down, do your work assignments, don't start any fights and get as much sleep as possible. You're both going to need your strength," she instructed, then walked over to a button that was on the wall and pushed it.

"I'll see you both on Monday," she said as she turned back just as the door opened.

A moment later, she left the room and Elsie and I were both escorted back towards my block. I thought we'd walk past the hospital wing, to drop off Elsie, but to the surprise of both of us, the C.O took us to where they hand out the welcoming kit, which consisted of a spare jumpsuit, a toothbrush, toothpaste, shampoo and conditioner, soap, a couple of towels, a couple sets of non-wire, non-elastic underwear and a pair of plain white sneakers.

After Elsie received her pack, we were finally led back to F block, where Elsie was put in a cell opposite mine. I would have much rather been put together, but she was sharing a bunk with Shorty, which gave me comfort that she was at least going to be protected at night by someone who knew how much I loved her and who I trusted.

Monday came quicker than I expected. When the lights were turned on and a baton was run along the cell bars, forcing me to wake up at the god-awful time of 6:30 in the morning, my heart pounded in anticipation at what the day was going to bring.

The cell doors automatically unlocked and I could hear the C.Os calling, telling us it was time for a head count. As if anyone could escape at night, considering we were locked behind cell doors, couldn't get past the building doors without a swipe card, and the guards on the outside walked above the prison walls with rifles in their hands. It would be suicide to even try.

I groaned as I pushed back my barely-thick-enough-to-call-a-blanket blanket and stood up. My cellmate, a woman called Floss, jumped down from the top bunk, causing my heart to pound faster as I hadn't expected her to be so chirpy so early in the morning. My hand went on my chest, just as my bracelet started beeping.

"Way to give a girl a heart attack," I muttered, just loud enough for her to hear. She glared at me for a moment, before looking at my bracelet. The truth was,

I'm pretty sure it wasn't her that was causing my heart to act up. I was nervous about today, considering what Elsie was about to go through.

"What the fuck is that?" Floss asked, reaching forward and grabbing my wrist to investigate it. We probably had about two seconds to get to the front of the cell before the C.Os gave us a shot for not being where we were meant to be, but I wasn't about to let this woman touch me, when she didn't have my permission.

"It's none of your fucking business, that's what it is," I snapped in reply as I yanked my arm out of her grip.

"Alright, grumpy, calm down," Floss replied and put her hands in the air in mock surrender.
I narrowed my eyes at her and she turned to walk in front of our cell.

I followed close behind her, trying to regulate my breathing to calm down my heart, but the mixture of annoyance, nervousness, and tiredness made it difficult.

I flicked my gaze across to the other side, feeling a calmness wash over me as my eyes landed on Elsie. She waved at me, putting her hand on her own chest just above her heart. I saw her mouth move and I could just make out that she was asking if I was okay. I nodded my head.

C.O. Rizzo stopped walking as she got in front of me

and glared down at my wrist, which was still beeping. Stupid fucking thing.

"Does that thing have a shut the fuck up button?" She asked.

"I suppose it will turn off if my heart decides to stop pounding because I had to look at your ugly face," I snapped back, cursing myself instantly.

Floss tried to hide her laugh by coughing instead.

I heard a groan, which I knew right away belonged to Elsie. C.O Rizzo's eyes narrowed even further and I was sure if she wasn't in front of several inmates and another correctional officer, she would have slapped me.

"That's another shot, Torres. If you didn't have your court appearance today, that comment would have put you in the SHU," she announced loud enough for the whole of F block to hear.

She continued to walk past me to carry on the count and it was a miracle that I felt my heart return to its normal beat and my bracelet stopped making the horrid noise. I looked over at Elsie who shook her head at me. I gave her a sly smile and a small shrug of my shoulders. The other correctional officer, C.O Wright, cleared his throat.

"Alright, hit the showers, ladies!" He called out and everyone, me included, went back into our cells to retrieve our toiletries, towels and a change of clothes. It wasn't long until I met up with Elsie in the bathroom.

"You're lucky she didn't send you to the hole, regardless of court!" she exclaimed, just as I pushed past another inmate, whom I didn't know, to get to the shower before her. Elsie slipped in behind me and I closed the curtain. The shower cubicle was small, but it was still big enough to share it.

"I know. I'm sorry. She just gets on my nerves," I replied, as I hung my towel up on the hook. Elsie followed suit and then began to take off her prison-issued pajamas. I watched her undress and she gave me a scowl.

"Stop watching me, Lu. We only have five minutes," she reminded me, causing me to let out a small moan of annoyance.

It was the only time we could get naked together these days. I hoped when we were put in the general population we would get more naked time together, where I could take all the time I wanted to watch her. Not to mention do other things, that kept me up most nights because I couldn't stop thinking about making her scream.

I got undressed as Elsie turned on the shower. We stepped in a moment later and started washing ourselves and quickly washed our hair. Not long after we both rinsed the conditioner out of our hair, the shower automatically shut off. That in itself was a crime. We quickly dried ourselves and got dressed.

The rest of the morning went by quickly, filled with breakfast and a quick check up by the nurse in the hospital wing, me for my heart from its earlier alert and Elsie because she had to take her meds.

We were then taken to a room that was similar to the one where we were strip searched when we first arrived, so we could get changed into normal clothes for court. Elsie wore blue jeans, a white blouse and a black jacket. I was given black jeans, a light blue blouse and to my amazement, a pink blazer. I was pretty sure Olivia might have something to do with my outfit, or even my father somehow.

By the time we were put in the back of the transfer van, it was 9:30 a.m. and we had half an hour until we were due in court. Elsie and I stayed silent on the way to the courthouse, as C.O. Wright was sitting in the back of the van with us. However, thanks to the fact that they had handcuffed us with our hands in front of our bodies, it didn't stop us from holding onto each other's hands.

Elsie was shaking with fear. Her legs were jiggling up and down and I could see that she was chewing on her bottom lip. I kept rubbing my thumb across the back of her hand, in hopes of calming her down, but she was just too wired.

When we got to the courthouse and stepped out of the van, the driver and C.O Wright recuffed us so our hands were behind our backs. C.O Wright took my upper arm, while the driver took hold of Elsie. I think his name was C.O Morgan.

They escorted us inside the courthouse and we were taken to a set of chairs outside a room that said 'Court Room One.' They cuffed us to the chairs, so there was no way were could even stand up without having to rip the seats out of the wall to escape. Now my legs were starting to jiggle as the time ticked closer to 10:00.

Camilla walked down the hallway, stopping in front of us, just as the court door opened and the same bailiff who was at our arraignment poked his head around the door.

"You can come in now," he told us, although he was looking at Camilla and the correctional officers.

We were uncuffed, which was a pleasant surprise, and escorted into the courtroom. Cooper Wyatt, the same prosecuting attorney, watched us as we walked in.

I focused my gaze on the public gallery. Once again, the room was already filled with people. I could see Briar Miller and her family. Ryleigh. Mrs. Moretti.

My mouth went dry when my eyes landed on her. She was staring straight at me, her eyes glaring. I swear, if looks could kill, I would be dead. Beside her was a scary looking man. You could tell that he was Italian too. He looked slightly younger than Mrs. Moretti - maybe her brother? He was holding onto her arm, whispering something into her ear, which made her look away from me.

I breathed out in relief and focused on walking behind the table, standing close to Camilla, with Elsie on my other side. Olivia was sitting right behind us again. She gave Elsie a quick hug and then turned to give me one too. She didn't say anything to us though – it looked like if she opened her mouth, nothing would come out but sobs.

Beside her was Mrs. Taylor, who hugged Elsie while Olivia had hugged me. She didn't have her baby with her. I guess you don't bring your baby to things like this. I was surprised when she turned to hug me, but I gave her a quick hug back before the bailiff stood in front of everyone and cleared his throat.

"All rise," he instructed. The room all stood up in unison and soon the judge emerged from his room. I zoned out as the bailiff spoke again, only hearing my heartbeat in my ears. I watched the judge as he made his way to his platform and sat down.

I felt a tug at my arm from Elsie and I realized I had missed the bailiff telling us to sit down. I swallowed and quickly sat down.

There was water on the table and I leaned forward and poured myself a glass. I went to take a sip just as I heard my name being called out. Damn it. My throat was dry and I didn't have time to drink it.

"Please stand," the bailiff instructed me. He sounded annoyed, so maybe he had to repeat himself. I gulped again, trying to lubricate my throat, as I stood up. My hands flopped to my side and almost immediately, my left hand was grabbed by Elsie. Camilla had stood up with me. The judge looked at me and leaned forward to talk into his microphone.

"Lucita Torres Alvarez, the prosecution has put to you an agreement of a reduced charge of manslaughter in the second degree with a sentence of one year, in exchange for a change of plea," the judge stated.

"Yes, Your Honor," I agreed, swallowing as if there was a lump in my throat.

"How do you plead to the charge?" he asked me. Elsie squeezed my hand as I leaned forward to the microphone in front of me.

"Guilty, Your Honor," I replied, my voice sounding

foreign.

"Mr. Wyatt?" the judge asked the other lawyer, who I had just noticed was standing up as well.

"The prosecution rests on the case of Lucita Torres Alvarez," Mr. Wyatt announced and the judge nodded.

"Very well. Officer, please escort Miss Torres Alvarez out. We will see you back here for the rest of your sentencing next week," the judge stated and I froze.

"Wait what?" I asked, feeling my heart pound faster.

Elsie gripped my hand tightly. Camilla leaned over to me.

"Please, Lu, don't start anything. Just follow the officer," she pleaded.

I looked at her, blinking away the tears that were threatening to leave my eyes.

"I'm not going anywhere. I'm staying here with Elsie," I whispered.

Camilla just shook her head. She didn't warn me about this. Why didn't she tell me I couldn't stay?

"Is there a problem, Ms. Moreno?" the judge asked.

Camilla gave me a pleading look, before turning back to him.

"No, Your Honor," she responded.

There was a problem. A *big* problem. Elsie squeezed my hand again and I looked down at her. She just mouthed that she would be okay and let go of my hand. I looked at her for a moment before giving her a small nod and then looked at C.O Wright who had brought out his handcuffs.

Olivia gently patted my shoulder as I walked behind Elsie's chair. I looked at her and she gave me a reassuring smile. Mrs. Taylor gave me the same look. When I reached C.O Wright, he made me turn and cuffed me behind my back and started to escort me out.

"You should get more than a year for murdering my boy!" shouted a very upset Mrs. Moretti.

I wanted to turn back to respond, but I was gently pushed forward. The judge had said something to her instead and soon I was on the other side of the courtroom, leaving Elsie to be tried by herself.

Chapter Thirty-Two
Elsie

With my heart pounding in my ears rather than my chest, the rest of the day went by in a blur. Glasses of water kept getting pushed into my hands and I drank them, not even aware of what I was doing. The twelve people who made up the jury had entered, gotten sworn in and the trial started and the whole time all I could think was that my heart was really loud.

Olivia and Mrs. Taylor had to leave, because they were witnesses for the defense. My defense. Ryleigh also left and so did a bunch of other people I didn't know

Mr. Wyatt started off by saying that there was no doubt that I had murdered my father, but I zoned out, staring at the glass of water that I had my hand around.

People came and went as witnesses to my crime. They told the jury what they had seen me do. Camilla sometimes stood up and shouted 'objection,' which was followed by a lot of talking, but most of it was just gibberish to me. The gun I used was shown as evidence. Pictures of Richard on the ground were shown. I zoned out of everything.

It wasn't until we were dismissed for the day that I finally came back to my senses. I was escorted out of the courtroom, handcuffed behind my back. As soon as I got out of the courtroom someone bowled into me from behind and squeezed me in a hug. The wind was knocked out of me and I had to catch my breath and pull back to realize that it was Olivia.

"Mom!" I said before bursting into tears. She tried to comfort me by rubbing my back and quietly shushing me in my ear, as I awkwardly leaned into her, my head on her shoulder. I wished I could wrap my arms around her too, but they didn't give me enough time to even move my arm, because I was pulled away just as quickly.

"Sorry, ma'am, but we have to get her back to the prison," said the man who was escorting me out of the courtroom. He was the driver of the van this morning. I moved my head and looked at his name tag. G. Morgan. Olivia quickly kissed me on the cheek and stood back.

"I'll see you tomorrow," she said quietly and I just nodded before I was taken away and led back to the van.

The correctional officer, Wright, was waiting in the passenger seat. Lu wasn't anywhere to be seen. I assumed she had already been taken back.

It didn't take long until I was reunited with her. She had spent the day in solitary confinement, because she had kicked Wright in the shin when he tried to get her in the van, but she was released from it that night, because someone else who had done something worse needed the cell. I didn't get to spend a lot of time with her though, only through dinner and an hour in the common area before lights out.

I couldn't wait until we were allowed to spend the day together. I missed her so much.

When we woke up the next morning, the count went off without a hitch. Lu didn't mouth off to Rizzo as she passed, despite Rizzo saying stuff to provoke her on purpose. We had a shower together and then had breakfast.

It wasn't long until I was sitting in the courtroom again. I kept ahold of the glass of water because, for some reason, this kept me calm. Camilla leaned over as she topped it off for me.

"I know yesterday was a lot, but today is about you and your defense. The doctor will be talking about your frame of mind at the time. Olivia will also be testifying," Camilla explained, as she put the jug back down. "Ryleigh will be testifying."

I looked at her with my eyebrow slightly raised.

"How did you manage to get her to agree to help defend me?" I asked, my heart skipping slightly.

"She wasn't really happy about it…" Camilla admitted and I let out a soft chuckle.

"I bet she wasn't," I retorted, picking up the glass and taking a sip. My hand was shaking so much that the water splashed up the sides and over my hand. Camilla handed me a neatly folded handkerchief, with a look of pity and was about to say something, but the bailiff stood up in the front and told us to stand for the judge.

I quickly wiped the water off my hands before standing up just as he walked through the door. He made us sit down and once again I stared down at the glass of water and heard nothing but my own heartbeat.

The doctor who had assessed me on my first day at the prison was the first to testify on my behalf. I tried to focus on what he was saying, what Camilla was asking him, but I just couldn't. What if he said nothing was wrong? What if he didn't want to agree that I was insane at that time? I glanced over to the jury and I could see by their intense faces that they were taking in everything he was saying.

Maria was next. I paid a bit more attention, because I knew she would be on my side. Camilla introduced my medical records through this testimony. I saw the jury foreperson flinch when the photo of my cut back was shown. A jury member in the back row looked like she was going to be sick. I could see the man sitting down in the front at the end clench his fists when they showed my black eye. When the finger bruises were shown around my upper arm, I saw a man in the back place his hand over his mouth.

After Camilla's questions, Mr. Wyatt stood to ask his questions.

"Did you see Mr. Neilson commit these alleged abuses?" he asked her.

Her answer was, of course, no.

"Did Miss Neilson report these assaults to the police?" he asked.

Again, no.

He sat back down and Maria was escorted from the witness box. She looked over to me and gave me a smile full of pity as she left the room.

Camilla called a doctor I didn't recognize next. He was old and it turned out that he was the doctor who had been at every incident when I ended up in the hospital. He was the doctor who had actually saved my life when I had a shard of glass in my lung.

Camilla asked him about Richard's behavior when he brought me in all those times. Asked how I had reacted and if it was the same as other children who were abused. He said yes.

Camilla asked if he had called the police on my behalf.

He said yes.

Did he call child protective services?

He said yes.

Mr. Wyatt asked if my injuries could have happened the way Richard had said they had happened. The doctor said no. I couldn't help but smile a little at that, considering it made Mr. Wyatt slightly flustered. After that, he finished his questions quite quickly.

Olivia was next. My heartbeat pounded more as she talked about my reactions being near him. How I would have a panic attack and throw up just being in the same vicinity as him. She was asked about what I had disclosed to her, about everything I had remembered about growing up with Richard.

Mr. Wyatt kept calling out his objections and something about hearsay, but Camilla kept reminding him that Olivia was the outcry witness, because she was the person who first heard an allegation of abuse made by a Child – me - so it was allowed.

Olivia kept glancing at me, giving me small smiles, which I returned, without actually feeling anything.

Mr. Wyatt questioned her about her relationship with me. Asked her if she was biased because I was her daughter. The jury lapped that up. I couldn't help but feel like that made them doubt that Olivia was a creditable witness.

Camilla then called Ryleigh. I sat up straighter as she walked up into the witness box. She put her hand on the Bible and swore that she would speak nothing but the truth. When she sat down she looked at me without emotion as if she didn't even know me.

"On the 14th of August 2016, did you witness an incident involving Richard and Elizabeth Rose Neilson?" Camilla asked her.

Ryleigh nodded and leaned forward, her hand slightly shaking as she held the microphone neck.

"Yes, I did," Ryleigh spoke, her voice betraying her nervousness.

"Can you tell us what happened please, Miss Atkins," Camilla requested.

Ryleigh nodded again.

"Elizabeth and I were playing with her late mother's clothes and wigs," Ryleigh started and my heart slowed to the point that I thought it was going to stop.

"Mr. Neilson had left us at their house, to quickly do something at the funeral home. He came home to find us in the room and he was really angry," Ryleigh continued.

She let go of the neck of the microphone and sat back a little. I could tell that her leg was jiggling. She was just as nervous about being up there as I was to hear her talk.

"He kicked me out and then started yelling at Elsie. Sorry, Elizabeth," she stated and she glanced at me, nervously. I looked away from her and took a sip of my water, being careful to not spill it on myself again.

"I didn't want to leave while he was still yelling, so I hid in the entrance way, which was just by the den where Mr. Neilson had dragged Elizabeth," she continued.

"I looked around the archway and watched. Mr. Neilson was really angry, yelling in her face. Elizabeth stood up from the couch and ran away from him, running straight into the closed glass door of their sliding door," Ryleigh stated so confidently, that I almost didn't realize she had lied. I put the glass down on the table, hard. I tried to stand up and Camilla quickly moved over to me.

"It's okay, Elsie. Calm down," she said to me, knowing I was getting upset. She turned back to Ryleigh.

"You do know it's a crime to lie under oath?" Camilla reminded her.

"I'm not lying. That is what happened," Ryleigh replied, confidently. Camilla walked backwards to her desk and picked up a report.

"I would like to put this police interview of Ryleigh Atkins conducted by Detective Olivia Swanson on the 19th of March 2022, into evidence," Camilla announced to the judge who leaned forward and grabbed the report that she was holding out to him. He read it over quickly and then nodded his head.

"Please put it down as exhibit H," he stated and the court clerk who was at a table filled with other evidence put a similar piece of paper forward. Camilla walked the report over to Ryleigh, who took it. Her hands were no longer shaking as she looked down at it.

"Please read the highlighted sections," Camilla instructed.

"'Mr. Neilson picked her up by her hair and threw her on the glass coffee table, so hard that the glass shattered,'" Ryleigh read. She paused and looked up at Camilla.

"Carry on please," Camilla ordered.

"'Blood started seeping from Elsie's chest and Mr. Neilson picked her up and I saw a large piece of glass sticking out of her,'" Ryleigh continued.

"Did you say this at the interview with Detective Swanson?" Camilla asked her.

"Yes I did," Ryleigh replied, putting the report down on the edge of the witness box.

"Why would you say that in the interview, if you're testifying today that something else happened?" Camilla asked, raising her eyebrow slightly.

I could see her as she was standing side-on, so she could

see me in the corner of her eye. I gripped the glass of water so tightly that my fingers were turning blue.

"You also told everyone on live television that is what happened; why would you change your story now?" Camilla continued.

"Earlier on that day of the interview, Elizabeth had broken my nose and threatened me," Ryleigh announced, looking around at the jury.

"She had threatened she would get her girlfriend, Lucita, to cut me if I didn't tell Detective Swanson that her father had hurt her. I was still thinking she would kill me after killing Richard if I didn't speak about it on TV," she explained.

"She's lying!" I shouted, just as the glass under my fingers shattered and water went all over the desk and my pants.

The glass cut my hands and blood started spreading everywhere. Camilla swore slightly under her breath as she hurried over to me. C.O Cooke, who was standing guard, hurried over too. I cried as the pain overtook everything I was feeling. I was pulled from my seat and my hands were wrapped in a white cloth that was saturated by my blood in seconds.

I heard the gavel being pounded over my crying and I saw people moving, but I was hurried out of the courtroom so fast that I didn't actually know what was happening. Everything happened so fast. One minute I was crying with pain, trying to get out of the tight hold of the C.O and the next minute I felt a sharp pain in my upper arm. The pain started to fade, but so did everything around me. The last thing I saw was the psychiatric doctor who had assessed me, who had clearly stayed behind after his testimony, in case I went crazy. Everything went black.

~.~

It turned out that they had ended court for the day after my outburst. I had woken up in the hospital wing, chained to the bed. Lu was beside me, her upper arm bandaged. She was watching me so intently I swear she wasn't even blinking.

"What happened to you?" I breathed, groaning as I tried to lift myself up, but the pain in my hands stopped me.

"Got in a fight. Floss stabbed me with her toothbrush shiv," Lu replied, with a small shrug of her shoulders.

"Lu! She could have killed you!" I said, my eyes going wide.

She shrugged her shoulders again.

"Nah. She only stabbed me 'cause I let her. I wanted an excuse to be in here. I could have stopped her if I wanted to," Lu replied, moving her body so she was closer to the edge of the bed, so therefore closer to me.

I couldn't help but wonder if the rest of the beds were already full, or if she had paid a nurse to get the bed closest to mine. That, or we were just incredibly lucky.

"They had to take twenty pieces of glass out of your hand," Lu said quietly. I winced, trying to move my hands to look at them. Of course, they were covered in bandages and it didn't help that my right arm was cuffed to the bed.

"I'm going to kill Ryleigh," Lu said so quietly that only I could hear her.

"Not if I kill her first. How do you know about Ryleigh?" I asked, my heart beating at the thought of even more betrayal by my former best friend.

"Olivia came to visit you while you were still out," Lu explained and I frowned slightly, wishing that she was still here.

"The warden made her leave, because the other inmates were complaining about your so-called special treatment," Lu added.

I nodded.

"Right. Was Floyd the instigator?" I asked, thinking of the inmate who kept calling me names and pointed that out the first time Olivia had come to visit me.

"Yes, actually," Lu replied with her own frown. "I don't like her."

I couldn't help but laugh.

"I'm pretty sure she doesn't like me either, considering when I first met her I was apparently 'fresh meat,' then too white and crazy for her. She's the one that started calling me Skittles, you know," I told Lu, who wrinkled her nose.

"They could have come up with a name that doesn't have anything to do with over-the-counter pills," Lu retorted and I laughed slightly, glad that Lu was with me, even though she had to get hurt to be here. It made the events of today seem less frightening.

"I like it. It reminds me of the rainbow," I stated and Lu smiled at me.

"How're your hands feeling?" She asked.

I lifted up the non-cuffed hand and turned it in front of me.

"Like I've been stabbed a dozen times," I admitted. Clearly, they hadn't given me any pain killers.

"I heard them saying they didn't want to give you anything strong, considering your history," Lu explained quietly.

"Oh," I replied, my hand falling to my side. I thought about how easy it was for me to get addicted to alcohol and that was only after drinking it every day for a single week.

"That makes sense," I added.

I leaned in further against my pillow and looked at Lu, who watched me carefully.

"Do you think the jury is going to believe Ryleigh?" I asked quietly. "That I threatened her to lie to Olivia? That he didn't push me into the table?"

Lu took a deep breath then shook her head.

"I don't think so. Olivia said they were going to continue questioning Ryleigh tomorrow. They are also going to recall Olivia, so she can testify about the interview. She told me that there was no way Ryleigh was lying in that interview, because she even apologized a lot for not telling anyone before now. They're going to show the jury the tape," Lu explained and I smiled.

There was no way Ryleigh was going to get away with her lie. Now she was going to be arrested for perjury.

"Do you think I fucked everything up by reacting the way I did?" I asked, my smile faltering.

"Well, considering you didn't take the opportunity to pick up a broken piece of glass and try and stab the bitch, no, I don't think you did," Lu responded, her smile picking up. "I think the jury got to see you in shock by her lies. If anything, I reckon it could have helped."

I smiled again.

"I hope so," I said quietly. I leaned back on the pillow and stared at the ceiling.

"Seeing all the pictures and hearing everything reported about what happened to me, is harder than I thought," I said quietly.

I felt Lu's eyes on me as I spoke.

"I think I made a mistake. I should have just pled guilty. What if my outburst did fuck all of it up? What if they say I'm guilty, despite the psychiatrist's testimony? Despite the doctor from the hospital telling them about my injuries?" I paused, feeling cold at the thought.

"What if they say I'm guilty and I get another twenty years?" I asked, turning to look at Lu, who was now sitting up on her bed with her legs crossed. The nurse was watching us through the windowpane of her office, so no doubt, if Lu tried to move to my bed, she would stop it in a hurry.

"Then those jury members are idiots and every one of them will have an unexpected visit from Fingers," Lu stated, her face full of seriousness.

I laughed.

"L! I'm being serious."

"So am I, babe," she responded, but she gave me a small reassuring smile. "If you are found guilty and have to serve another twenty years, then you have to serve another twenty years. I promise you, you won't have to serve them alone."

My heart pounded.

"But you're going to serve less time than me, because you only got one year for that crime," I reminded her and Lu shrugged her shoulders.

"Doesn't matter. There's plenty of things I can do in here that will get time added onto my sentence. You won't be alone," she said so defiantly that I chose not to argue.

"I love you," I said quietly and she smiled.

"Not as much as I love you, *mi esposa*," she replied.

My wife. I grinned.

"When we're put in the gen pop, I will buy us some rings from the commissary," Lu promised. "They're not as beautiful as the ones we had for, like, two seconds, but they're still something, right?"

"They'll be perfect," I countered and Lu smiled.

We heard a service cart being pushed into the room and moments later, Lu and I both had trays of food that were meant to be our dinner placed in front of us. We ate in silence and not long after, I found myself too exhausted to talk anymore.

I drifted off to sleep, despite how anxious I felt about the next day, but at least it made the pain from my hands go away.

Chapter Thirty-Three

Olivia

"Do you swear to tell the truth, the whole truth and nothing but the truth, so help you God?" the bailiff asked me as I had my hand on the Bible and my other hand up in the air, looking at him as he spoke to me.

I had stopped believing in a god the moment I found out that the love of my life had perished in a fire. I stopped believing in a god when my child was ripped out of my arms only an hour after giving birth to her. Yet I stood here today, testifying for the second time on her behalf, to try and get her off of a charge of murdering a man who was supposed to keep her safe, but who abused her instead. If God was real he must have been laughing at us up above.

"I do," I stated, bringing my hand down to my side. I took my hand off the Bible and sat down on the seat that was raised up high enough that the jury members and those in the public gallery could watch me as I answered whatever questions were thrown my way.

I gazed over at Elsie, who was staring down at her bandaged hand, plucking at a loose thread that had come off the cotton.

Ever since I left the correctional prison yesterday, I

had a feeling that she had lost all hope in receiving a not guilty verdict. It was the first time in my whole life I really wanted to murder someone. Sure, I thought about it in passing with Jorge, but I swear to the laughing God, if I got my hands on Ryleigh Atkins…

"Detective Swanson, could you please tell me: on the afternoon of the 19th of March 2022, did you interview Ryleigh Marie Atkins regarding what she witnessed on the morning of the 14th of August 2016?" Camilla asked me, bringing my focus back to her.

I blinked a couple of times before nodding my head. I leaned forward towards the microphone.

"I did, yes," I replied.

"Can you please tell the court what you remember about the interview please?"

"Ryleigh came into the station, around 4:30 p.m. that afternoon. She had been an hour later than expected because she had just come from the hospital getting the damage to her nose taken care of," I started, internally hitting myself for confirming that she had a nose break.

"She had told me she had gotten in a fight with Elizabeth that day in school and Elizabeth had broken her nose," I continued, giving an apologetic look towards Elsie who had lifted her head to look at me. She gave me a small nod, which I took to mean that she understood. I turned to look back at Camilla.

"After I got her settled into the interview, I asked her what she remembered about that morning of August 14th, 2016. She immediately broke into tears and told me how she had witnessed Richard Neilson push Elizabeth into a glass coffee table," I stated. "I asked her why she hadn't told anyone this and she told me it was because she was scared of what Mr. Neilson would do to her and Elizabeth if she said anything."

"At any point, did you believe that she was telling you all this because she had been threatened earlier in the day?" Camilla questioned.

"No, I did not. Everything she told me felt genuine. She said she regretted keeping it a secret all this time and she had even said she had always worried about Elizabeth's safety and didn't want to do anything that would comprise her safety even more," I responded.

Mr. Wyatt stood up.

"Objection, hearsay," he countered and Camilla walked over to her desk and picked up a tape.

"Everything the witness has just said is on the interview tape," Camilla retorted, looking straight at Mr. Wyatt, who looked slightly lost for words.

"Overruled," the judge responded, which made Camilla look back at him.

"May I enter this tape into evidence, Your Honor?" Camilla asked the Judge.

"Granted. Exhibit I," the judge responded.

Camilla gave the Judge a smile and walked the tape over to the court clerk who was taking care of all the evidence.

"That is all the questions I have for Detective Swanson," Camilla concluded, then went to sit down.

"Mr. Wyatt?" The judge looked over to Mr. Wyatt, who stood up again and stood in front of me.

"Did Ryleigh tell you what the fight at school was about?" he asked me.

I nodded and leaned forward again.

"She did. Ryleigh thought she was being called in to see me because of an incident that happened a couple of weeks earlier, when Elizabeth went to the hospital with a torn ligament in her wrist. Ryleigh told me she had poured paint all over Elizabeth's artwork in retaliation for the thought of being told on, which prompted Elizabeth to hit her," I explained, my heartbeat accelerating as I repeated what I had been told. This definitely wasn't helping Elsie.

"So, Elizabeth has a history of retaliating with violence when someone offends or hurts her?" Mr. Wyatt asked, raising his eyebrow.

My heartbeat went so fast, it felt like it had stopped completely.

"Only that one time," I said quietly.

"Twice, if you include the fact she shot her father," Mr. Wyatt argued. He went to stand near his desk again.

"No further questions," he commented.

I looked at the judge who nodded his head at me and I stood up to leave.

Now that I had finished testifying, I was allowed to stay in the courtroom, so I stood and walked over to the seat behind Elsie. She watched me as I walked, with tears in her eyes. I would have given anything to hug her. Too bad I would be arrested for contempt of court if I even tried.

When I sat down, the bailiff called for Ryleigh again. I saw Elsie tense up at her name and those tears started rolling down her cheeks as she watched Ryleigh walk into the room and back up on the pedestal.

Ryleigh was sworn in and Camilla asked the clerk to play the tape recording of the interview.

Everything that I had said on the stand was played out loud, with Ryleigh's cries about how sorry she was for not telling anyone sooner. I watched Ryleigh as she paled. She knew the interview was recorded. I had told her at the start. Why did she think lying was a good idea?

"What do you have to say about that?" Camilla asked, when the interview was finished playing.

I looked over at the jury, some looking at Ryleigh with disgust. I hoped that meant that they were on the not-guilty side of the vote.

"I'm a really good actress?" Ryleigh replied, her face turning bright red. Then she burst into tears.

"I'm sorry, I lied. She killed my best friend's grandfather. She shot the headmaster in front of me. I've had nightmares every night since prom. It was meant to be the best night of my life, but she ruined it because she shot someone in front of me!" Ryleigh cried.

My fists curled up. Sure, seeing someone shot was traumatic. But I'm pretty sure being raped was worse.

"So, you admit, you were lying?" Camilla asked, ignoring her tears. Too bad she couldn't ask her about setting Elsie up with Dante.

Ryleigh sniffed and wiped her eyes.

"Mr. Neilson pushed her into the glass coffee table. He pushed her and didn't even care that she was hurt. He just yelled at her for getting blood on his carpet," Ryleigh sobbed.

"I didn't know what happened next, because I ran away after that. Elsie and I stopped being friends, because she didn't want to believe what happened to her.

She believed she walked into the glass door, so I let her believe it, because it was easier than having to remind her of the truth," she continued, sniffing more.

The judge leaned over and handed her a box of tissues. She took one and blew her nose loudly next to the microphone.

"No further questions," Camilla commented, moving back to her desk.

"Ryleigh Marie Atkins, you are under arrest for perjury," the judge commented and Ryleigh cried even more. One of the court officers moved up to the pedestal to help her down and then she was handcuffed. She was read her rights.

While that was happening, I took the opportunity to lean forward and put my hand on Elsie's shoulder. She looked back at me, her face just as red and splotchy as Ryleigh's, but at least she was a quiet crier.

"Are you okay?" I whispered and she nodded.

Camilla handed her a tissue and she blew her nose. She then wiped her tears away with her sleeve.

"I'm just glad she told the truth and is about to see the consequences of her lies," Elsie whispered.

The judge cleared his throat and Elsie turned to pay attention, while I leaned back on the chair.

Edith Taylor was called next. I didn't really get to talk

to her at Lu's change of plea hearing, but as I watched her walk up to the witness box, I could tell that she was struggling with being a single parent. She looked exhausted, like she hadn't slept properly in days. I would have to remember to check in on her after all this was over.

Camilla stood after she was sworn in.

"First of all, I'm sorry for the loss of your partner," Camilla started, but Edith leaned forward, looking rather confident.

"There's no need to be sorry; I'm not," she answered, causing a few members of the jury to let out a shocked gasp.

"What do you mean by that?" Camilla questioned.

"What I mean is, I believe everything Elizabeth has been trying to tell the court. He was an awful, manipulative man and I wish I had seen it earlier," Edith stated.

Elsie looked at me over her shoulder a second, the look of shock clear in her face. Clearly, she hadn't expected that. Neither had Camilla, because she took a while to respond.

"Getting back to Elizabeth. On the early morning of April 16th, 2022, you told the Sutton Police Captain, Captain Swanson, that you overheard Richard Neilson say something to Elizabeth moments before she shot him, is that correct?" Camilla asked, grabbing a piece of paper off the table.

"That's correct," Edith replied.

Camilla asked for the paper to be put into evidence, which was granted. Once everyone had a copy of the form, Camilla looked at Edith again.

"Do you recall what he said?" she asked and Edith nodded and looked straight at the jury.

"I recall exactly what he said, because I replay it in my head every night. If he could say that about his daughter, who he had raised for eighteen years, what could he say about our son?" Edith said to them.

I could tell that Mr. Wyatt wanted to object to her comment, considering it had nothing to do with the question, but Edith continued before he could even think about it.

"'It's a pity that I didn't kill you when you fell into that table. Maybe then I wouldn't have a murdered student in the girl's bathroom,'" Edith quoted.

Some of the jury members gasped. Considering the day before, both the psychiatrist and Maria had testified that only moments prior to that, Elise had just been sexually assaulted, I had a feeling that most of the jury was now on Elsie's side.

I couldn't help but feel that there was hope yet. I just hoped Elsie felt the same, even though she looked like she had just seen a ghost after hearing those words again.

Chapter Thirty-Four

Lu

So, it did turn out I really did need Elsie to remind me to behave. With her away at court and with me being left to my own devices, it seemed I could get myself in a lot of trouble. Already I had been put in the SHU for trying to get back into the courtroom after I was forced out of it, I had offended Floss to the point where she stabbed me in the arm with a toothbrush (which to be fair, I did do on purpose), and I had gotten about ten shots from different C.Os because I couldn't keep my smart mouth shut. It was like I didn't have a filter. No matter how hard I tried, I had to say the first thing that popped into my head and a lot of the time, the C.O.s didn't appreciate it. I didn't know if it was because I was worried about Elsie and how her court case was going, or if it was just becoming more of a bad habit because I knew I was doomed in here anyway.

I was mopping the food hall's floor while Shorty and Floss were cleaning the tables and wiping down the chairs, and the rest of the F block cleaned the inside of the kitchen and the adjacent corridor.

Because Floss had just got out of the SHU for shivving me and I was still sporting the bandage, C.O

Rizzo was assigned to watch over us, in case another fight started out. She was not happy about it. Add the fact that I kept looking up at the clock on the wall, every five minutes to see if it was 4:00 p.m. yet, and she was livid with me.

I knew I had to hold my tongue, because I knew she was just itching to send me to the SHU. I couldn't risk that happening because I had to be with Elsie tonight. I didn't care if I had to break out of my cell and into hers. I would find a way to make it happen. I couldn't do that if I was locked away in solitary.

"Focus, Torres!" snapped Rizzo, I looked up at the clock for the seventh time.

"Watching the clock isn't going to make your girlfriend appear any quicker," she continued, leaning against the wall with her foot up on it, as if it was saving her back.

"Wife, actually," I retorted as I pushed the mop back and forward with a little more grunt.

"Is that right? Could have fooled me, with no rings," she replied and I heard the amusement in her voice.

I gripped the handle of the mop. I must not rise up to her baiting. It was what she wanted.

She would have known that any wedding rings would have been confiscated at the police station, especially if they were expensive. She would know exactly who the Los Dragones were and how many of them were inmates in this prison. She would have heard of my family, so she would know how rich we were. She knew I would have had expensive rings.

"Fair enough. It'll be much clearer once I can get to the commissary in the gen pop," I replied, trying not to put any tone in my voice.

I continued to mop the floor, thinking about anything other than what it would be like to turn the mop into a weapon and whack the bitch over the head with it. Sure, it wouldn't do much damage, but considering how disgusting this floor was, hopefully she would get a mouth full of something gross.

Once I had finished, I picked up the mop and bucket and went to the kitchen cleaning cupboard to get rid of the dirty water. I could feel eyes on the back of my head, so I knew Rizzo was watching me carefully. Once I had put everything away, I walked over to Shorty who handed me a cloth to help her wipe down the rest of the tables. I absentmindedly started wiping the table next to the one she was doing, so I could talk to her.

"How long do trials usually last?" I asked her. I hadn't had much time to talk to her lately, but I knew if anyone would know about the court system, it would be her, considering she had told me she'd been arrested a number of times.

"Depends on how much evidence they have to put forward to the jury," Shorty answered, as she continued to wipe down her own table. She looked cautiously at Rizzo, who was now watching Floss carefully as she moved to a table closer to mine.

The thing with Floss was that she was over her anger the moment she stabbed me. We didn't hold a grudge towards each other and considering we were both alive after spending the night in the same cell, I'm pretty sure she was over me calling her a tweaker.

She was coming off meth and had just gotten over her withdrawal symptoms before being put in F block. Even though people didn't talk about what they did to get in here, I had to only take one look at her to know her story. I ignored her and turned back to Shorty.

"Sometimes it can go for a few days, or it could go for the whole week," Shorty continued.

I moved along the table to reach the middle as I continued to wipe it.

"As well as the evidence, there's the witnesses. Usually the defense likes to put as many witnesses as possible in the box. Mostly for character. They seem to think the more people they can get to talk positive about their client, the more they'll feel sorry for them. Especially young ones, like your girl," Shorty offered.

I gave her a small smile. I sure hoped the jury felt sorry for Elsie. They would be idiots if they thought she really did it with malicious intent. Just one look at Elsie and you could tell she was a quiet, shy girl. Even over these past few months she still looked innocent.

"If the trial is going well, they could be doing closing statements tomorrow. Then it's up to the jury to come up with a decision. That usually takes the longest, because there is always one fucker who wants to do the opposite as everyone else. One time, the jury took three days to come back with a not guilty verdict for one of my friends. For me, they usually take ten minutes. I don't even know why I bother pleading not guilty."

Shorty then let out a relieved sigh when she finished wiping the end of her table. I quickly finished wiping mine and soon Floss declared that she was finished too, so Rizzo had us put the dirty cloths into a bag and escorted us to the laundry room.

Since it was still part of the 'work' day, there were inmates from the gen pop working the laundry. When we entered the room, several pairs of eyes turned and stared at us.

I heard wolf whistles near the corner of the room and I

turned slightly red, knowing that it was directed at me. No offence to Shorty and Floss, but there was no way anyone thought they were hot enough to call out.

I grabbed the bag from Shorty and walked over to the giant laundry basket, which I knew held all the still-to-be washed stuff. I emptied the bag and turned back around to leave the room, but I froze on the spot as my eyes landed on a familiar face.

Shit.

Wearing a beige colored jumpsuit, with the top folded in a knot above where her belly button was revealing the white tee everyone wore, with half her red hair shaven off and the other side in a short bob cut, stood my ex-girlfriend. My heart pounded, setting off my bracelet as I watched her. She was fuming.

"You," she said, dropping the sheet that she was folding and storming over to me.

I flicked my eyes to the corner, to where Shorty and Floss were watching in interest and Rizzo was standing behind them, pretending she didn't see what was happening. I flicked my eyes back on my ex just as she grabbed the front of my shirt and pulled me closer.

"I always knew you would end up in here, Lucita," she hissed.

Izabella Spencer. Spencer to everyone who knew her.

Spencer was my first. My first girlfriend, my first kiss, my first consensual sexual partner. She was also the first person I got sent to prison.

My bracelet was beeping loudly, making the other inmates whisper and point. My heart was pounding so intensely, that for the first time since it had stopped, it actually hurt. I tried to even out my breathing, tried to settle my heartbeat, but it was proving to be difficult, considering all I could see was Spencer being escorted from the courtroom in handcuffs, after being found guilty of larceny in the first degree.

She had been sentenced to the max time of twenty years, with a chance of parole in fifteen. I had been fifteen years old at the time and she had just turned eighteen. It was my testimony that got her convicted.

Even though it was me who broke into the four-million-dollar Lamborghini Veneno Roadster because I was bored. Even though it was me that crashed it into a wall, lucky to get out alive, because I had no idea how to drive. I guess that's what happens when your father could get someone to make sure her prints were on the wheel instead of mine. That's what happens when you have someone who could make the footage look like a certain redheaded young adult picked the locks and hotwired the vehicle instead of a teenager.

I gulped as I looked in her eyes, noting how they were dark and empty compared to the loving woman I had known three years ago. I guess that's what prison can do.

"Spencer … fancy seeing you here," I said, breathing in and out slowly and trying to make it look like I was not freaking out.

I looked down at the arm that was holding my shirt and noticed that it was covered in tattoos. They weren't professional-looking and I knew she didn't have them before. She had gotten prison tatts. Considering how painful I heard they were to get and how many she had on just this one arm, I knew she had gotten tough. A few inmates snickered at the name. Spencer smirked.

"The name is Rott, now," she informed me.

I couldn't help myself. I let out my own snicker, though it was very much in a what-the-fuck-kind-of-name-is-that way. Spencer - Rott, now I guess - leaned her face in closer.

"As in Rottweiler. As in, I will bite your fucking nose off if you fuck me off," she elaborated, then bared her teeth and growled at me.

I leaned back from her as the other inmates laughed. What the fuck?

I saw someone move out of the corner of my eye and I turned to look at who it was. My eyes went wide as I saw an inmate turn her head to look at me. Where her nose was meant to be was a scarred, horrible looking mess. It was half the length it should have been, with two long slots which I assumed were her nostrils. She turned away, her eyes blinking away tears as more laughter followed. I looked back at Rott.

"I'm not the same girl you used to know, Lu. You killed her the moment you told that jury that she was the one to break into that car. She died the minute her heart broke into a thousand pieces when her girlfriend betrayed her," she sneered, and instead of being afraid I rolled my eyes.

I found that I was over the shock of seeing her and I was now just pissed that there was a C.O. standing a few feet away who was doing nothing, even though Rott was clearly threatening me. I was going to show these inmates that I wasn't one to be messed with.

My bracelet had finally turned itself off now that my heart had returned to its normal rhythm.

"That's what you fucking get for loving a fifteen-year-old girl, you fucking freak," I retorted, bringing my arm up and hitting the bone side of my forearm hard on hers, to force it away from holding me. I stepped forward and head butted her in the face, causing her to shriek out in pain. Instantly her hands went to her face and blood started pouring out between her fingers. She took a step back from me, her eyes wide.

The other inmates started moving towards me, like they were going to gang bash me, but I held my arms up with my fists balled tight in a fighting stance.

"Come on then, let's see what you've got. I'm not afraid of you," I declared, bouncing on the balls of my feet. I suddenly felt exhilarated, ready to fight.

The inmates stopped walking towards me and I wondered why for a moment, but then I felt a sharp pain in my side. I turned to look at what had hit me, but before I could even move an inch there was another hard whack. I doubled over, bringing my hands to my side. I looked up to see Rizzo holding a baton. She was hitting me to bring me down.

Sirens sounded around me and all the inmates went flat on their stomachs. Moments later, I was forced onto my own stomach and my hands were roughly pulled behind my back. It felt like they were being pulled out of my shoulder sockets. I tried to resist, but I got another whack along the base of my back.

"Stop resisting, Torres, or this is going to get a whole lot worse for you," Rizzo shouted over the wailing sirens.

I was forced to my feet and shoved forwards, just as

several other C.O.s entered the laundry room. Wright hurried over to Rott, who was trying to stop her nose from bleeding, but it just kept pouring out.

"Fuck you!" I shouted as I turned back to look at Rizzo and spat in her face. She whacked me in my side again, this time so hard that I doubled over. Another C.O. grabbed me and I was pretty much dragged away from the laundry.

"She's a Pitbull," I heard someone say, as I struggled not to start crying because of the pain. I smirked at the comment. It wasn't long until I was thrown into the SHU, with a single bed and a toilet and sink. The door was bolted shut and I was left alone in the darkness, with nothing but my thoughts and pounding wounds on my back and ribs where I had been hit.

Fuck. Now I couldn't be with Elsie.

Chapter Thirty-Five

Elsie

I was mad. I was mad and upset because when I got back to the prison, I found Lu had gotten herself put in the SHU again for breaking a woman's nose.

I needed her now more than ever and I was sure she knew how this trial was making me feel, but she couldn't even behave for one day without starting a fight or keeping her mouth shut.

For the first time since our relationship started, I wondered if she cared more about herself than she did me. Did she even care that I was constantly replaying the final words that man said to me? Did she care that all I could see in my mind was all the blood coming from his chest? She couldn't behave for a few hours without me being there. Lu was hopeless.

I sat next to Shorty at dinner while we ate the stuff they called food. She tried to make me laugh by pulling funny faces at the correctional officer when he wasn't looking, but I really wasn't in the mood.

I kept pushing the food around with my fork, my head leaning on my hand with my elbow on the table.

I was told tomorrow would be the closing statements. That was when the prosecution and the defense would tell the jury what they thought would be enough to win their case. Since it was the last thing the jury was told before they went into a separate room to deliberate the outcome of the rest of my life, I hoped what Camilla told them was enough to convince them that I was temporarily insane at the time.

As I pushed at my food, I couldn't help but think that it was ironic that I was pretty much completely insane now. I absentmindedly ran my finger along the raised scar on my throat. Even though the tattoo hid it, it was still a constant reminder of just one of the terrible things that happened to me that plagued my insane mind.

The correctional officer walked back past our table. Normally they stayed on the side of the room, leaving us to eat without interfering, so when he stood in front of our table, it took a couple of seconds for anyone to realize that he was staring at me. Shorty nudged me. I stopped pushing the peas to the side of the plate and looked up.

"Is there a problem, Skittles?" he asked me.

My face warmed at the name. Everyone had started calling me that. I honestly didn't mind it, but everyone knew that I needed heaps of different medication to help me function and without them, I was pretty much a crazy suicidal maniac. It made it easy for people to judge me and watch me to see if the drugs they gave me were really working or if I would somehow spontaneously combust or something.

"I'm not very hungry," I muttered, looking back down at my tray.

"You have two options. One, you eat the goddamn food or two, you will be taken to the ding wing," the correctional officer stated and I cringed slightly at how loud he was talking. Everyone was looking in our direction now.

The ding wing was the mental health ward. I had learned that when Floyd insisted that she didn't want to catch whatever crazy I had, because I was in the general hospital wing and not the 'ding wing,' as if what was wrong with me was contagious.

"I'll eat," I mumbled and then quickly proceeded to stab the food with my fork and hurriedly put it in my mouth. He watched me for a few minutes, making sure I actually ate it before going back to his post by the door.

He continued to watch me from where he stood, so I didn't dare stop eating. Once I was done, I looked up to find that everyone on my table had finished too and was waiting for me to finish.

"Sorry," I mumbled, before we all stood up and walked to the front of the room where we had to put our empty trays for the kitchen staff.

Once we were done, we were escorted back to F block. The rest of the night consisted of free time, when most people played card games, but I chose to stay in my cell until lights out, reading a book that Shorty had given me about how to survive prison for the first time. So far, I was doing a stellar job, considering the first chapter had mentioned not to hide away and to involve yourself with other prisoners.

Once it was close to lights out, I went to the bathroom, along with most of the others to brush my teeth and use the toilet. There was no point trying to shower, considering there was no way I was going to get naked in front of the other inmates without Lu.

I knew I had to stick up for myself and I knew how to, thanks to Lu's lessons in self-defense, but I didn't want to risk anything when my trial was so close to ending. It would be just my luck if I got injured or was put in the SHU myself.

At lights out, I fell asleep almost immediately, already feeling the effects of the melatonin medication that helped me sleep.

~.~

The next morning, I was a bundle of nerves. I couldn't stop thinking; what if the prosecution was more convincing? What if the jury believed I had done it all out of malice, that I had acted with the actual intention of killing him?

I ate my breakfast, because the same correctional officer was watching me carefully. I ate all of it even though I felt like I was going to be sick with every mouthful.

After we finished eating, I was taken to the hospital wing to get my medications and to have the dressings on my hands changed. The nurse watched me carefully, making me show her my mouth to make sure I actually swallowed my pills, like she did every morning. Correctional Officer Rizzo came in just as the nurse finished looking in my mouth, allowing me to shut it.

Rizzo took me back to my cell to get my showering gear. She had a pile of clothes for me, which she gave me once we were in the bathroom. I was relieved to find that the bathroom was empty. Apparently since it was my last day of the trial, I got special treatment.

I showered and washed my hair in the five minutes that I was allowed, which I found awkward to do, considering I had to wear bags around my hands to keep my dressings dry. I got changed with Rizzo watching me, making a sound like she was sucking in her breath when I turned my back on her and she saw my scar. It was the same sound the jury made when they saw the photo of it.

I picked up my pace and soon I was in a suit that made me think of Lu, who loved wearing dress pants and jackets instead of dresses. My heart ached as I thought of her, alone in solitary confinement. I hoped she was all right.

Soon, after I had finished dressing, I was escorted to the transfer van. Once we were on our way to the courthouse, I spent the remainder of the time staring at a rust mark that was shaped like a heart, thinking about what it would be like if I was found guilty. No doubt I would be sentenced for the whole twenty years.

I had done some stupid, reckless things since prom night, including escaping the country, so I was sure they weren't going to be lenient on sentencing. I was already looking at roughly fifty-one years for all the other crimes I had already pled guilty to. And that was if they didn't give me a life sentence for being involved in killing Keith Miller.

If I was found guilty today, then I could be looking at seventy-one years in prison. I wasn't going to get out until I was eighty-nine. Even if they didn't sentence me to life in prison, I was going to be spending the rest of my life in it anyway. If I was found not guilty, fifty-one years was still a long time. There was every chance I would die in prison.

Why did I think that stealing was fun? From the moment I ran from the diner that day, instead of paying, I had changed the course of my life. Every decision I had made, every item I stole, led me to this exact moment. It was devasting that several minutes of fun turned into this lifetime of confinement and regret.

When we arrived at the courthouse, Olivia was waiting just inside the door. Since Rizzo was the one escorting me today and not Cooke like it had been the last two days, I figured that was the reason why she was allowed to be there.

Olivia greeted Rizzo like an old friend, giving her a hug before turning to me and giving me one too. My hug was far longer and I swear a tighter one. Rizzo actually had to clear her throat and attempt to pull me away from Olivia to get us moving again.

Olivia walked ahead of us and continued walking as we stopped by a door that led into the courtroom. She had to go the public way, since she wasn't the counsel or the defendant. Camilla stepped up beside me a moment later and gave me a reassuring smile. She seemed confident, which I suppose was a good thing.

"How are you feeling today?" She asked and I just shrugged my shoulders, not bothering to verbalize how I felt. I'm sure she already knew.

When the door was opened, I took a deep breath as I was escorted into the courtroom. Olivia was already seated next to Mrs. Taylor, who, surprisingly, looked very nervous. Olivia reached over and grabbed Mrs. Taylor's hand to try and comfort her.

It was in that moment that I realized that Mrs. Taylor could have been my stepmother if things hadn't turned out the way they did. I hadn't thought about it before, but maybe Mrs. Taylor looked nervous because for a long time she thought I was going to be her stepdaughter. She had always treated me kinder than any other teacher at school. So maybe I was like a daughter to her, more than I realized?

I breathed out again before I passed out due to lack of oxygen and walked to my normal seat behind the table and next to Camilla. I turned and put my hand on the banister, which Olivia and Mrs. Taylor both reached for. I laughed quietly as Olivia ended up holding onto my pinky finger, while Mrs. Taylor held onto my thumb.

They looked at each other and laughed too and I couldn't help but wonder if, after all this, they would be friends.

"Thank you for coming," I said quietly, mostly to Mrs. Taylor, because I knew there was no chance Olivia wouldn't be here. That and the fact that Mrs. Taylor would have had to find someone to look after Noah.

"Of course I came. I wouldn't have missed this for anything," she replied, giving my thumb a quick squeeze. I gave her a small smile and then looked at Olivia, whose eyes were filling up with tears.

"Don't cry, Mom. If you start, I will too and I don't know if I will be able to stop them," I pointed out.

Olivia let out a half-hearted laugh and wiped away her tears with her sleeve of her other arm.

"Sorry," she announced, just as Camilla gently put her hand on my shoulder, to get me to turn around.

Olivia gave my pinky a squeeze and they both let go of my hand and I turned just in time for the bailiff to direct everyone to rise.

Once the judge had sat down and told us all to sit, my heart picked up its pace in anticipation. The jury walked in through their allocated door and sat down, each looking over in my direction to, I suppose, gauge my feelings. It hadn't been as dramatic after the first day, so I guess they were feeling tired of my trial by now.

Once they were all seated, the judge explained that today was closing statements and that we would hear from both the prosecution and defense. He explained that after that, they would then go back to their jury room and deliberate on their verdict. They would be given all the evidence shown in court the last few days, from both sides and they had to come to a unanimous vote.

I had been told previously that it could take anywhere from minutes to several hours and in some extreme cases, days. I hoped my fate was decided in minutes because I didn't know how long I would last.

Mr. Wyatt was up first. His statement was all about how I had planned to kill Richard. How he was trying to derail my plan with Lu, so I had to get rid of him. The only thing I hadn't planned in killing him was the use of the gun, which was convenient at the time of the shooting. He was clutching at straws and for once since this whole thing started, I was actually feeling optimistic. When he sat down, even I knew the jury wasn't convinced.

When Camilla stood up, my heart pounded like crazy. This was her moment to say everything she could in my defense. This was the moment where she could make or break my future.

"Ladies and gentleman of the jury. Was Elizabeth Neilson the one who shot Richard Neilson on the night of August 16th? Yes. There is no doubt of that – even she has admitted to killing him that night and not once has she tried to say it wasn't her," she started, pacing along the front of the jury panel and looking back at me. I was watching her carefully, my heart continuing to pound at her words.

"Did she shoot him out of malice? Did she plan to kill him that night? No, she did not. Was Elizabeth a victim of his abuse over many years, both mentally and physically? Yes, she was. Evidence and witness testimony proved that," she pointed out.

I bit my lip and leaned forward to grab the (now plastic) cup of water in front of me to lubricate my ever-drying throat.

"On the night of April 16th, when he had told her that he wished she was dead, only ten minutes after she had been sexually assaulted, did she snap, grabbing the gun that moments earlier had been pointed at her own head and turn it on Richard Neilson? Yes. Again, we are not denying that fact," she continued.

I took a sip of my drink, trying not to think about what it felt like to have that cold metal against my forehead, believing I had seconds to live.

"Elizabeth Neilson acted out of fear, out of desperation after years of mental and physical abuse. She did not plan or decide weeks earlier that he had to be killed. Both his comment about him wishing she was dead and the fact that he had just announced to the whole school that she wasn't even his daughter, made Elizabeth flash back to when she was twelve with a shard of glass in her lung. To when she was six with a broken wrist. To when she was eight and he broke her ribs. She flashed back to every moment in her life when she felt degraded, worthless, not worthy of love. In her mind she had no other option but to shoot the man who had just threatened her again. In her mind her only choice was to hurt him or get hurt herself, yet again. Yes, she killed Richard Neilson. But we put to you that she was, as medically proven, temporarily insane at the time. Ladies and gentlemen of the jury. Do the right thing. Find her not guilty due to temporary insanity," Camilla concluded.

She gave a small nod to the judge to announce she was finished and walked over to the table and sat down. She put her hand on my back and leaned in to talk to me.

"Are you all right?" She asked me and I nodded, putting down the now empty cup of water.

She gave me a small reassuring smile, just as the judge started talking to the jury again. When he stopped talking, they were dismissed and the bailiff instructed us to rise again. The judge left the room and then Rizzo came up to the table, along with one of the court officers.

I was taken out of the courtroom with just enough

time to turn and wave goodbye to Olivia and Mrs. Taylor, who were still holding each other's hands. It gave me a warm feeling in the pit of my stomach to know that they had each other for this.

I was taken into a small room with a few seats, a table and a little coffee station. Camilla sat me down and Rizzo stood by the door, guarding it so I couldn't try and run. Camilla walked over to the coffee station.

"Would you like one?" She asked me, but I shook my head. If I had caffeine it would only make me more jittery. As it was, I was already a nervous wreck, bouncing my legs like I always did when I felt like this. I folded my arms on the table and put my head down on them, closing my eyes.

I didn't know how long we would have to wait, but I knew I didn't want to be awake for any of it. Thanks to the medication the doctor had put me on, I no longer had nightmares the minute I closed my eyes. I drifted off to sleep moments later.

~.~

"Elsie?" I felt a hand on my shoulder gently shaking me awake. I opened my eyes and blinked a few times, trying to remember where I was. In the waiting room. To wait for my future to be spelled out. That's right.

I looked up at Camilla, who was giving me her

reassuring smile again. It wasn't quite warm, but she meant it all the same.

"The jury has made their decision," she explained and I sat up properly and looked around the room for a clock. There wasn't one.

"How long has it been?" I asked, my voice harsh due to my throat being dry. She pushed a plastic cup filled with water towards me.

"Thanks," I stated, before picking it up and taking a gulp out of it.

"It's been an hour," Camilla told me and my heart skipped a beat. An hour to decide on my fate.

"Right," I said, before downing the rest of the water. "Do I have time to go to the bathroom?"

Camilla looked over to Rizzo who looked at her watch.

"Hurry up about it," Rizzo demanded and I nodded before moving to the door that was labeled 'restroom.' I walked in and closed the door behind me.

The room reminded me of the jail cell in New Zealand, as it only had one window and it was up way too high for anyone to try and escape, plus it had bars on it. I sighed before making my way to the toilet. I relieved myself, but even after I had finished, I sat there, bringing my hands to my face. I started crying into them.

I didn't want to know what my fate was. I already knew they were going to find me guilty. Why wouldn't they? I had killed him. I had taken the gun and I had shot him. I had done that. I was guilty.

Knowing my luck, they wouldn't believe the abuse. Knowing my luck, they probably thought it was all fabricated to look like it was real. I was going to be found guilty. I was going to prison for the rest of my life. There was a knock on the door.

"Hurry up, Torres!" Rizzo called out and I couldn't help but feel a wave of happiness go through me at being called Lu's name. It took a few weeks, but finally I was officially Elizabeth Rose Torres Alvarez. Only, I guess not in this trial.

I quickly wiped myself and stood up, flushing the toilet. I pulled my pants back up, then walked up to the sink. I washed my hands and splashed some water on my face before drying both my hands and my face with a paper towel. I looked like I had been crying, but I didn't care. I was beyond caring now.

I unlocked the door and Rizzo took my arm and led me out of the waiting room. I must have taken longer than I should have, because I found myself practically running to keep up with her quick strides. Camilla was walking just as quick in front of us.

Soon I was standing behind the table again, waiting for the judge and the jury to enter the room. I remained standing as the bailiff asked the foreperson to stand up. She was holding a bit of paper, her hands shaking slightly at being the center of attention. The judge looked over to her.

"Were you able to reach a verdict, Madam Foreperson?" The Judge asked.

"Yes, we were, Your Honor," the lady responded.

"Was it unanimous?"

"Yes, it was."

"What is your verdict?"

My heart stilled.

"On the charge of manslaughter in the first degree, we the jury, find the defendant, Elizabeth Rose Neilson, not guilty, due to temporary insanity."

It wasn't until I felt a clap on the back of my shoulder and heard Olivia crying with happiness, that I realized what had been said.

My heart started beating again and again my tears fell from my eyes, only this time they were from happiness too. I turned around and gave Olivia a huge hug, which, for once, I was allowed to do. I felt several other hands on my back, probably belonging to Camilla and Mrs. Taylor, congratulating me.

I heard a few cries of unhappiness coming from the prosecution side of the public gallery, but in that moment I didn't care. The jury believed me. They believed the evidence.

There was a hit from the gavel, trying to get our attention and I pulled away from Olivia, wiping away my tears as I turned around to look at the judge and everyone in the room who was standing sat back down.

He turned to the jury and thanked them for their service. They were asked to leave and a lot of them looked eager to do just that. Once they had left the courtroom, the judge looked back at me.

"I understand that you are on medication now and are to receive weekly counseling sessions in the correctional facility, is this correct?" He asked me.

"Yes, it is, Your Honor," I replied, trying not to grin like an idiot. I was so happy but at the same time I knew that this situation was not really one to boast about.

"You are aware that with an insanity defense, any changes in your mental state or behavior can cause you to be transferred to a psychiatric hospital for the remainder of your sentence?" He questioned.

I wasn't actually aware of that, but good to know. I cleared my throat slightly as I leaned forward to the microphone.

"Yes, Your Honor," I replied, because there was no point saying anything different. He nodded then hit his gavel again. The bailiff got everyone to stand again and we were dismissed.

I gave Olivia, Mrs. Taylor and Camilla each one final hug goodbye, before I was escorted back to the van and back to the prison, where I couldn't even share my good news with Lu because she was still in the SHU.

~.~

Monday morning came around slowly. I suspected it had to do with the fact that Lu had been in solitary confinement this whole time, so I had to fend for myself. I had Shorty with me most of the time, for which I was grateful for, but I knew she was only looking out for me, because of Lu.

I hadn't made any connections with any other inmates because most of them kept their distances from me. Apparently, everyone in the entire prison had heard about Lu attacking the top dog and breaking her nose. She was now being called Pitbull and no one wanted her to attack them, so they stayed away from me. I didn't mind. It meant that I was safe. For now.

Finally, Monday arrived. It was the day that Lu and I were going to find out the length of our sentences. Luckily, it was decided that Lu had been in the SHU for long enough and she was being brought out after she had breakfast, so our sentencing day didn't need to be postponed.

I finished my breakfast early, so I was escorted to the showers by Rizzo again, who was holding my change of clothes. When I got there, Lu was brought in by another correctional officer that I didn't know. She left pretty quickly after she gave Rizzo a nod of acknowledgement and Lu's change of clothes.

I shrieked as I saw Lu and ran to hug her, only to stop when I was inches away from her and pull myself back.

"You stink," I declared, screwing up my nose as I took a step back.

She merely laughed, ignoring the snigger from Rizzo, as she proceeded to get out of her clothes that I was sure hadn't been changed in the last six days.

"That's what happens when you are stuck in a cell for six days with no shower and have to sleep in a room with your own shit particles floating around," Lu stated and I wrinkled my nose even more.

"That's gross and really not healthy," I pointed out, moving my eyes over her body.

I couldn't help but let out a gasp. There were bruises over her ribs and on her stomach. There was even one that started on her side and moved around her back.

I winced at the sight of it.

"Move it," Rizzo snapped and I blinked a couple of times, before doing the same as Lu and took off my clothes. We were about to step in the same shower, but Rizzo tutted.

"No. Separate showers. This isn't sexy time," she declared and I turned red as I moved to the shower next to the one I was going to enter.

"Maybe if you had more sexy time, you wouldn't be such a bitch," Lu muttered under her breath, causing me to let out a small giggle. Rizzo must not have heard her, because she stayed silent.

We showered, got changed and soon were on our way to court again.

Even though this was for our sentencing, I wasn't nervous like I had been last week. I was with Lu and I would be for the rest of my life. I wasn't worried.

When we got to court, Camilla was sitting at her seat at the end of the table. Mrs. Taylor and Olivia were standing in the public gallery as always, but so was Elena. Lu actually cried when she saw her. Lu pulled Elena into a hug and didn't care that Rizzo was trying to pull her off of her. Elena cried too, trying to reassure Lu that everyone was all right and that she would be able to see her again once we were allowed visitors at the prison.

It wasn't until Rizzo threatened that she would have Lu put back in the SHU, if she didn't let go of Elena, that she did what she was told and turned back around. I took hold of her hand instead and she gave my hand a squeeze, while wiping the tears from her eyes with the other.

The bailiff had everyone rise again. The judge entered and I squeezed Lu's hand in anticipation.

I couldn't help but feel nervous now, seeing the judge in his black robe, walking up to his pedestal and taking a seat.

"You may be seated," he announced and everyone sat down.

My heart pounded and I couldn't help but notice even Lu's hand was feeling clammy.

"We are here today for the sentencing of Elizabeth Rose Neilson and Lucita Torres Alvarez," he started, looking around the room, then his eyes landed on us.

"Please stand," he instructed to the two of us.

We did. I gripped Lu's hand tighter.

"On the charge of robbery in the first degree, you are both sentenced to five years," he declared.

Lu squeezed my hand.

"On the charge of larceny in the second degree, you are both sentenced to fifteen years, being five years for each count," he continued.

I bit my lip. Twenty years so far.

"On the charge of escape of custody, you are both sentenced to another ten years," he told us.

Thirty years.

"On the charge of criminal impersonation, you are both charged to another one year," he added. He paused and looked up over his glasses to look at us for the final sentence.

"On the charge of felony murder, you're both sentenced to twenty-five years," he stated and my heart plummeted. At least it wasn't life.

"You are to carry out these sentences consecutively," he added. And with that he hit his gavel and dismissed us.

I was going to prison for fifty-five years, Lu for fifty-six. We were going to be seventy-three when we got out.

That is if we weren't killed first.

TO BE CONTINUED.

If you enjoyed my book, please leave a review!

Goodreads

Follow me on Instagram!

ACKNOWLEDGEMENTS

First of all, I would like to thank each and every one of you for purchasing and reading my book. The fact that you're here for book two means the world for me.

Thank you for sticking by Elsie and Lu as they deal with the consequences of their actions, as well as figuring out their emotions.

This book means a lot to me, as, like book one, it has a lot of my own experiences in it.

Thank you so much to beta readers - Katy, Kimberley and Libby.

A huge thank you to my editor Kristen. Your suggestions and input meant a lot, and it really helped shape my book more. Thanks for putting up with my repetitive gulping.

If you enjoyed my book, I would really appreciate it if you left a review on Goodreads, Amazon, or any other platform that works for you. Reviews help my book and get it out to the world.

In 2023 I will be focusing on writing book three, Locked Up In H.E.L.L

Much love,

JC Rowe

Books In This Series

They Are H.E.L.L

The adventures of Elsie and Lu.

553

We Are H.E.L.L

Running From H.E.L.L

Locked Up In H.E.L.L (2023)

9 780473 648886